The Cambridge Introduction to
Modern British Theatre

SIMON SHEPHERD

CAMBRIDGE
UNIVERSITY PRESS

CAMBRIDGE UNIVERSITY PRESS
Cambridge, New York, Melbourne, Madrid, Cape Town, Singapore,
São Paulo, Delhi, Dubai, Tokyo

Cambridge University Press
The Edinburgh Building, Cambridge CB2 8RU, UK

Published in the United States of America by Cambridge University Press, New York

www.cambridge.org
Information on this title: www.cambridge.org/9780521690188

First published 2009

Printed in the United Kingdom at the University Press, Cambridge

A catalogue record for this publication is available from the British Library

Library of Congress Cataloguing in Publication data
Shepherd, Simon.
    The Cambridge introduction to modern British theatre / Simon Shepherd.
        p.   cm.
    Includes bibliographical references and index.
    ISBN 978-0-521-86986-7 (Hardback)   1. Theater–Great Britain–History–20th
    century.   I. Title.
    PN2595.S44   2009
    792.0941′0904–dc22   2009035019

ISBN 978-0-521-86986-7 Hardback
ISBN 978-0-521-69018-8 Paperback

For Mick,
with my love

The Cambridge Introduction to
Modern British Theatre

British theatre has long been regarded as a world leader in terms of its quality, creativity and range. Starting in 1900, this book introduces the features that characterise modern and current British theatre. Topics covered include experimental performances under motorways, plays by Stoppard and Ayckbourn, amateur theatre and virtual spaces, the emergence of the director, the changing role of writers and political and community shows. The book is clearly divided into four sections: where it happens, who does it, what they make, and why they do it. It discusses theatre buildings and theatre that refuses buildings; company organisation, ensembles and collectives; and different sorts of acting. A large section describes the major work done for the stage, from Shaw through to Complicite, via poetic drama, different sorts of realism and documentary drama. The *Introduction* stands apart from other accounts of modern British theatre by bringing together buildings, people and plays.

SIMON SHEPHERD is Deputy Principal and Professor of Theatre at The Central School of Speech and Drama, University of London.

Contents

Illustrations

Foreword

In this book, 'modern' is defined as everything after 1900. It is an 'introduction' not a history, so it aims to explain the sorts of activity and thinking that seem characteristic of the modern period. Most slippery of all, it deals with 'theatre'. Theatre can include a very wide range of artworks and companies and here a number of exclusions have been made.

I am the sort of person that picks up a book like this and goes straight for the index, to check out what is said about favourite shows and companies. I would probably find myself triumphantly disappointed by the gaps. The book doesn't aim to do coverage, and it doesn't seek to reproduce accepted lists of the great and the good. Some pretty obscure work comes in for analysis, on the grounds that it tells us something significant about the modern period, and, by way of the reverse, some wonderful theatre art is ignored.

I have cut brutally short my accounts of two very large areas – theatre scenography and music theatre. Clearly these areas are deeply connected with the subject matter of this book, but they also spill over way beyond it. They are rather too large and significant, I think, merely to bolt on, and have crucial differences as well as connections – in modes of work and production, and in relationships with other artforms and disciplines. Properly considered, an account of theatre scenography in the modern period would range across genres of visual culture, production of visual pleasure, and changes in how we look. So too an account of music/theatre would move from cantata and folk song through dance and interlude to revue, musical and opera. Each account is a book of its own.

Meanwhile this book is written so that you can begin at the beginning and go straight through, or alternatively use the headings and index to criss-cross it. The structure of the whole thing is explained by the Contents list.

Acknowledgements

Thanks to Bette Bourne for checking through the material on BLOOLIPS, to Claire Macdonald for looking through the material on Impact, to Matt Adams for looking at the Blast Theory bits, to Mischa Twitchin for reading through the material on Shunt, to Mick Wallis for putting me straight, as it were, on the facts of inter-war amateurism. And big thanks to Kate Harris for researching all the illustrations and permissions.

Modern Theatre: two characteristic arrangements for performance from around the middle of the modern period. Of these the second is the more ancient, with its roots in the medieval pageant wagon.

1. The Library Theatre, Scarborough, 1955, designed by Stephen Joseph, although 'no-one really designed the Library Theatre; it just happened' (Joseph 1968: 114).

2. Inter-Action's Fun Art Bus, Festival of London, 1972.

Chapter 1

Where it happens

This section is about buildings, spaces and their management; about the money that pays for them; and about the people who visit them. It begins with one particular project, the story of which touches on a number of issues in all that follows.

National theatre

The twentieth century saw the aspirations towards a national theatre turn into concrete.

The vision of a theatre which was 'national' had been alive since at least the middle of the preceding century. But on the journey towards its realisation in concrete and glass this vision went through a number of changes. At different points in time there was new thinking about location, design, costs and programming. More fundamentally there were shifts in the definition of what a 'national' theatre might be and do. These shifts were products of differing ideas about the relationship between theatre and nation.

When they began in the early twentieth century, debates about the national theatre were shaped by two dominant attitudes to the contemporary theatre. One of these was that the period from about 1880 to 1914 was 'the new great age of English drama' (Pinero in Whitworth 1951: 78). The other was that theatre was threatened to a greater extent than ever before by commercialisation.

If the story of the campaign for a national theatre involves definitions of what the nation is, it also involves declarations as to what good theatre is. In the account that follows we shall see how the changing arguments about theatre and nation position national theatre in relation to different allies and opponents.

A central theatre

In 1904 William Archer and Harley Granville Barker published *The National Theatre: A Scheme and Estimates*. This was a huge leap forward beyond the previous campaigns. The book presented a cogently argued case supported by detailed costings of the organisation and materials, together with suggestions about personnel and programming.

Archer and Barker proposed a theatre that would be 'the property of the nation' (Archer and Barker 1907: xviii). The model for this had been specified by their predecessor Matthew Arnold, who wanted to imitate the idea of the Comédie Française. More recently Edwin Sachs had noted 'there is a growing feeling, both in London and in many of our provincial theatres, that the presentation of plays merits the recognition and encouragement of the public authority ... There is even some hope that the London County Council may soon seriously consider the advisability of officially supporting Opera and Drama' (Sachs 1898: 9). Sachs said this in the context of a general survey of European theatres, where a number were 'national'. These Archer and Barker saw as reflecting the power and dignity of the state. For them the building that housed the national theatre should naturally be in London, and its funding was to come from endowment. It was to be run by the Director, assisted by the Literary Manager, Business Manager, Solicitor and Reading Committee Man. The company would perform the classics of English-speaking theatre, major European works (such as *Pelleas and Melisande*) and some of the established modern drama (*Trelawny of the 'Wells'*, *The Importance of Being Earnest* and *Countess Cathleen*). The site would be given by government or public authority, one major donor would provide the building, while the Guarantee Fund would come from a large number of private contributors.

Its selection of plays makes clear why the national theatre was necessary. Barker's preface to the book talks about the commercialisation of contemporary theatre. He calls it the 'American invasion', since, for him, much of the damage was being done by American, or American-influenced, entrepreneurs, interested only in theatre for profit. The opposite of commercialism was 'art'. The Archer–Barker national theatre would be 'ample', 'dignified' and 'liberal', but it would not be an 'advanced' or avant-garde theatre. It needed to remain in touch with the mainstream, yet at the same time avoid a 'democratisation' that amounted to 'standardisation'.

In being 'endowed' the national theatre would have public responsibilities for its repertoire, which would underwrite its artistic authority. This then would set a benchmark for imitators. In the Archer–Barker vision a string of provincial theatres would be modelled on the national theatre. They would all be organised on the 'repertory' model, which aimed at a programme in which, in any one week, no two performances were of the same play (see Repertory). On this model, the national theatre is at the centre of a network of similar theatres. And indeed that's how they refer to it: 'The Central – or National – Theatre'.

That choice of word – 'Central' – indicates a particular attitude towards the culture Archer and Barker were living in. When they originally wrote their proposal for a National Theatre it was privately distributed. In published form (1907) it contained the names of a small group of highly influential supporters. This suggests a single network of people who are able to make things happen simply by taking action among themselves. They are thus culturally central, in two senses: they are the main driving force in theatrical activity and they don't need to seek a popular mandate for what they do. They are both forceful and select. This view of how culture and politics are done also shaped the economic scheme for the theatre. It was to be supported by 'private liberality' (Archer and Barker 1907: xviii, xix).

It is characteristic of Edwardian culture that a relatively small group of committed theatre workers should feel that they could design a repertoire worthy of, and appropriate to, the whole nation and that such a scheme can only be initiated by private donors. The problem was that these private donors did not materialise in sufficient quantities to enable the scheme to progress. The flaw in the model of a 'Central' theatre is that it was dependent on individual willingness to support good causes. At a time when big money was being made out of the formation of chains of theatres doing variety and popular hits, the economic logic was more on the side of commercial theatre for undifferentiated customers rather than a central theatre for the 'nation'.

But this was not the only way in which the scheme came unstuck.

A racial theatre

When Archer and Barker designed their repertoire they were very clear as to what was, and was not, English drama. When the company from the Irish National Theatre Society visited London in 1903 they created a huge impact through the quality of their performing. But, although this company was given a home at the Abbey Theatre by the tea heiress Annie Horniman, and Ireland was still officially ruled by the English, to Archer and Barker this was work from Ireland. It was not the English national theatre.

One of the functions of such a theatre was to sustain Englishness. The reason for performing the classic works of the dramatic canon was to keep English drama alive. That intention had particular force in the early years of the century. For alongside the development of the scheme for a national theatre there was a separate movement to raise funds to build a memorial to Shakespeare. In the years following the Archer–Barker proposal in 1904, the two campaigns became entangled with one another. A scheme whereby the national theatre would itself be the Shakespeare memorial was overseen for a period by a joint – and much distracted – steering committee. But all were nominally united by 'common reverence for the great spiritual heirloom of our race' (Archer and Barker 1907: 89).

That race was, in the years prior to the First World War, stretched across the world, with London the centre of a British empire. As seen by a supporter of the scheme, speaking in the debate on the National Theatre in the House of Commons in 1913, it would preserve English standards – not just a national but an imperial theatre. Archer and Barker, however radical their liberalism, were caught up into this rhetoric. Their national theatre would have a role to play in strengthening the bonds between 'Anglo-Saxon peoples' (Archer and Barker 1907: xvii). But actually, whatever the rhetoric, by this period the Empire was past its glory days. London had not resisted the American invasion. A national theatre could not really function to sustain something in place. Instead it was more of a crusade, a focus for all those elements in society – or is that Society? – which recognised the role that could be played by a revitalised English drama.

Writing in 1910, P. P. Howe justified repertory theatre on the grounds that it was a form of 'racial self-expression' (Howe 1910: 69). But, as he realised, this conception of theatre was available to a wide diversity of races. The Irish drama seen in London was conspicuously Irish in its concerns. And even as the arguments for an English national theatre were being developed there emerged, some distance to the north, a concerted effort to express the race of the Scots.

That a national theatre was, temporarily, established in Scotland before England may have had something to do with the fact that the aspiration was connected with the formation of companies, whereas in England much of the energy was spent in planning for a building. The first step was the founding of Glasgow Repertory Theatre in 1909. This had as one of its aims 'the initiation and development of a purely Scottish Drama' (Howe 1910: 66). The other three aims were all to do with producing high-quality drama. It was apparently influenced by Barker's season at the Court, although it is also suggested that it followed on from Annie Horniman's company at the Gaiety (Bannister 1955). For Horniman in Manchester had similar consciousness of region, and her work led to the flourishing, and recognition, of a 'Manchester school' of playwrights (which included Brighouse and Houghton). These two potential influences mark the division at the heart of both the Rep and later enterprises, for the insistence on standard of work sometimes came into conflict with the emphasis on Scottishness.

The Rep folded in 1914. Its assets went to the St Andrew's Society, which, in 1920, sponsored the formation of the Scottish National Players Committee. This had as its aims:

> To develop Scottish National Drama through the production by the SNP of plays of Scottish life and character; to encourage in Scotland a public taste for good drama of any type; to found a Scottish National Theatre.
>
> (McDonald 2004: 200)

In 1922 the Scottish National Theatre Society was formed. It was an amateur group. But it was the amateurs who, by Jan McDonald's account, sustained the ideal of native Scottish theatre in the inter-war period. The same can be said of Ulster, where the Ulster Literary Theatre was, in Guthrie's words, 'at that time [around 1926] outstandingly the most important group of its kind in the North of Ireland. After the Abbey it was the most important Irish company' (1961: 40–1). Some of that importance surfaces in the playfulness of the Ulster writer George Shiels, whose *Paul Twyning*, done at the Abbey in 1922, opens with a joke about the North being 'more democratic' and later pastiches quaint Irishness (Shiels 1945: 99, 133). Whether in Ireland or Scotland the tension was between race and standards. Tyrone Guthrie, who toured Scotland with the SNP from 1927, suggested that some of the board 'considered it their duty to press for plays by Scottish authors, and advocated the presentation of even feeble and amateurish scripts if they were written in sufficiently broad vernacular. Others were for good theatre' (Guthrie 1961: 45).

Certainly there was a preferred view of what constituted Scottishness – it had to do with glens and hills, not politics and mines. When Joe Corrie submitted *In Time o' Strife* (1927) it was rejected. So he went on to tour the play with his own company, scoring a huge success with it and thereby extending the range of what theatrical Scottishness might be. Indeed when Glasgow Unity was founded in 1941 its successes included McLeish's *Gorbals Story* (1946) and Stewart's *Men Should Weep* (1947), about a woman with seven children and an unemployed husband living in a Gorbals tenement. But Unity, emerging from a gathering of leftist amateur groups in the city, had as precedent London Unity and shared its conception of its role and target audience. If its theatre work aimed to be natively Scottish, it was in a much more pronounced fashion also for the 'people', conceived, here, as 'working' people.

Unity folded in 1951. By that time there was in existence a theatre that has often been regarded as Scotland's real, if unofficial, national theatre. While Unity pitched itself at working people, the management board of the Citizens' Theatre consisted of Glasgow's artistic and corporate notables. Founded in 1943 by the dramatist James Bridie its aims, as McDonald says, were 'to present plays of didactic and artistic merit; secondly, to establish a stage for Scottish dramatists and actors; and third, to found a Scottish drama school' (McDonald 2004: 207). For its founding the Citizens' received money from the

London-based Council for the Encouragement of Music and the Arts (CEMA). Its emphasis on standards and education, alongside a generalised Scottishness, enabled it to be subsumed, without any rough-edged nationalism, into what was by then a British set of values.

But, back in the 1920s, what the developments in Scotland suggest is that, if the national theatre is, in part, a 'racial' theatre, this compromises its role as a central theatre. For when the Scots got close to establishing their own national theatre, it was as if something on the rim of one wheel started to become a hub of another. So, in reviewing those early years of the campaign for a national theatre from the distance of 1930, Barker came up with a rather different model for it. He suggested that a national theatre can be likened to a public corporation such as the BBC.

A people's theatre

The concept of the BBC was that it was public and British. This is not the language of 'private liberality' and 'Anglo-Saxon peoples'. The world had changed since then.

The major event that had intervened between Barker's first call for a national theatre in 1904 and his return to the topic in 1930 was the world war of 1914–18. The war was hugely destructive and traumatised many people. While it did not substantially change the basic economic organisation of the country, at its end a different language was being spoken about social and cultural issues. In 1904 the campaigners for a national theatre envisaged an institution which was ample, dignified and liberal … but not necessarily 'popular'.

That word was associated with an already existing theatre, the Old Vic on the south of the Thames, near Waterloo station, 'a People's Theatre in the broadest sense' (Marshall 1947: 136). The theatre had a moral mission in relation to the socially and economically deprived area around it. It specialised in playing grand opera and Shakespeare, but with low ticket prices the shows were done on the cheap. When the campaign for the national theatre began in earnest there were those who suggested that the Old Vic itself could be such a theatre, but their opponents noted that the work was not of high enough quality. There was perhaps too much emphasis on the diversity of the audience and not enough on the standards of the shows. While it was all too popular, there was not, it seems, enough art.

That said, the Vic was clearly different from the commercial managements, both in its social mission and its commitment to the classics. It was far from being the enemy envisaged by the national theatre campaign; indeed it was a potential ally. But the fact that the Edwardian campaigners didn't feel it was quite right as a national theatre indicates in itself the social and cultural bias which governed their thinking. At the end of the war, in 1918–19, this social bias had altered. From the late 1930s onwards the Vic company moved closer to being seen as a national company. Its work was backed by CEMA and then the Arts Council through the 1940s in an explicit attempt to sustain it as a company which did the classics, and possibly prepare it for National status. From 1963 onwards the theatre was the home of the formally established National Theatre company.

But the concern with theatre's relationship with the 'ordinary' people of the nation went well beyond the Vic. During the 1914–18 war, while commercial theatres cultivated audience taste for 'light' entertainment, others went out to meet the troops. Lena Ashwell, actress and theatre manager, organised expeditions to mainland Europe, taking to the troops repertoires that included Shakespeare and other classics. This was the model for the later Entertainments National Service Association, overseen by the producer Basil Dean, in the Second World War, though by then it was, symptomatically, state sponsored.

Ashwell's motivation came from a firm ideological commitment to keeping theatre art dignified, for the sake of preserving the Empire. Back in London in 1919 her 'Once A Week Players' did tours of the town halls of the London boroughs, offering art theatre to 'ordinary' people. For these 'ordinary' people seemed to be hungry for serious theatre. In his book on the campaign for a national theatre Geoffrey Whitworth tells a story of lecturing to the troops and then staying on to hear 'The Crayford Reading Circle' read a short play by Stanley Houghton. For Whitworth this experience crystallised his thoughts about what a national theatre might do. It would be something that had the spirit of the Crayford Reading Circle – and all such groups – at its heart. A national theatre would be 'a Community Theatre writ large'.

Whitworth on 'The Crayford Reading Circle'

… here were no actors in the proper sense of the word. They were not dressed for their parts. They had not even memorized them. With books in their hands, and with a minimum of action, they did not do much more than read the words of the play, pointing them with a few gestures. And yet, through the emotional sincerity of their interpretations, the characters came to life, and as I watched and listened, I felt that I was coming close to the fundamental quality of dramatic art in a way that I had never understood it before. Here was the art of theatre reduced to its simplest terms, yet in this very reduction triumphant. Devoid of grace, and of the simplest gadgets of stage appointment, the agonists on the platform found the right echo in the hearts of the audience. And they were in no way expressing *themselves*. They were denuding themselves of all the normal attributes of their selfhood, depending for the effect they made almost wholly on a microscopic rendering of the playwright's thought, achieving at the same time that unity between reader and audience whereby both reverberate in unison as a couple of tuning forks when one is struck. Thus they vindicated the existence of that common soul in which we live and move and have our being. And at Crayford this vindication was achieved for its own sake alone. Not for private gain, not even in the cause of charity, these players were simply following their own instincts, satisfying their own need. That was all they knew and all they needed to know. But in so doing they were satisfying also the need of the community. Givers and receivers were one.   (Whitworth 1951: 148–9)

Instead of throwing himself into a renewed campaign for a national theatre, Whitworth stepped sideways. In December 1918 he founded, as a private venture, what was to become known as the British Drama League (BDL). This was formally launched at a public meeting in June 1919, where Whitworth described its origin and argued that 'as this was a time when the art of theatre was moribund, the contrast between that deadness and the promise of vitality outside suggested a scheme whereby a theatrical revival on democratic lines might be stimulated'. Note the opposition to moribund – and commercialised – theatre now comes not from a 'centre' of leading people of the theatre but from a revival on 'democratic' lines. The scheme of the BDL was that it should 'include representatives of every interest involved – not artists only and not social workers only' (Whitworth 1951: 150).

The first conference of the BDL in August 1919 was, claims Whitworth, the first occasion at which were assembled amateur and professional theatre people, educationists, social workers and members of the public. The aim was to do something bigger than create a national theatre. The BDL wanted to reach into 'the small community, the village and the home'. Its first conference established two main objectives: 'A National Theatre policy adequate to the needs of the people'; 'A faculty of the Theatre at the Universities of the country, with the necessary colleges' (Whitworth 1951: 153, 156).

Recalling the history of the campaign, Whitworth listed the various names given to it: National Theatre, Exemplary Theatre, Ideal Theatre. To these he adds a new phrase – the 'amateur theatre' will provide the audience for a National Theatre. Here, now, we are no longer looking at the model of a centre and its ring of imitators. The centre is dependent on, and committed to, a wide amateur drama movement dispersed through the communities of *Britain* (see Amateurs).

While the BDL started its work, the formal campaign for a national theatre during the 1920s put pressure on various governments, seeking bequests of land on which to build. When a Labour government was elected in 1924 there was a concerted attempt to restart the campaign. In yet another parliamentary debate the Opposition asked whether anyone really cared about a national theatre, and whether it meant anything to those who were not an elite. Putting it in those terms was to recall the Edwardian situation – in a Britain where the divisions between poverty and wealth were still clearly marked. But outside Parliament, and indeed outside the national theatre campaign, the theatre activity of the nation was galvanised by new energy. For a young theatre worker at the time, Norman Marshall, the commercial theatre of London had been reduced to 'a dead level of mediocrity' by the 'timidity' of the theatre managers and the 'tyranny' of the Censor. The struggle against it led to exciting experimentation which, says Marshall, was at its height in 1925–6 (Marshall 1947: 13). It was this range of activity which anticipated the next major development.

A nationalised theatre

Charles Landstone, of the Arts Council, tells how in 1943 Robert Digby and friends from Colchester Repertory Company approached the Arts Council's predecessor, CEMA, with plans for a new building: 'it was one of those magnificent plans for a new England cherished all over the country at that time by people of all interests and in every walk of life' (Landstone 1953: 103). The request chimed with the BDL's proposal to the Prime Minister in 1942 for a 'Civic Theatre Scheme'. This argued that, in order for high-quality drama 'to be preserved for the benefit of all classes, and fairly distributed', the theatre should be supported by state aid (Whitworth 1951: 231–2). For, as the Minister of Labour, Ernest Bevin, said, theatre was a national institution which expressed the character of the 'ordinary' British people.

> In this mechanical age we look to the theatrical world to preserve the characteristics of our people – not merely national characteristics but (and this is what most appeals to me) local characteristics. In the British people there exist great divergencies of character which are endangered by the current tendency to uniformity, and I look forward, at the end of this great struggle, to the living theatre not only coming into its own as a means of livelihood, but to its becoming one of our great national institutions to convey to the peoples of the world the real character of the ordinary British people.   (Ernest Bevin, at the inaugural meeting of the Provincial Theatre Council, in Whitworth 1951: 232–3)

The plans for a new England came somewhere nearer to reality when, at the end of the Second World War, the Labour Party was elected, by a landslide, to government. This was the most left-wing of any Labour government, indeed in parts actually socialist, and its plans for a new England envisaged nationalisation of various industries. As Landstone says, there was a craze for nationalisation. This craze extended, among those on the left, to the theatre. In the spring 1947 issue of *New Theatre* its editor, Ted Willis, argued that 'a great national art like the British theatre is being cheapened and may be ruined for years to come, because its resources have been cornered by private interests'. Or, as the director André van Gyseghem put it later that year, in Britain 'theatre has become a place of speculation every bit as profitable as the stock exchange', with a consequence that there is little experimentation with dramatic form (van Gyseghem 1947: 13). Willis's solution was government intervention either directly or through the Arts Council in order to stop very long runs and prohibitive prices in theatres; to give powers to local authorities to build theatres; to convene a national conference of local authorities; and to convene a meeting of theatre organisations, which would include the Trades Union Congress (Willis 1947a: 2).

The campaign against private monopoly in the theatre moved fast in 1947. Beatrix Lehmann, president of the actors' union Equity, proposed state control to guarantee the right to work of all 'genuine' members of the profession and to raise 'artistic and economic standards' (Lehmann in Willis 1947b). J. B. Priestley and Basil Dean put their names to a scheme for a National Theatre Authority which would replace the Arts Council, form four national companies similar to that at the Vic and encourage the building of civic repertory theatres, 'as part of the public amenities and not as anybody's private property' (Priestley and Dean 1947: 12). From this followed the great British theatre conference in 1948, the 'Parliament of the British Theatre', which proposed abolition of censorship, establishment of Chairs of Drama in universities, better qualifications for teachers of drama, drama education for adults, state aid for students of theatre and the founding of an experimental children's theatre centre. The same year the Local Government Bill empowered local authorities to provide theatre.

Through all this there was debate as to the nature and function of theatre as art. The proposition was that it is the job of theatre to take sides in politics, that 'always the best theatre has been a weapon' (D'Usseau 1947: 12), that art can never be neutral (Hamilton 1947: 2). That concept of theatre as political weapon reaches into the mid-1920s, when Miles Malleson argued that the dramatic societies of the Independent Labour Party had a mission to do 'propaganda' in order to show the 'facts' of society to those living in misery. This ILP initiative would create the break with a theatre that 'up to now … has been entirely capitalist run' (Malleson 1925: 4, 12). With the title 'The Theatre is our Weapon!' van Gyseghem prefaced a wartime publication of two one-act plays with the call for theatre to whip up support for 'our Soviet Allies' (van Gyseghem n.d.: 2). In 1941–2 Soviet resistance to the Nazis was seen, on the left, as drawing strength from the mobilisation of art and culture, with actors touring into battle zones (Settle 1941). This logic of theatre in warfare pointed towards new organisation. The WEA educationalist, A. J. J. Ratcliff, spurned amateur shows for 'frivolous cliques' and called for 'the drama of the profession-als and the services, and always of the schools' (1941: 10). In the Soviet Union theatre was relevant and mobilised because, as van Gyseghem said, it was, 'for the first time since the days of the ancient Greeks', state-controlled: 'The Soviet regime saw the theatre as an important educational and recreational stimulus to their new world, and it had a place in each successive Five Year Plan as important as education or heavy industry' (1947: 13). In Britain, immediately post-war, there was an effort to involve organised labour in theatre produc-tion. In 1946 the Scala theatre in London hosted a series of plays sponsored by trades unions. It was, as Willis put it, an attempt to establish a 'cultural Left' in general, and, specifically, a theatre that had a 'social purpose' and a 'mass audi-ence' (Willis 1946: 18, 20). Or, as others put it, 'propaganda'.

> What place should theatre occupy in our society?
> Has the State any responsibility in this matter?
> Is the theatre an art or an industry?
> Would any form of State aid be of service to it in either capacity?
> (from van Gyseghem 1947: 17)

The 'weapon' debate assumed broad cultural engagement in a divided soci-ety. While this differed somewhat from the positioning of Archer and Barker it nevertheless gave a new twist to their model of a distributed theatre which was national because it included a chain of venues across the nation. In the years 1945–52 the Arts Council oversaw directly managed and associate companies in Coventry, Nottingham, Ipswich, Colchester, Chesterfield. This then provided a base for London and big-city theatre, which in the early 1950s was attracting an audience 30 per cent larger than in the 1930s. The ultimate plan, according to Landstone, was that these companies should be linked to 'one great cen-tral creative theatre in London' (Landstone 1953:107). But the Arts Council's vision and role were not entirely adequate to the job. Nor was the Soviet model workable. The way to national theatre lay through local authorities.

For this version of national theatre the main ideologue was J. B. Priestley. His 1946 book *Theatre Outlook* (published 1947) was designed to 'take its place among works considering the problems of our democracy'. It was written, he says, because in the post-war world 'this particular art meant far more now than it could have done fifty years ago'. His model for national theatre is a 'pyramid' with, at its top, 'as a shining example and inspiration to the whole theatre of the nation … several companies of the highest possible excellence … Each of these companies should be a public corporation, financed in the first place, and afterwards guaranteed against loss, by the State' (Priestley 1947: 13, 70, 54–5: my ellipses).

For Priestley civic theatres 'should be part of a national scheme' and backed by, among others, the Ministry of Education, through the Arts Council, and local educational authorities: 'Each of them should be a public and not a private enterprise, a truly civic affair', 'rooted in civic life'. While the little theatre may be a gesture of defiance against commerce, the civic theatre should be big. It gains power by being 'a properly financed public corporation, with some civic authority behind it' (Priestley 1947: 60).

These theatres should have drama schools attached to them, from which touring companies will visit smaller towns. Throughout the smallest outfit is linked through to 'higher levels' of the art. It is this mutual responsibility and interconnectedness which give strength, says Priestley, to the current Soviet theatre. So, 'clear away all the silly nonsense, the muddle, the gambling, the insecurity, the exhibitionism, the cheap inflated egos, and start with a clean bare stage, solidly set in the community and linked with hundreds of similar sensible organisations, a stage on which something good and true and glowing can be created' (Priestley 1947: 53).

The interest in dissemination of culture through civic mechanisms connected with a vigorous programme of regional theatre building between 1950 and around 1970. Within the context of making theatre public, if not nationalised, these regional theatres declared their purpose in their bricks-and-mortar – or more likely concrete – form. As the architect Richard Leacroft put it in 1947, 'The theatre is one of the few places where a natural communal spirit is aroused' (Leacroft 1947: 18).

By the mid-1970s, however, these very same regional 'reps' came to be regarded not as the buzzing point of artistic energy but of a theatre comfortably settled into corporation aspic. For these regional developments were indeed still subject to the judgements of those who, while they may have 'understood theatre', knew what they liked and liked only what they knew. It was both a contradiction of – and yet, somehow, an extension of – Ernest Bevin's belief that theatre was a way of preserving the 'local characteristics' of 'our' people, sustaining the diversity of the nation in all its richness. By the mid-1970s there was little that was particularly 'local' about the art being seen in the regional reps. What was arguably local, however, was the resistance to practices which were unknown or experimental.

That problem was written deep into the heart of the project from the mid-1940s onwards. While it didn't have at its centre a tight Edwardian network, it still conceived of cultural production being led by an artistic, or more likely political, vanguard. This began to unravel when the points of cultural energy were materially distributed. The centre came into tension with that which, in several different ways, was de-centred. The tension became very obvious when the national theatre vision became, so to speak, a concrete reality.

A concrete building

The official National Theatre building opened in October 1976, at a site on the south bank of the Thames very near the spot suggested by Granville Barker. That, however, was probably its only substantial link with the past.

The story of how the building got there is a complicated account of factions arguing through committees, of sites identified and then relinquished. The nearest thing to a national company was based at the Old Vic. In the 1940s it was principally run by actors, Laurence Olivier and Ralph Richardson, but, as the finances looked like going into deficit, they were sacked and a new manager imposed. With the formation of a properly National company Olivier returned to front it, but in preparation for entry to the new building a 'co-director' was appointed at the beginning of 1973 to work alongside him. This was the younger Peter Hall, from the Royal Shakespeare Company. On the eve of his appointment Hall discriminated, in *Theatre Quarterly*, between '*theatre*, which is pure … and *theatricality*, which is technique, trick, custom, that which is easily accepted' (Hall 1972: 7). Behind the prose seems to hover the contrast with Olivier. He was an actor, with famous technique, and, according to Elsom and Tomalin, while no manager, he operated as a paterfamilias in the National company. Hall was a director who embraced management with energy and decisiveness; on his management team he had no actors. Coming from the RSC, he was associated with a company that had developed a radical image in the 1960s and was characterised as full of 'university men', in the eyes of the traditional theatre world. When the power shifted decisively towards Hall, it seemed – in the narrative promulgated by Elsom and Tomalin two years later – that an older mode of theatre was being painfully eased out.

Hall identified himself with change and vitality, proposing that 'the theatre is a living element of our community'. What sort of 'element' it was became clear when he repudiated the 'idea of Granville-Barker and Shaw, who saw the National Theatre as an adjunct of further education, as a kind of library with a repertory of forty plays'. This was consistent with Hall's rejection of the authority of the writer (Hall 1972: 7). Rather than education or library, the National should open its doors 'to the fringe, to musicians, to poets, to the young with their experiments'. For the theatre, he averred in 1973, is 'a small part of our democracy' (in Elsom and Tomalin 1978: 251, 255). To encourage the young and the democratic he commissioned the National's first new play from a rising 'fringe' dramatist, Howard Brenton, to be directed by David Hare, himself associated with the 'experimental' company Joint Stock.

In this new play, *Weapons of Happiness* (1976), two people ride on stage on a motorbike. A young communist, Janice, has as her pillion Joseph Frank, a Czech socialist who has met Stalin. It is London's dockland.

> FRANK: What is this place?
> *Janice gets off the motorcycle.*
> JANICE: Wharf. Before they knocked it down.
> *She shouts into the dark.*
>   Ken! Liz!
> *A pause.*
>   Played here when we were kids. Mothers and fathers.
>   Vietcong meet the Daleks. First boy I fucked was here.
> *Janice laughs.*
>   That's the River over there. Low tide. Tell by the smell. Sh!
> *A slight pause.*
>   Hear the rats?
> *A slight pause.*
>   Smashing London apart, you see. Ruins and holes.   (Brenton
>   1976: 33)

Brenton and his director, echoing Peter Hall, felt that the new National Theatre was all too narrowly middle-class, or, to use the favourite word of the 1970s, 'bourgeois', in its culture and interests. It excluded the sorts of people who lived in the poorer areas adjacent to the theatre. So by way of opening the doors Brenton put on stage what was seen at the time as the reality of Britain, with the derelict docks a sign of past glory gone to rust. It was, perhaps, now less important to stage a young communist than a deep decay.

This decay penetrates the class structure of contemporary Britain. At the bottom end are the workers in a factory that makes crisps. The choice of product is typical of its time: while there were still factories in the mid-1970s, there was a sense that Britain no longer had a genuinely productive industry able, for example, to build machinery on a large scale. When the factory workers enter in scene 2 they are playing cricket in the yard. Their dialogue is barbed with references to which a middle-aged middle-class audience would be sensitive: references for people who listened to Dylan ten years ago, people that their children think of as old, people anxious about ageing. And then the fictional middle-class characters are made difficult to relate to: the factory owner vicious, drunken, maritally unfaithful; his wife aggressively tough.

These aspects of the play are typical of drama of this period. But, in making a 'play for our time', Brenton conceived it as 'Jacobean' and 'epic'. This was made possible, almost uniquely, by the facilities of the National. While the Lyttleton stage was one onto which a motorcycle could be ridden, the technical kit allowed for a scene such as that where Josef Frank meets Stalin. He and his friend are stopped in a wintry street and taken to Stalin 'for a drink':

> *A choir sings. The portrait of Stalin, huge, glows through the snow. Stalin advances, smiling, smoking a pipe. A Waiter walks at his side, a step behind, carrying a tray set with glasses and a vodka bottle. Behind Stalin a crowd of men in a long line, all in dark suits and smiling and carrying vodka glasses, advances. Stalin stops. The entourage stops. The snow ceases to fall. A silence. Stalin takes a glass from the Waiter's tray. He knocks the drink back in one. The entourage knock their drinks back in one. A silence.*
>
> STALIN: The Union of Soviet Socialist Republics.
> *A pause.*
>   Has a very great.
> *A pause.*
>   Ice-hockey team.
> *Stalin laughs. Everyone laughs. A silence. Stalin and his entourage as a tableau. It fades as Josef Frank speaks aside.*
> FRANK: What do you expect me to see when I look in that mirror? The empty world. Like a room from which all human beings have fled. Leaving filth upon the walls, a few torn newspapers upon the floor. Oh we had the world to remake. The universe in our hands, history was water in a cup, we had only to drink. Who could have, then, imagined this dereliction.   (Brenton 1976: 31)

The technical apparatus of the spectacle – the production and dissolution of the tableau, the orchestration of a large sound – is simultaneously required, in physical terms, yet labelled as fiction in narrative terms. The reality for the audience is Josef staring out at them, speaking of failed dreams and lost history. But there is also the actual excitement of big stage effect.

The bigger the spectacle of Stalin, the more powerful the impact of historical irony. And this spectacle was brought into being by the resources of the National's technical facility. That's to say, the savagely ironic sense of decay and loss could best be produced, not in poor, but in well-equipped, wealthy, conditions. Brenton's desire to show the National's audience an excluded class was combined with a desire to use its rich resources. This combination leads to the sort of theatre work which became characteristic of subsidised 'serious' drama of the mid to late 1970s. That theatre work specialised in spectacle as irony, where scenes of social and industrial decay were juxtaposed with large – impossible – fantasies of grandeur. It produces an overall image of human ineptitude caught up into a wider and always ironising frame.

The National in the mid-1970s lent itself to this imaginary. Its position in London could be problematised; its facilities allowed for most demands of spectacle; its apparently middle-class audience could be challenged. At this period the National, together with city reps across England, generated a particular theatre for the nation. It was a story of decay, big effects and help-lessness.

Although Brenton celebrated his entry to the National as a sort of fringe writer's putsch, it was a putsch at an open door. He and his work fitted very nicely into the scenario whereby the ageing actor-manager was ousted from the national limelight by the modern director-manager. *Weapons*, with its group scenes and big effects, is much more of a director's than an actor's vehicle – and it fully intended, in those effects, to capitalise – if that is the word – on the National's expensive resources. For expensive they were. In 1976 the theatre received 25 per cent of the Arts Council's annual budget. This would later rise as the Arts Council struggled adequately to fund what was turning out to be, in its size and complexity, an expensive machine. Seeing its disproportionate share of national funding, some began to ask how national the National was.

If his entry onto the big stage seemed a necessary step for the radical fringe dramatist, that is not how it was seen by political radicals. A press release from the Independent Theatre Council (ITC) / The Actor's Theatre Company (TACT) Joint Action Committee in 1976 argued that there were really two national theatres:

> One stands on the South Bank of the Thames, cost £16 million to build, is subsidised to the tune of £2 million per year and will eventually employ 500 staff and just over 100 actors. The other exists in workshops, community centres and short-life premises all over the country. It performs everywhere and anywhere from parks and art galleries to schools, trades union halls and arts centres, taking theatre to people where they want to see it.   (in Itzin 1980: 268)

Quite apart from eating up a large chunk of available arts funding it seemed that the National was doing little for the artform itself: as a reviewer in *Time Out* put it, it 'shows no capacity whatever for genuinely transforming the the-atregoing practices of the masses, nor does it seem interested in promoting new or experimental talent' (in Itzin 1980: 271). Within two years of the official opening the Arts Council launched an enquiry into what the National Theatre was doing with its money.

But that enquiry is fairly peripheral to the major development of modern British theatre. As too, perhaps, is the National Theatre itself. For the irony is this: once the National Theatre campaign reached its goal, as soon as the company entered a building, the building became the problem. As a building it was a static showpiece gobbling up money. Companies, on the other hand, were flexible, dynamic, could play to different people in different places. That ITC/TACT press release neatly put its finger on the issue: when the National building went up, thinking about theatre had changed, its practices were culturally dispersed, people engaged in new ways. When Hall imagined he could simply open the doors to admit them to the National, he showed his distance from the attitude to culture and society that was really emerging at this period. For the concept of an identifiable point of cultural leadership, so important to the modernist Edwardian educators, was giving way to an emphasis on networks, fluidity, transitory gatherings, dispersed points of energy.

The greatest impact of the National Theatre on the development of British theatre may perhaps have to do with the fact that it gave new intensity to a rumbling question, namely: does theatre actually need a building?

Buildings and their people

Actor-managers

Archer and Barker's scheme for a national theatre is prefaced by a list of supporters. Heading the list is Henry Irving. Having that name there was something of a coup. For Irving represented a form of theatre which was the antithesis of that proposed by Archer and Barker. He specialised in spectacular pictorial productions encrusted with ornament and detail. At the centre of the picture was Irving himself, not simply the star of the production but also its originator. He was, in short, an actor-manager.

The early twentieth-century actor-manager had two sorts of authority, both within the world of the play, as its lead part and star, and over the theatrical apparatus that put on the play, as its manager. Irving was one of a group of actor-managers that included Charles Wyndham who owned three theatres, Cyril Maude who did comedy at the Haymarket, and Irving's successor in spectacular theatre Beerbohm Tree at His Majesty's Theatre. Each actor-manager had a specialist characteristic – or, more properly, trademark – which shaped their image as a celebrity. This image was reinforced, much as it is in the movies, by the shows they elected to perform. For example George Alexander at St James's Theatre was famously fashionable. He maintained his stage stylishness outside the theatre, and insisted that his company did likewise, issuing rules as to their standards of dress offstage.

While the actor-manager Irving was the first knight of the theatre, Archer, Barker and their regular supporters could be characterised as upper-middle-class intellectuals, some of whom were not theatre professionals in any sense. The newer sorts of theatre were championed by these people, most famously through the agency of the Stage Society. The first meeting of the Society, in the middle of 1899, was organised by Frederick Whelen, who worked in the Bank of England. Others who attended included Janet Achurch, famous for pioneering the staging of Ibsen in England, Grant Richards, the publisher of Shaw's *Plays Pleasant and Unpleasant*, and the author William Sharp, who wrote under the name Fiona Macleod. By its 1904–5 season the Society had 1,194 members; the entrance fee and the subscription fee were each one guinea (£1.05).

Stage Society principles

To promote and encourage Dramatic Art; to serve as an Experimental Theatre; to provide such an organisation as shall be capable of dealing with any opportunities that may present themselves or be created for the establishment in London of a Repertory Theatre; and to establish and undertake the management and control of such a theatre.

We should note that Tree himself supported new drama, and had staged Ibsen, but on the whole there was a basic opposition: on the one hand, an established arrangement of actor-managers inherited from the late nineteenth century; on the other, a much smaller, and perhaps more coherent, group of intellectuals who were arguing for change. The shape of this opposition is characteristic of the broad cultural movement that is modernism.

By the mid-1970s those intellectuals were dominant. When Britain eventually got its National Theatre building, the last great actor-manager, Laurence Olivier, was superseded.

Owners

Innovative and articulate as Archer, Barker and the members of the Stage Society were, it was not their opposition which ultimately saw off the actor-managers.

The demise of the actor-manager and the main change in the organisation of theatres were brought about by developments in ownership. The year after the plans for a national theatre were privately circulated, Horace Edward Moss was knighted and Irving died. Moss, as much as Barker, was a new face of theatre. By the time he was knighted he owned a string of theatres in major cities across the country. The first notably successful venture had been in Newcastle in 1884 with the opening of the Gaiety Variety Theatre, and thereafter more acquisitions followed in Newcastle (1890), Edinburgh (1892), Birmingham (1893), Sheffield (1895), Liverpool (1896), Glasgow (1897), Hull (1897), Nottingham (1898), Leeds (1898), Bradford (1899). Moss gave brand identity to his string of theatres by calling them all the same name – Empire (unless there already existed an Empire in the town, as at Hull). He also gave them a deliberately exotic architectural style and interior decoration, favouring the 'Moorish' or oriental, produced for him most often by the architect Frank Matcham. The look of the theatre was part of the selling-point: at the opening in Edinburgh before the curtain went up the house lights were put on full – to display the auditorium. The theatre was itself part of the show. And what these theatres expressed, in their rich and exuberant decoration, in their 'twice-nightly' variety programmes and in their large-capacity houses holding anything between 1,750 and 3,000 people, was deliberate and confident plenty.

When most of the exotic new theatres opened, older theatres were demolished or closed. With his competitors, however, Moss formed alliances – with Richard Thornton in Newcastle and later, more famously, Oswald Stoll in Nottingham. By these means Moss established one of the most powerful theatrical organisations ever, and in 1899 the empire arrived in London. Empire Palaces appeared in New Cross (1899), Stratford (1902) and Finsbury Park (1910) – not in the heartland of London's theatre scene but instead opening up the suburbs. The empire expanded significantly in 1942 when Prince Littler became chairman, for Littler was already chairman of Stoll Theatres. By the early 1950s Prince Littler Consolidated Trust controlled over 50 per cent of the seats in the West End (Rebellato 1999: 54). Later, as theatregoing habits changed, a number of theatres eventually closed, but a relic of the empire's approach to theatre entertainment lived on in the London Palladium.

The Moss Empires specialised in 'variety'. In the licensing arrangements controlled by the London County Council theatres, music halls and theatres of variety were distinguished from concert halls, dancing rooms and other places of entertainment. While smoking was permitted in a variety theatre, stage plays were not. The legal boundaries were tested in the matter of the 'sketch', which offered speaking on stage. In 1905 the rival groups of managers came to a compromise on numbers and lengths of sketches, together with a ban in variety houses on any stage play licensed within fifteen years. The ban was invoked later that year when the licence of the Oxford Music Hall was opposed by the Suburban Theatre Managers' Association because the Oxford did a stage play (details from Hunt 1906).

Variety, though, was on the ascendant. As an alternative perhaps to the horrors of war, audiences watched shows such as *Chu Chin Chow* (1916) and *The Maid of the Mountains* (1916), feeding a dynamic growth of the revue and musical which strengthened the grip of the commercial owners and managements. It brought into being a new power base of entrepreneurs who specialised in serving up what one of their leading figures, George Edwardes, called 'harmless entertainment' (Howe 1910: 14) – musical comedy. From here, all the way through the century, 'harmless' entertainment was to prove profitable entertainment and 'musicals' in particular were to be the lucrative form for entrepreneurs, achieving in the Thatcherite 1980s the globally sellable product developed most famously by Cameron Mackintosh.

Alongside musical comedy, American capital was pouring into London. Indeed Granville Barker was only able to stage his experimental season in 1910 through the patronage of an American, Charles Frohman. The tense Edwardian relationship between commercialism and emergent, but more or less powerless, champions of serious 'art' seems to inhabit at least one play of the period, Elizabeth Baker's *The Price of Thomas Scott*, done by Annie Horniman's company at the Gaiety Theatre, Manchester in 1913.

Baker had come to fame with her stridently realistic – as contemporaries saw it – play about middling clerks and marriage, *Chains*. Horniman's company was an example of successful repertory programming, the model recommended by those embattled with commercialism. In the play, Thomas Scott is a draper whose shop is failing economically. He is a man of profound religious faith, opposed to drinking, dancing and theatre. He wants the best for his children and is desperate to sell the shop to release them all from their hard-pressed circumstances. Chance comes his way with an offer from Courtney's Halls, an entertainment company that would turn the shop into a dance hall. Once Thomas realises the nature of this prospective buyer, and what would happen to the shop, he refuses to sell. His daughter, trapped in the business, had been desperate for a sale. In the event of her father's refusal, disappointed as she is, she admires his pride.

The first description of Courtney's Halls catches the sense of a fast developing chain of profit-making entertainment venues: 'We charge one shilling or two shillings, according to neighbourhood. It pays, I can tell you. One of our chaps was over this way the other week and he came back and says: Strike oil over West' (Baker 1913: 47). Wicksteed, who is proposing the idea, is an old friend who has already left the locality. Alongside him Thomas, with his opposition to dancing, looks old-fashioned and stuck in his ways. The play has Wicksteed clearly set out the commercial logic for selling up, together with suggesting ethical compromises. It's both financially logical and yet slippery. The dramatic energy here is given to Wicksteed, who does most of the talking, while Thomas says less and indeed in one pause stands alone, thinking. The logic, dynamism and perhaps inevitability are with the commercial enterprise, the deep but difficult seriousness belongs to the failing shopkeeper.

In a climactic scene in Act 3 Thomas Scott refuses Wicksteed's offer on religious grounds. Wicksteed says Scott is acting on 'prejudice':

> you are throwing away an opportunity of setting your wife free from the drudgery of a business that is going to pieces; you are tying that fine girl of yours up in a little back room like this; you are keeping your boy from a career which he shows himself fitted for.

Against this destructive 'prejudice' he places 'progress' and broadmindedness, for 'Times have changed since you and I were Sunday school teachers together' (Baker 1913: 78, 79).

The audience at the Manchester Gaiety may have had little problem rejecting Wicksteed's logic because of its links with the spreading commercialism of entertainment. But Thomas's resistance is also rather difficult to take, because he is opposed to theatre – and the audience at the Gaiety is, well, an audience at the theatre. The apparently absent position is that of a resistance to commercialisation coupled with a belief in the usefulness of serious – as opposed to entertainment – theatre. That would be the minority position of those arguing for a national theatre.

And at one moment the play does seem to articulate, albeit metaphorically, that position. Annie is showing her parents a hat she has made. Putting aside with contempt an elaborate creation such as most customers demand, she holds up *'with exultation'* the *'smart hat'* which is the sort of thing she really wants to make: '*Mrs. Scott sits petrified with astonishment. Scott stares.*' He says he doesn't like it. Annie, '*with a little gesture of defiance, puts it on.*' Her father orders her: 'It's not a fit hat for you to wear' (Baker 1913: 40–1). Clearly not an ornate hat, there is nevertheless something deeply wrong with it. It is neither properly submissive nor inappropriately ornamental. It is simply 'smart'. Annie, demonstrating her defiance in it, is occupying a space somewhere between her father's fundamentalism and her customers' vulgar tastelessness. It amounts to a performance that is somehow inappropriate without being obviously unnecessary, tasteful yet somehow aggressive. Annie is a craftswoman who knows her own skill and judgement. She, like the makers of the new drama, refuses both anti-theatricality and commerce.

In opposition to new drama, as later events show, those two latter positions slide together. In the mid-1960s an owner, Emile Littler, joined forces with a representative of the theatre ticketing agencies, Peter Cadbury, to mount a campaign against Dirty Plays. Governed by a concept of 'family entertainment', the ticketing agencies undertook to assure their punters about suitability. Both Littler and Cadbury thus argued that Dirty Plays were bad for theatre because they alienated audiences (Jones 1971). The sort of things they had in mind were Orton's *Entertaining Mr Sloane* and Rudkin's *Afore Night Come*, both new plays. Meanwhile, on the stages run by the old, and powerful, company of H. M. Tennent Ltd there were language and sex a good deal more explicit than anything in Orton or Rudkin. But Tennents were a vehicle for a figure who turned out to be as powerful as any owner, the manager Hugh 'Binkie' Beaumont.

Managers

The relationship between actor-managers, owners and managers was described, cynically, in 1908 by Borsa. Noting that 'proprietor-managers' often owned restaurants and hotels, he called them '*restaurateur*-proprietors' since they 'adopt for the stage the standards that prevail in their kitchens', giving audiences what they want. The manager then combines 'the artistic pretensions' of the actor-manager with 'the culinary crudeness' of the '*restaurateur*-proprietors' (Borsa 1908:5). By 1946 relations between producing managers and owners were, as Priestley saw it, very one-sided: while managers guaranteed a weekly minimum that covered all the owner's charges and expenses, they also bore the cost of salaries and royalties (1947: 29–30). The income to the theatre-owner (as opposed to the producing manager) for one week of a play was £1,300, where a ticket price at a provincial theatre in 1944 was seven shillings and sixpence (37.5p), recently raised from six shillings.

H. M. Tennent were famous for glamorous productions, costume designs in the height of Paris fashion, the production of 'stars' and an apparent stranglehold on West End theatre. Beaumont the manager was hugely successful and powerful, and reviled as the epitome of the coterie – and to make it worse the homosexual coterie – that appeared to run the commercial theatre. Some of his deals were dodgy, as when he invented an offshoot company which supposedly did productions that had an educational purpose and thereby neatly avoided Entertainment Tax. But there was no actual corruption here and the profits allowed Tennents to run the Lyric Hammersmith – in what was then a working-class district – as an experimental theatre. Indeed, the left-wing *Theatre Newsletter* praised Tennents as a management company. Similarly, in

1971, in the heat of the explosion of 'alternative' theatre, *Theatre Quarterly* noted that the Society of West End Managers was an employers' organisation that had strict rules about proper payment of actors, as opposed to 'the clubs and cellars of the avant-garde' (Jones 1971).

And Beaumont's power also allowed artistic risk. He achieved general popularity for the twee verse plays of Christopher Fry, by use of star casting; but much more importantly he introduced to London some of the heavyweight American drama, Miller's *Death of a Salesman* and – more scandalously – Williams's *Streetcar Named Desire*. It is one of those delightful ironies that the commercial homosexual introduced to London a play that showed the alienations of commerce and one that unpicked the structural insecurities of gender.

Neither play would probably have been promoted by the woman described by Tyrone Guthrie as 'the most important theatrical manager in Britain, probably in the world' (Guthrie 1961: 193). Lilian Baylis was manager of the Old Vic. She succeeded her aunt, Emma Cons, who had bought the Old Vic and turned it into an alcohol-free 'music hall'. While Cons was principally occupied with social reforms, Baylis transformed the Vic artistically. She convinced, or otherwise browbeat, her governing body to replace lectures and recitals with grand opera. She founded the Vic's Shakespeare company in 1914. Then she bought the dilapidated Sadler's Wells theatre and reopened it in 1930, launching from there a third Vic company, doing ballet under the control of Edris Stannus, otherwise known as Ninette de Valois. This commitment to art was in the face of financial difficulty: the Vic was obliged by its charter to set ticket prices affordable by artisans. There was no lucrative income to offset costs. Yet the Vic came to be regarded as an artistic leader.

The career of Baylis suggests that there is something more to management than returning profits to the theatre or company. She had a view of what theatre should be doing in society – the audiences it should play to, the repertoire it should offer. Another manager who similarly used the role in order to define theatre's place was George Devine, who became manager of the new English Stage Company in 1955. He brought to the theatre what Wardle claims was a new method in Britain 'of running his theatre with a small technical and artistic team', with multi-skilling on the technical side (Wardle 1978: 174). Devine and his co-director, Tony Richardson, went on to write a prospectus, on a model derived from Devine's previous colleague at the Old Vic Theatre School, Saint-Denis, for a new sort of theatre (1963). This would have a permanent company, a permanent setting, an audience-building organisation, training for writers and actors. From this, they believed, a modern style would emerge. But not, of course, just an artistic style: the theatrical director fuses with company-manager.

The bringing together of those two roles is important, for the manager deals with a range of interests that bear on the work of the theatre. By the 1970s it was customary even in the subsidised theatre for the theatre manager to have control over the art (Gooch 1984: 29). In this situation aesthetic choices are taken by someone who knows the importance of the board and the funders. As the twentieth century went on more interested parties emerged: civic authorities, state and private sponsors, educational bodies – all that range of folk that are gathered up in the cover-all word 'stakeholders'. This diffusion of interests is culturally characteristic of the later twentieth century. For, as many have noted, the emphasis on monolithic hierarchies of structure and thought gave way to an emphasis on networks and diversity. Management of theatre is management of theatre's social connections.

Buildings

The Edwardian age's sense of itself as one of the great periods of theatre was made manifest in bricks and mortar. In the period from the 1860s to 1914 there was huge, if not unprecedented, activity in the building of new theatres. The growth of Moss's empire is but one example of this. Larger, conspicuously elaborate, and with modern facilities such as electricity, the buildings had in common with their predecessors the arrangement of an end-on stage, a proscenium arch and an auditorium in levels. Borsa, writing in 1908, said that in London there were fifty-nine theatres, sixty-one music halls and 630 other halls.

This activity was prompted and made possible by two main economic drivers: the expansion and remodelling of cities, especially London, which gave opportunities for property speculation; and the activities of emergent theatre entrepreneurs who saw that theatre could be exploited for profit. In the first case the theatre now called the Gielgud, on Shaftesbury Avenue, London, sits in an area opened up in the mid-1880s. It was originally designed in 1906, as the Hicks theatre, in part of an architecturally coherent block which included the Queen's Theatre (1908). Similarly the Aldwych theatre was designed in symmetry with the Strand theatre – originally called the Waldorf – in 1905. Each theatre, together with the hotel that was designed between them – the Waldorf Hotel – was part of a scheme to develop a great curved highway (Aldwych/Kingsway) which would be appropriate to the new monumental London, as capital of Empire.

By contrast the activities of the theatre entrepreneurs were driven less by visionary planning than by a desire to capture increased audience numbers. Their theatres thus opened wherever demographic opportunity offered itself.

The Hackney Empire was built for Oswald Stoll's theatre chain in 1901; the Hippodrome was built in 1900 for Edward Moss – as a venue, initially, for circuses. Both of these were designed by Frank Matcham, whose most famous work is the London Coliseum (1904), commissioned by Stoll as the showpiece of his theatre enterprise, and designed deliberately as a variety theatre to capture a new West End audience. And note: if the Edwardian period was that of the theatre entrepreneur, so too it was the great age of the theatre architect. Alongside Matcham was the figure of W. G. R. Sprague, who designed all the other theatres mentioned above – Hicks, Queen's, Aldwych, Strand.

While the entrepreneurs searched for new audiences the architects learnt how to deliver structures which were both flexible and – in their ornament – entertaining. Outside London the major towns and cities already had established civic theatres, often dating from the eighteenth century. The impact of the entrepreneurs and their architects was perhaps most felt in a new demographic area, the suburbs and hinterlands. Some indeed specialised in the suburbs: Herbert Campbell built the Granville (Walham Green), Camberwell Palace and the Grand Theatre of Varieties in Clapham (1900, designed by Woodrow). A Hippodrome went up in Camden in 1901 (designed by Sprague), Middlesbrough got one in 1903, and Golders Green in 1913.

Many of the new buildings were being designed explicitly as variety theatres, with the capacity also to incorporate circus. The drive to maximise audiences required a free-ranging, capacious concept of theatrical entertainment, and one that went well beyond servicing the scripted play. But this commercially driven flexibility pushed forward to associate theatre even with non-theatrical activities. Sometime around 1911 two multi-purpose halls were built in Stepney, one above another, with the upper one probably designed to double up as a cinema. In the same year Margate got its Winter Gardens, in which an amphitheatre blurred with a dance and concert hall. In this arrangement it is uncertain that theatre is the main attraction. Indeed in Nuneaton in 1909 the building was expressly designed as a skating-rink, with an added-on possibility of accommodating variety performances. By 1912 it was known as a Picturedrome.

Just as with the external appearance of the theatre, the interior architecture defines the relationship between actor and audience, and thus how performance is to be both viewed and done. Thus, Marshall notes, at the Cambridge Festival Theatre of 1926 'conventional realistic production was almost impossible':

> It was difficult to find any definite point at which the stage ended and the auditorium began. There was no proscenium. The width of the stage was the width of the auditorium itself. The broad forestage merging into

a great fan-shaped flight of steps extending to the feet of the audience sitting in the front row abolished any boundary line between actor and audience.   (Marshall 1947: 54)

At the Festival Terence Gray had created a theatre that, almost uniquely in Britain in the late 1920s, engaged with European experiments in Expressionist and anti-naturalist staging. He had developed a combination of block-like scenic modules and lighting that could, very speedily and by abstract means, suggest different atmospheres and settings.

But the most consistent form of reaction against – and attempt to prevent – picture-frame spectacle drew on a home-grown 'pre-realist' mode. William Poel's archaeological reconstructions of Shakespearean platform staging in the 1890s were known by Tyrone Guthrie, who had also worked at the Festival Theatre in 1929–30. Doing *Hamlet* at Elsinore in 1937, Guthrie found himself needing to turn to the Poel model. For bad weather compelled the company to abandon their outdoor performance. They moved into a hotel ballroom: 'There was no stage; but we would play in the middle of the hall with the audience seated all around as in a circus. The phrase hadn't yet been invented, but this would be theatre in the round' (Guthrie 1961: 170). The experience confirmed Guthrie in his direction, and led to his famous production of *The Three Estates* at Edinburgh in 1948.

Guthrie on *Three Estates* at Edinburgh Assembly Hall in 1948

The audience did not look at the actors against a background of pictorial and illusionary scenery. Seated around three sides of the stage, they focused upon the actors in the brightly lit acting area, but the background was of the dimly lit rows of people similarly focused on the actors. All the time, but unemphatically and by inference, each member of the audience was being ceaselessly reminded that he was not lost in an illusion, was not at the Court of King Humanitie in sixteenth-century Scotland, but was, in fact a member of a large audience, taking part, 'assisting' as the French very properly express it, in a performance, a participant in a ritual.   (Guthrie 1961: 279)

It also led to experiments in theatre design, where Guthrie pioneered his 'open stage'. It was this sort of staging that he described on a visit to Sheffield as they were considering plans for a new theatre in the mid-1960s. The theatre director, Colin George, wanted something which would have the same effect as work done outside theatres for children in schools. This aim, given substance by the open stage model, led to the Crucible Theatre. Very much a product of its time, the Crucible is a theatre building that embodied the contemporary turn against theatre buildings.

But its architects did not reference a perhaps more radical experiment that had already taken place. In 1955 Stephen Joseph founded Studio Theatre Ltd. His intention, like that of the contemporary English Stage Company, was to revitalise theatre. But, whereas the ESC at the Royal Court saw the answer in a renewed emphasis on writing for the stage, Joseph wanted to change the physical form of theatre. His first experiment was in the Vernon Road Library in Scarborough where, using rostra funded by the Pilgrim Trust, he turned a square room into a theatre with an audience of 250 sitting around an acting area. This was the model which then shaped the Victoria Theatre in Stoke-on-Trent (1962) and then Michael Elliot's Royal Exchange in Manchester in 1976. It also paved the way for experiments which make the audience–performance relationship even more flexible, by removing most of the seating. Promenade theatre encourages audiences to move around the space, adopting their own position in relation to the changing location of performance. At the same time it extends and reinforces the performance's impact on the audience. From early on a favoured promenade tactic was to drive entries through the audience, to spill over onto them, to make them feel more physically vulnerable. In the National Theatre's modern version of a medieval mystery cycle audiences at the Lyceum in the early 1980s were enabled to feel that their rough handling took them back to traditional, democratic, yea even working-class, 'roots' of theatre. It was a powerful affirmation of the ideological strength of this new element of modern theatre's spatial vocabulary. And taken together with performance-in-the-round it suggests that Joseph's staging initiative may have had a deeper impact on the artistic development of modern theatre than the experiments at the Royal Court.

Meanwhile, for theatres that could not formally abandon the memory of the picture frame, there remained an interest in positioning the audience. For example, in the Nottingham Playhouse (which opened in 1963) the auditorium curves around the audience space, giving the stalls a sense of being centred. While such design may not have substantially altered a traditional view of the stage, it did work towards positioning the audience in ideological terms. In the publicly funded civic playhouse, the audience – as burghers of the town – have a central place in the activity of the theatre.

That comfortable centrality came under pressure when Trevor Griffiths's *Comedians* (1975) opened in the theatre. The play shows the culmination of evening classes in comedy, the presentation of the acts to an agent in a club setting, and the reflective aftermath of the adjudication. It's a story-line that allows Griffiths to reflect on money, art and, in particular, challenges to liberal reformism. When the comedians hear that the agent has no time for jokes that unsettle received attitudes, a couple of the acts revert to material which is sellably racist and sexist. In the second act the Playhouse audience is assumed to be the club audience, but that assumption is tense. For the Playhouse audience does not necessarily share the cultural position of a traditional club audience. As the jokes turn sexist and racist, laughter begins to stop. And, while others laugh on, those who have stopped get a strong sense that this apparently coherent, centred, body of people is riven with deep divisions of attitude and politics.

This is one example of a show playing against the effects of interior architecture to reveal the assumptions literally built into the auditorium. Of many others, one of the most notorious was John Arden's *Serjeant Musgrave's Dance* at the Royal Court in 1959. In the final stages of the play (see p. 156) a Gatling gun is pointed at the audience while Musgrave asks them what modern weapons are used for and alludes to the little country where his regiment is based, which in 1959 might be read as Cyprus. The Royal Court was a cosy version of the late nineteenth-century auditorium, with an audience in layers circling the front of the stage, always within fairly intimate range of the actors. Here is where the Edwardian Stage Society launched new work in front of a well-heeled intellectual audience. When the English Stage Company relaunched the Court as an intellectual theatre in the mid-1950s, under George Devine, a similar audience gathered. Radical it may have been, but its image was middle-class (McGrath 1981). By having them suddenly stare down the barrel of a gun Arden repositions these educated liberals. But he was doing something more. We know, from Dan Rebellato's (1999) account, that Devine encouraged in his company a general contempt for the audience. Arden makes manifest this opinion and in doing so reveals the contradiction of a theatre practice which both encourages a community around itself and yet feels morally superior to that community.

The internal arrangements of the theatre building, then, like its external architecture and its positioning in the town, work to situate theatre art in relation to society. This 'society' is more than those defined as customers of theatre. Even in the nineteenth century the management of the Britannia in Hoxton acted as charitable patrons to their immediate geographic community. In a viciously competitive market it makes sense to treat people as something more than customers, encouraging them instead to feel they have some ownership over the theatre. When it is not entirely governed by the market-place, when indeed it is part of a set of civic amenities, then a new claim is made upon theatre. If society as a whole pays for it, then, whether it goes to it or not, society can have a view on what the theatre does. This is the prospect which opened up when the twentieth century created one of its great innovations, state subsidy for the arts.

State funding

The immediate motivation for introducing state subsidy was, as Dan Rebellato (1999) argues, the onset of the Second World War, and, with it, the fear of seeing again the cultural collapse during the First World War, which witnessed a boom only in musical theatre and revue. The concern about sustaining people's cultural education had roots which went back into the Edwardian period if not earlier, to the 1880s. This expressed itself largely in the movement for adult education which was active between the wars. W. E. Williams's vision of 'Art for the People' (1935) had direct impact on Thomas Jones, Secretary of the Pilgrim Trust, a charitable endowment supporting artistic activities. Jones began a dialogue with the government in 1939 and produced an arrangement whereby the Treasury and the Pilgrim Trust would together provide funding for a central body to promote artistic activity. The body was called the Council for Encouragement of Music and the Arts (CEMA); it was directly overseen by the Board of Education, and it formally came into being in January 1940.

CEMA's initial two aims reflect its own cultural and political origins. These aims were to mount regional tours, particularly to areas without cultural facilities, and to place an emphasis on amateur work. To mark this emphasis it appointed a leading national specialist, L. du Garde Peach, as the Honorary Director of Amateur Drama. When in late summer 1940 CEMA gave support to professional theatre, the companies it supported fitted within this ethos. The first was E. Martin Browne's Pilgrim Players – Browne pioneered the Religious Drama Society and later was Director of the British Drama League. CEMA also supported the Old Vic, which at this time sent out two companies on tour – to South Wales (with Lewis Casson and Sybil Thorndike), and to the North-west. In his account of these years, Charles Landstone, an officer with CEMA and the early Arts Council, suggests that state-subsidised touring was to become a crucial barometer of the healthiness or otherwise of state support for the theatre. Touring was associated with a deliberate decentralisation, a movement of theatre towards all regions of the country. When conditions of wartime bombing forced the Old Vic to move to Burnley, its season opened in January 1941 with a programme note by Tyrone Guthrie and Jess Linscott that welcomed 'the dispersal of the treasures of art and culture throughout a wider area of the land, and a wider range of the people' (in Landstone 1953: 23). CEMA itself set up tours to wartime hostels in late autumn 1942. According to Landstone 'They were, at that time, simply emergency measures of succour for the isolated areas ... but they were to prove an important factor in the Arts Council policy of the future: the policy of providing drama for the theatre-less towns, and thus building up a taste for the art throughout the country.'

These tours laid the basis for 'the solid repertory work' in the post-war years (Landstone 1953: 50).

Landstone also notes, and this was a sign of the shift that was to come, that CEMA found the touring performances insufficiently spectacular. For within about three months of the founding of CEMA questions were being asked about the emphasis on amateurism, and over the next ten years CEMA's founding aims were reversed. The principal agent of this change was the politician and economist John Maynard Keynes. Keynes became Chair of CEMA in April 1942 and direct funding for amateur drama very soon ceased. Keynes had founded the Arts Theatre, Cambridge but also, as Landstone neatly puts it, he 'loved glamour, he loved success' (Landstone 1953: 67). These tastes were articulated in regular invocations of 'standards'. In his account of the early years of the Arts Council, which emerged from CEMA in 1945, Dan Rebellato (1999) shows how the repeated assertions of 'standards' cleared the way for a new emphasis on professionalism, buildings and building-based companies. More money went into buildings than tours. CEMA acquired the lease of the Bristol Old Vic in September 1942, and provided funds for the Glasgow Citizens company to open its theatre a year after. But it wasn't just about buildings.

As the first Drama Director of the Arts Council put it in 1950, if there was too much concentration on 'something for everybody, we shall probably end by lowering standards' (in Rebellato 1999: 44). This set the pace for Arts Council policy documents, which in 1954 announced the need to concentrate on fewer 'high-quality' centres of theatre. In other words, enhancement of 'standards' justifies the downgrading of the mass and the popular. And it opens the door – once again – for commercial interests. When CEMA became the Arts Council it ceased to be run directly by the Board of Education and Treasury assessors could attend meetings. The glamour-struck Keynes himself allowed one of the largest theatre management organisations in London's West End, H. M. Tennent Ltd, to develop a scheme to dodge Entertainment Tax (see Managers). While Tennents did nothing illegal, their exemption flew in the face of the spirit of arts funding at the time.

So on the one hand there was professionalism and 'standards', and on the other an ideal of popular involvement in the development of new theatre. In its manoeuvrings between these the early Arts Council began to develop its character. Its incipient commitment to vested interests and vulnerability to commercial glamour were exemplified most strikingly by its refusal to support properly the leading British theatre company of the 1950s, the East End-based and politically radical Theatre Workshop, thereby destroying the company. The 1970s reversed these tendencies by creating regional arts associations and increased funding to small and touring companies. Joint Stock was funded to allow uncommercially long rehearsal periods; the explicitly political activity of North West Spanner was underwritten. It also supported Foco Novo's *Nine Days and Saltley Gates* (1976) which linked the General Strike of 1926 and the miners' victory of 1972. But this show prompted questions from politicians and the right-wing press as to the proper use of public money. As a member of the Drama panel suggested, rupturing the traditional silence, the Arts Council's deliberations, with panels implementing decisions taken by others, were cloaked in mystery. Was it time, he asked in 1977, 'to democratize the Arts Council, or should a completely new organization to fund the arts be devised?' (Griffiths 1977: 13)

Change was in the air, but it wasn't towards democracy. While an editorial in *Gambit* in 1977 noted that 'it is salad days for playwrights, who have never had so many theatres, some of them small and improvised, but theatres nevertheless … By 1980 we shall probably be looking back with envious nostalgia' (Calder 1977: 3), by winter 1980, indeed, one of the editors of *Theatre Quarterly* spoke of 'the grey economic and social conditions in which we at present live'. A new right-wing government under Margaret Thatcher had got itself into power in 1979 and things began to change fast. The other editor of the journal commented that 'economic necessity is already driving individuals and companies to a more rigorous rationalization of what it is that they are actually doing'. This was Clive Barker, who had already experienced 'rationalization' in the treatment of Theatre Workshop. Now he noted that the main area of 'rationalization' was touring (Barker 1980: 7). This was highly significant, for, as we have seen, touring was associated with a democratic vision in the days of CEMA. The strangulation of touring seemed to mark the end of this vision. And, indeed, while the 1990s embraced the idea of a range of 'stakeholder' interests to which theatre was responsible, these did not necessarily include a democratically conceived audience.

Audience

Crucial to so much of the thinking about buildings, about funding – and indeed about dramaturgic form – is the audience.

There are two main issues about audiences: who the audience is and what an audience is. The first has to do with demographic, social and sometimes geographical facts. The second is more about concepts, assumptions, definitions. Explorations of audience response are usually dependent on sorting out these two issues, for response may well be governed both by socially based codes of conduct and by the way an audience is regarded – by others and itself. This attitude to an audience can be evidenced both in formal effects onstage and in arrangements of the relationship between the performing and watching elements at an event.

Who is the audience?

The audience that arrives at a theatre building has already been selected, as it were, by its ability successfully to negotiate various barriers to its approach and access. The development of a public transport system, and in particular trains, in the nineteenth century meant that audiences were no longer necessarily constrained by their geographical positioning with regard to a theatre. It remained the case, however, that some people could not afford the costs of public transport and were limited to visiting their local theatre, if there was one. Later, as we shall see, this sort of localism was cultivated as a way of maintaining an audience.

Alongside transport costs the other obvious cost is the ticket for the show. An audience can be priced out or happily accommodated. But Edwardian ticket prices were, according to Wade (1983), lower than they later became. It was, however, a thoroughly class-divided theatre. So there are other factors besides cost which work to select the audience.

We have already noted above that the architecture of a theatre can send signals as to openness, or otherwise, of access. When the new Edwardian theatres were designed as variety houses or hippodromes, and even more so when they doubled as dance halls or skating rinks, they were assuring their audience that this was something comfortingly 'popular'. Similarly the internal arrangements and design have their effects. Complex passages from entrance through foyer and promenades into a hierarchically organised auditorium offer something different from a platform at one end of a bar.

Signals sent by the architecture connect with, are sometimes reinforced by, two other sets of signals. The most obvious of these derives from the behavioural codes adopted by users of the building. The less obvious is connected with the place of the building within a larger, more intangible arrangement which is, crudely speaking, the functioning of everyday urban and civic life. We'll begin with this.

In 1903 the dramatist Pinero noted that serious drama was affected 'by the lateness of the Londoner's dinner-hour'. Rather than eat earlier to get to the theatre in time for curtain-up, the spectator goes to a music hall which can be visited at any time. If people ate earlier, said Pinero, the show could begin earlier, and people could eat afterwards (Borsa 1908: 29). Curtain-up for the main show in 1903 was 20.30. This was designed to suit those who would occupy the more expensive stalls and dress circle. They would probably leave work early to go home and change in order to get back on the train to go to the theatre.

But that was only possible if you could leave work early. The whole programme would finish about 23.00, after which there was time for 'supper' – unless you had to be up for work at dawn.

Change to these timings occurred during the Second World War. Curtain-up in the 1940s and early 1950s was at 18.00. This had the effect, as Dan Rebellato says, 'that it was going to the theatre, rather than a meal or a drink, that marked the move from work to leisure' (Rebellato 1999: 104). The later move of curtain-up to 19.30, the time suggested by Pinero, reflects a compromise position, allowing for quick pre-show meals if not a return home. Thus as the relationship between work, eating and theatre shifts, theatre becomes differently positioned in the rhythm of daily life.

This positioning then connects with behaviour in the theatre. The 20.30 start was designed to allow for a lengthy but necessary return home. What took the time was that audiences, the patrons of stalls and boxes, had to change into evening dress. (Ladies at matinees likewise, much to the annoyance of the people behind them, wore hats.) This costume, combined with their manner of arrival, distinguished them. On most nights of the week, says Borsa, there were queues of people waiting patiently for the doors of West End theatres to open. They were a mixed crowd but the dominant presence was young women – 'shopgirls, milliners, dressmakers, typists, stenographers, cashiers of large and small houses of business, telegraph and telephone girls', patiently waiting through fog or rain. Meanwhile there appear from the great smoky railway stations 'delicate visions of white, pale blue, or pink, in hoods or wraps of Japanese silk, embroidered slippers and fleecy boas, wrapped in their brocaded opera cloaks, beneath which stray glimpses are caught of the lace and chiffon of evening bodices'. These with their male escorts are the patrons of the stalls and boxes, on their way to the theatre 'to see and to be seen' (Borsa 1908: 3–5).

Only people who could afford to dress this way would be eligible as an appropriate audience for the main play. When the manager of St James's Theatre, George Alexander, suggested abandoning the convention of evening dress, there was a shriek of protest from the *Daily Mirror*, 'the ladies' newspaper': its scandalised reaction to Pinero's suggestion that they 'should abandon their dinner' for the sake of the theatre was as nothing compared to Alexander's proposal: 'Is it for this, we would ask, that the stalls of the St. James's Theatre have so regularly been thronged with beautiful and devoted women? … Is it for this that young gentlemen engaged in the study of fashion have nightly attended if haply they might find some new secret in the rolling of a collar or the adjustment of a scarf-pin?' (Borsa 1908: 31–2). Even allowing for the *Mirror*'s playing up to its readership, it is apparent that there was something more than respect for theatre that is enacted in the wearing of formal dress. It makes the audience as it were present to itself, activates desires to do with seeing and being seen; it specifically eroticises – indeed fetishises, through the details of cuffs and pins – that gathering of carefully clothed bodies which is the theatre event.

When an audience is mainly interested in the theatre as a social event, then the play matters less. This becomes clear in conventions of audience behaviour. In his account of audiences in the late 1940s Dan Rebellato (1999) notes how noisy they were. In part this noise was a learnt response to the play – applauding the entry of star performers, big speeches and impressive sets, or disapproving. But alongside this noise there was evidence of behaviour that simply disregarded the stage. More than the systematic munching of noisy sweeties under cover of darkness, conversations between audience members were conducted in everyday voices. As a consequence efforts were made to teach audiences how to behave. But while such teaching might imagine there is a norm of audience behaviour appropriate to all theatre, it actually effaces specific cultural differences governing play-going activity. These differences become apparent where theatre seeks out 'new' audiences. Famously the black audience doesn't respond like a middle-class white one.

Playing to a black audience

BRIAN BOVELL: 'Doing a Black play at the Royal Court, for instance. You get the regular *Time Out* reader, you know what I mean, they come from Islington. And it's a quiet night. At the end of the evening they go. Basically I believe their reactions comes off of guilt. The next day if you are doing the play for a black audience, I like to say a colourful richness, the play becomes a different play. It is live. You are getting response and participation. Vocalisation.'

TREVOR LAIRD: 'That is even more likely to happen if you play a club like we did in Peckham. The audiences were not professional theatre-goers.'

BRIAN BOVELL: 'Much more interesting.'

ROLAND REES: 'Lines and scenes were discussed whilst the next scene was in progress. There was an altercation outside, and we had to stop the play for a moment.'
(from Rees 1992: 122–3)

While audience reaction can make a difference to the impact of the theatre event, all codes of behaviour, even the most silent, provide a frame for the play's work. Take, for example, one of Lena Ashwell's great successes at the Kingsway Theatre, Cicely Hamilton's *Diana of Dobson's* (1908). Ashwell, the actress-manager, played the lead. It opens in a shop assistants' dormitory in a suburban drapery store. A woman enters the bare, dimly lit space, followed by another. Each begins to remove her assistant's uniform. Tie, collar and dress are taken off. The 'waist' laid over the bed, the pins removed from the switch and puffs (ornamental, often artificial, hair arrangements), the real hair let down. Miss Smithers holds a puff in her mouth as she talks; while her own hair hangs down she focuses her attention on combing her artificial switch. The elements of the smart female are turned into extraneous objects as the undressing, for most of the act, continues. Meanwhile their audience sits in formal evening dress, the women fastened and pinned into the very same sort of shapes as are being dismantled in front of them. The smarter the audience, the more tense is the relationship created by what we could call theatre's sartorial narrative.

What is an audience?

Dress, behaviour, pricing, architecture, transport: all these are material factors which select and shape the audience. Dramatists, managers and architects have also wondered if artistic form and design can have effects on an audience. These lead us to ask about the artistic construction and management of an audience.

This issue became pressing for theatres as the twentieth century unfolded. It began with the demolition of 'neighbourhood' theatres, most noticeably in the East End of London. In the mid-century, 'civic' theatres were built, often among other public buildings, as part of the planned public life – and image – of the town, central but not necessarily neighbourly. And then there was the impact of film and later television. So theatre makers needed to explore how to reconstruct an organic connectedness between theatre and audience.

The main emphasis was on building an audience that was somehow 'local' to the theatre. In the amateur movement (see Amateurs) there was less of a problem, for the community were often both show and audience. It was in professional theatre that relationships could be reduced to the seller–buyer contract of the market-place. Various strategies were used to alter this contract. There are shows done on 'local' issues, drawing on community experiences, as in the work of the Victoria at Stoke; the politically inspired shows were often played to those who espoused the same political cause. Some theatres and companies developed around themselves a less explicit, but nevertheless still defined, community which shared artistic values and cultural competence – a case in point here might be the 'new audience' in the late 1950s at the Royal Court, which in John McGrath's words, were 'university-educated, perhaps in origin non-middle class, perhaps non-public school, perhaps even from Manchester' but all 'absorbing as many of the values of the middle class as possible' (McGrath 1981: 11–12). An extension from this model of 'artistic' community is the formalised, and financially underwritten, scheme for 'friends' of a particular theatre or company.

It is on the stage of the Edwardian Court, with its intellectual audience, that we can begin an exploration of the work of defining what an audience is. In the suffragist play *Votes for Women* (1907) there is a scene where a speaker addresses a crowd in Trafalgar Square. In the production at the Court Theatre the director, Granville Barker, ensured that the crowd was orchestrated in vocal terms – each member of it had something to say. The onstage audience became, as it were, a dynamic sonic entity. While Barker was motivated largely by the demands of realistic representation, if we come forward several decades, to 1967, we find in Peter Terson's *Zigger Zagger* an onstage audience that combines theatrical with social reference points in order to create an entity which is so dynamic as to become the leading presence in the play. This audience is the crowd in a football stadium. It sings football chants about the action; characters step out from and go back into it. By 1967 football crowds and their behaviour – 'hooliganism' – had become the objects of media attention, which produces loaded associations. Describing the rehearsals the director, Michael Croft, notes that the stadium crowd was 'both a backcloth to the action and a permanent chorus line', it is 'continuously present, Greek-style' (Terson 1975: 23, 20). The reference to the classical Greek chorus anchors this crowd within a theatrical tradition, even if it is a somewhat crude variation of it. And in physical terms it was one of the most striking features of a reportedly exciting production. This 'backcloth' was composed of the entire company of the National Youth Theatre. It was both the scene and the actors in the scene. This is audience as crowd, as chorus and as company.

Its effects were part of the rhetoric of the show – the collective chants, the rhythmic energies. But it was also crowd as aesthetic spectacle, the pleasure not in individuals but in a company. This was 1967. While 'hooliganism' may have been the dark side of energised crowds, there were other political and cultural forms of mass action and mass pleasure. In *Zigger Zagger* the theatre audience sees an image of audience as energised mass entity, always there, larger than the individual actors, bigger than the play.

This image logically linked with, and became labelled by, the concept of a 'popular' audience, meaning those who did not normally go to 'high' art theatre, who enjoyed that which was 'entertainment' more than art, who were not part of a cultural elite. The theatre makers' interest in this sort of audience was very much of its period, for academics and cultural commentators in the

1970s were much focused on 'popular' culture, at a time when the organised working class was a powerful presence in the political sphere. The popular audience seemed to be large but outside the normal operations of professional theatre. To connect with this audience would apparently, then, give access to a way of doing theatre that was no longer boxed in by discriminations founded on class and money.

And there's the issue. While the theatre could invoke, in its language and physical arrangements, a particular sort of audience, it could not always definitely know that it had made connection. The need for this assurance led, I think, to the restless interest in the audience's identity and role. Clearly most shows know when they have made connection because you can feel it, the quick laughter, the straining silence. But if you are opposed to dominant theatre, and looking for hard evidence of your organic connectedness, other things have to be tried. For a time in the late 1970s/early 1980s there was a fashion, in 'alternative' theatre, for scenes representing meetings. This was a favoured technique of Red Ladder. Their play *Strike While the Iron Is Hot* (1974) presented the case for equal pay for women. In its penultimate scene the women, who have gone on strike and closed the works canteen, put their case to the union. George on stage addresses the audience as the meeting, men seated in various parts of the room raise objections, pandemonium periodically erupts. At the end George asks all those in favour of the women to raise their hands, while Helen holds up a placard with a question mark on it (Red Ladder 1980: 56–8). The impact of this sort of scene is attested by John Hoyland, who used the technique for the Councils of Action which structure the show he wrote with Jon Chadwick, *Nine Days and Saltley Gates* (1976): 'Audiences adored the way that we made these meetings come alive. The actors placed themselves around the auditorium, amongst the audience, and argued at each other from many vantage points. The audience love being part of the meeting' (in Rees 1992: 88). Thus, while some experimental groups assaulted their 'bourgeois' audiences, the meeting scene treated audience members as individuals who were interested in the debate, who might take a position on the issues and who might, by implication as it were, take responsibility for their position.

That implication, indeed that state of being implicated – and knowing it – could be described by another word … 'Shot at close range in the arm by a friend and rushed from a gallery in Venice, California to hospital for his 1971 performance *Shoot*, the artist Chris Burden described those watching him that night not as an audience or as spectators but as witnesses.' This is Tim Etchells, founder member of Forced Entertainment, in a short overview of changes in theatre practice through the 1980s and 1990s. Here he links changes in artform to the 'drive to make witnesses or participants not spectators'. One example of this drive is his company's *Speak Bitterness* (1995). By the simple means of keeping the watchers gently lit, 'the performers, whilst speaking the great litany of confessions both real and imaginary that made up its text, could see the public easily and as individuals, not as a mass.' Just as with other contemporary artists, the work offered

> an invitation to be here and be immediate, to feel exactly what it is to be in this place and this time. In *Speak Bitterness*, itself a textual form of bearing witness to the dreams and failings of a culture, the light on those watching meant, above all, that eye-contact was possible, so the two-way nature of every line was emphasised – something spoken, something heard – eye-contacts made and then broken again, eye contact offered, rejected, then offered again – a series of complex negotiations about complicity – about who has done what or who is implicated.   (Etchells 1998: 33, 37, 35)

The desire to conceive of audience as witness is no less politically interested than the drive to connect with the 'popular' audience. Indeed by 1995 it seemed to some that it was politically important to resist assumed ideas about the popular, to position the individual against the mass. This view was articulated by the dramatist Howard Barker when he attacked the 'imperative to enlighten, amuse and stimulate good thoughts of a collective nature' which was shared by both the 'carnival' left and the moral right (Barker 1989: 54). The date of this essay is 1988. Politically British culture had sashayed to the right. The re-election of Margaret Thatcher as Prime Minister in 1983 had been a landslide following jingoistically reported military success over Argentina in a contest over some islands in the Atlantic. The left, for all its attempts to embrace popular culture and mass audience, was powerless to resist, rhetorically eviscerated. The disenfranchised popular had become the triumphal populist. In the face of state-sponsored arrogance it seemed politically important to insist on the privacy, intimacy, difficulty, indeed the individuality, of the individual. Theatre, and its witnesses, had a new duty to perform: 'It has seemed that performance itself is both the memory and the chronicler of what might otherwise pass unrecorded or unnoticed in a broad public forum, an extraordinary open space in which the connections between personal history and the broader sweeps of cultural life can be mapped and documented' (Etchells 1998: 37).

But we have to pause and note that in, say, *Speak Bitterness*, the audience was witness to confessions which were both real and imaginary. While Chris Burden's arm had an indisputable bullet hole in it, while Franko B's blood pumped viscously out of his body, the manufacture of stage confessions could still float on the undecideable edge between real and imaginary, retaining for itself the ancient privilege of theatre to muck around with illusions. And the confessional mode itself soon settled into a set of formal triggers, fragmented syntaxes, intermittent amplifications of the voice, electronically elegiac sound-tracks, choreographed stage mess. Witness or not, the familiar division of makers and watchers was still apparent, and increasingly the witnessing was merely a formal convenience. It was not to be blurred with the other word that Etchells uses, 'participant'.

The movement towards audience as participant was driven forwards in the late 1960s as a political project, with companies trying to 'liberate' audiences from the prejudices which they had brought with them into the theatre. The people who attended the performance of the Ken Campbell Roadshow at the Royal Court's *Come Together* Festival of emergent art in 1969 would have found themselves being smeared with custard. An audience for the Pip Simmons *George Jackson Black and White Minstrel Show*, named after the American black rights activist, would have found themselves individually chained to a 'black' (that is, deliberately blacked-up) slave. Somewhat less coercive, the shows at Ed Berman's Inter-Action would often end by inviting the audience to join the performers – in a swimming pool or taking their clothes off perhaps. In all of these cases, there is a sense that the aim of the show is to force the audience to confront their own inhibitions, to take risks. Pip Simmons and Inter-Action explicitly invited audiences to make a step away from the assumed norms of daily life – in Pip Simmons's case this amounted to a declaration, by action, of a political choice, joining the performers in 'rioting' through the auditorium, for example. At Inter-Action there was an emphasis more on the personally therapeutic potential of theatre, a freeing of the body which would, at the same time, free the mind. It was theatre, to use the word of the moment, as liberation.

The limits of that liberation were clear, however: joining a fictional protester to storm a non-existent White House seems like nothing much more than joining in with the play acting. Being on the receiving end of exhortations or custard is still to be on the receiving end. But the cultural work was done cumulatively rather than as one-off shows. Late 1960s experimental theatre was remorselessly interested in performer–audience relationships. New roles and spaces were opened up for audiences. The work of one of the earliest experimental companies, The People Show, founded in 1965, provoked a live audience in order to use their responses in developing the performance. The space that opens here for an audience is one where they are more like co-creators of the event.

They remain, however, physically in seats, watching performers on a set. That spatial discrimination was to be more thoroughly blurred in events which did not organise themselves as theatre performances. For example, the visual art company Welfare State organised journeys and processions. In this context, the job of the company is that of curator or facilitator, and the 'performers' at the event are volunteers who have been prepared and organised: they are also witnesses to the event. In these respects a curated procession is much like an already-existing cultural form, the demonstration or carnival. It also links back to the more formally organised entity of the pageant. By contrast with such events, the specialness of much theatre performance, perhaps its intensity, often derives from the particular set of conventions that obtain only in that place. Performance is rule-bound activity. So the task in developing audience as participant may be less to do with dissolving the rules so completely that the experience of 'theatre' evaporates than with developing a form of rule-bound activity that allows for both intensity and participation. This is the territory of Blast Theory.

In *Uncle Roy All around You* (first done June 2003) two sets of players, in the streets and online, collaborate with the objective of finding Uncle Roy's office. The event – the 'game' – lasts sixty minutes. Street players start with a formal process, buying a ticket, being photographed, handing over possessions, being instructed in the use of their handheld computer. This device has a map, and receives messages as to where to meet Uncle Roy. When the street player indicates their position this establishes connection with the online players, who are also roaming a virtual equivalent of the same city. If the street player gets to the office, the online player(s) are invited to join them. Before they do so they are asked questions, including whether they would be prepared to commit themselves to being available for the next year to a stranger in the event of a crisis.

The event can only happen once people participate, and they can step out when they wish. Blast Theory's ongoing project has been to bring the audience into the work in such a way that the category of audience itself begins to dissolve. So too they are seeking to problematise the extent to which the company is seen as the creative force, thus, while they invent the game and its rules, they are dependent on participants for the thing to happen at all. By using the model of computer gaming they have, in a sense, retheatricalised non-theatre space. In the computer game, the player enters and inhabits a role with which they often intensely identify. By playing the game across real streets as well as virtual streets, the rules are extended into new spaces and the interdependence of those spaces makes each more vulnerable and intensely present. Furthermore, while *Uncle Roy* may have a formal start, it doesn't have as definite an end. Where there is commitment across a year to a stranger, the game's rule has extended beyond the time-limit of the game and into non-matrixed space, penetrating the private world even as it is secret from the public one.

In this respect Blast Theory's replacement of audience by participant has unearthed the deeper matter here. The 1960s experiments assumed an audience needed to be 'liberated', taken from their repressed private into the public domain of shared feelings. This was part of a general attempt to change culture and in particular the culture of theatregoing, with the radical companies leading the way. Blast Theory's exploration of the 'participant' has begun to question the divisions of public and private and has got there by intensifying, rather than relaxing, the rules. This makes for the creation of new, 'theatrical', intensities in supposedly anonymous non-personal spaces. But, more importantly, it creates new possible connections between people, connections facilitated by rules. This leaves the participant ethically positioned, with the power to choose to follow a rule which connects them, in however fragile a way, to another.

It also leaves us wondering where the place of theatre actually is.

Against the theatre institution

There is a version of theatre history which argues that as the art of theatre became organised into a capitalist business so it became 'institutionalised'. Once, touring players worked wherever they could get a paying audience, on village greens, in pub yards, in country-house halls. When investors later put up the money for purpose-built spaces, they required a return on that investment from the business done in those spaces. In these circumstances the players are no longer fully in control of their own activities. They are caught up into something larger, institutional.

Institutional theatre is often characterised by, though not confined to, its expression in real estate, the theatre building. The case against it was most eloquently argued in the late 1960s and 1970s. Before this time actors had taken shows into non-theatre spaces – parks, streets – in order to do politics rather than theatre. But in the new activism of the end of the 1960s the organisation of culture, and hence of theatre, was a focus for politics. The shorthand word for this historical moment is '1968', although it's a group of years. 1968 itself saw workers and students marching against the government on the streets of Paris and disruption of the Democratic Convention in Chicago. It saw widespread regular demonstrations against America's war in Vietnam, with 30,000 at London's Grosvenor Square demonstration. It saw the vision of a liberalised Czechoslovakia crushed by the Soviet Union and the assassination of Martin

Luther King. And it saw student riots and revolt from Japan to Mexico, with college occupations in Britain.

'1968' was a coming into being, across several years, of a new leftism. In France the relationship between workers and students had been tense because, while the workers were organised on a model of workplace politics and unions, the students, and more particularly the intellectuals, were engaging in a critique of cultural practices which included the 'personal' as well as the economic. This approach contrasted sharply with the brutal activity of the imperialist Soviet Union and those it influenced. For cultural activists in Britain the issue can be summarised in the words of John Hoyland: 'There was a gap between the left and cultural work which needed to be filled. There was a dissatisfaction with the straight left at that time, as being unimaginative and puritanical, and a dissatisfaction with underground [artistically 'experimental'] culture as being socially irrelevant and separate from political realities'. At a meeting held at Unity theatre in spring 1968 the AgitProp Information Service was founded to coordinate a range of disparate radical activities and to promote 'the application of the imagination to politics and the application of politics to the imagination' (in Itzin 1980: 39).

'1968' produced a drive for new alliances – which were sometimes difficult to establish. Theatre groups seeking new working-class audiences, or even collaborators, had to overcome much initial suspicion and hostility. But this effort to make new connections, and to rethink the old ones, set apart the 1968 moment from the activities of the previous decade. Cultural activity, and even everyday life itself, were seen as domains of political action. This attitude was heavily influenced by the philosophy then circulating in Paris. Situationism suggested that contemporary life was lived in a Society of the Spectacle. The gleam of consumer commodities combined with the unstoppable flow of the media's version of reality together constructed an illusion which veiled the true alienated and oppressed conditions in which most people exist. The job of revolutionaries was to disrupt the illusion, to interfere with the texture of 'ordinary' living, in order to unveil the truth.

The new political activity, combined with new attitudes to such activity, led, together, to the scepticism about traditional methods and sites of 'culture'. From this feeling was born the antipathy to institutionalised – profit-driven, building-based – theatre. One of the earliest of the post-'68 theatre groups, Red Ladder, saw itself as non-theatrical in origin and aim: 'The general feeling ... was that they did not come out of the theatre tradition; they did not see themselves as theatre workers for a long time. They saw themselves as doing political propaganda in a particular form. The main impetus was political rather than theatrical' (Hoyland in Itzin 1980: 43). In this respect Red Ladder continued the tradition of the Workers' Theatre Movement. But soon they were joined by others who had a more consciously 'artistic' direction. The founder of Welfare State (1968), John Fox, said that most of the company 'had a fine arts background … either as lecturers or students in art colleges. They tend to be very non-university, non-verbal, very much about making images. And certainly with no theatrical experience at all' (Itzin 1980: 69).

Welfare State can be defined as a visual art company, but it emerged at a time when distinctions between different artistic media were being consciously blurred. Those with a 'fine arts' background would have known of artistic experiments with sculpture and installation, where the artist's own body was used as part of the sculpted work. When the artist did not remain still but engaged in, say, repeated mundane activities, then it began to look like performance. More obviously framed as performance were the events – the 'happenings' – which, in tandem with contemporary sociological work, took apparently non-theatrical material, daily-life behaviours, structures of game and routine, and viewed them afresh as performances. If this work happened in a building it might be in an art gallery rather than a theatre. And even for those who were engaged in what was more conventionally theatrical, the label of 'art' declared their separation from the mainstream. In 1967 Jim Haynes founded a café-cum-studio space in Covent Garden that helped the emergence of groups such as Freehold, People Show, Pip Simmons, Portable Theatre: the space was named the Arts Lab. Other contemporary venues also abjured any reference to the conventional arrangements of theatre. Marowitz founded the Open Space in 1968; Ed Berman presided over Inter-Action and, more whimsically, Ambiance.

While it may have rejected the theatre institution, much of this 'art' performance still focused itself on special places which had their own behavioural customs and values. There were, though, two other drivers which pushed groups away from institutions and special buildings. The first of these was an interest, often politically motivated, in engaging with a wider range of people than those who normally watched theatre or viewed art. When he formed a theatre group which arose from his work as a teacher in a secondary modern school, William Martin declared his two main aims were: 'a company working within a style on a repertory of plays which had a relevance to a wide social spectrum, outside the institutionalized theatre' and 'a series of drama activities involving people in the community using relevant material' (Martin 1972: 18). With these aims the company based itself in what was to become one of the seminal venues of the 1970s, a youth club run by the visionary Peter Oliver, called Oval House.

This was a building made attractive by its facilitation of community contacts. More often, however, the drive to reach communities of varying sorts – and to make work which was, in the key term of the period, 'relevant' – led groups to spend much of their time on the road, taking theatre to audiences. For most alternative theatre groups work was structured both physically and ideologically by touring. For touring, from the early1940s onwards, was associated with a democratic arts mission. This combined, in the late 1960s, with another model – the rock band. A number of theatre groups, including Pip Simmons, compared themselves to rock groups. This analogy takes us to one more reason for repudiating a theatre confined to special buildings. The maintenance of a building is expensive, as too is its staffing infrastructure. Through the 1960s the Arts Council had tended to support companies in buildings and was uncertain how to fund the emergent work (Itzin 1975). So new theatre groups spared themselves the costs of maintaining a building by touring out to their audiences, and they reduced costs of commercial staffing structures by developing cooperative or collective organisations. Rock groups had demonstrated that it was possible to get audiences, money and even celebrity without having a building.

In the mid to late 1990s, in a very different culture, the arguments against institutional theatre from '1968' and after were authoritatively, and influentially, restated in formal academic terms. In *The Radical in Performance* (Kershaw 1999; see also Kershaw 1992) Baz Kershaw formulates the argument against institutional theatre and its real estate on the following lines. Theatre, he says, operates in the closing decades of the twentieth century as a 'disciplinary system'. It is a system in that it is a self-renewing structure of physical manifestations, discourses and ideas. It is disciplinary in that it works to reinforce a set of social values in its audience which has the effect of perpetuating exclusions from itself. As Kershaw summarises:

> a theatre building is not so much the empty space of the creative artist,
> nor a democratic institution of free speech, but rather a kind of social
> engine that helps to drive an unfair system of privilege. The theatre
> achieves this through ensnaring every kind of audience in a web of
> mostly unacknowledged values, tacit commitments to forces that are
> beyond their control, and mechanisms of exclusion that ensure that
> most people stay away.   (Kershaw 1999: 31)

This effect is caused by three elements: firstly, theatre's participation in the mechanisms of 'consumerism and commodification' (the tourist apparatus around shows, celebrity culture); secondly, a cultural policy that conceives of theatre activity as a service industry where authority resides with audience as consumer; thirdly, theatre conventions that produce 'pleasurable submission' to a system of values and to norms of behaviour which are embedded in, and reproduced by, the spatial arrangements of the building itself.

The process of theatre's transformation into this disciplinary system has, says Kershaw, been going on over the last forty or so years, namely since the end of the 1950s. It was accelerated by the developments in social and economic organisation which are collectively referred to as 'Thatcherism'. This was the point at which much more of theatre was forcibly opened up to the forces of the market-place, as subsidy was cut back. In consequence it needed to sell itself along the lines that other products were sold, and to spawn related selling lines, such as souvenirs of various sorts. In a discussion of 'Theatre in Thatcher's Britain' Rob Ritchie noted 'a whole new administrative class developing inside the building-based theatres which is learning the language in terms of Thatcherism. They are exerting more and more force on the artistic directors, whose room for manoeuvre is getting smaller and smaller' (Ritchie 1989: 118; see Managers). The experience of theatregoing was gradually remodelled, Kershaw argues, into the consumption of a commodity similar to other consumables sold in the market-place. Art was being defined as a cultural product, available through a process very like accessory shopping. Indeed by the 1990s it was the visual artists who were once again in the vanguard of another cultural movement, with the young 'Brit Art' generation arranging fashionable viewings in chicly post-industrial settings, where reviews slid across from the arts pages to the news columns and, more usefully, the gossip pages. Visual art stood once again at a cutting edge, this time between art and commodity. And like the words 'cutting' and 'edge' novelty was produced as cliché.

Looking back from his 1990s critique, Kershaw places his own artistic origins in the very late 1960s. The relationship between origins and critique which he foregrounds here can be paralleled with that of Norman Marshall, who, in the mid-1940s, looked back to 1925–6 as the years of energetic experiment in the theatre. These years saw the emergence of 'small' theatres such as Oxford Playhouse (1923), the Gate (1925), Cambridge Festival Theatre (1926). For Marshall, as for Kershaw, the damage to theatre activity was caused by a dominant system structured by commerce and housed in (large) buildings. In 1947 Marshall conceived of the opposition to this system as a small group of activists whose blatantly experimental work would make a difference. In 1999 Kershaw conceived of the opposition not as one active group but as a network of interconnected activities with flows of energy between them. In shorthand, Marshall's conception is classically modernist, Kershaw's postmodern, albeit somewhat sceptically so. While in 1947 there was a politically progressive government that was establishing the welfare state and arts subsidy, in 1999 the 'market-place' version of society and culture had come to be the norm. Concerned commentators at the end of the twentieth century were much more claustrophobically embattled than they were in the days of possibility in the mid-century.

While there is little new in the concern about commerce's effect on theatre, at different periods, in different circumstances, the solutions seem to lie in different places. They were debated with hottest energy in the mid-1970s.

On one side of the argument was the dramatist and founder of 7:84 theatre company, John McGrath. In a series of articles, and then in his book *A Good Night Out* (1981), he argued the need for theatre to engage with working-class forms of entertainment, which included assumptions about where a show is done and how it is watched. To exemplify this different way of doing things he described a typical evening in a working-men's club in an inner suburb of Manchester and then the experiences of 7:84 playing a miners' social club in a coalfield in Scotland. In each case the dramatic work had to compete for attention with the activities around the bar and the general social chatter. This was important not only for learning a language of theatre but also for discovering how theatre could exist in new venues. One of the barriers to a newly energised theatre practice, McGrath suggests, is, quite apart from the general sterility of institutional theatre, its expression in material terms, 'the close-carpeted blandness of the National Theatre's product range' (McGrath 1981: 65).

One of the targets in McGrath's book was the dramatist David Edgar, who had claimed that popular culture, as seen in club acts, was 'grossly reactionary' and 'bourgeois in essence' (in McGrath 1981: 33). He had also said that it was difficult to do a 'committed show ' with rep actors. Caught between the 'atrophied' popular and the uncommitted rep, Edgar outlined the development of a new sort of drama which was to be explicitly about public subjects and played on large stages (Edgar 1979). Of course large stages tended only to be available in theatre institutions. Edgar's own *Destiny*, about the rise of the fascist right, was eventually played by the Royal Shakespeare Company at the Aldwych theatre (1977). Similarly Howard Brenton talked about the necessity of building a mainstream socialist theatre, but also had his work staged by the National Theatre. For McGrath this accommodation with the 'trendy, experimental bits' of the RSC and National did not eradicate their 'bourgeois' values (McGrath 1981: 95).

The logic of the Edgar/Brenton argument was given a name by the playwright Trevor Griffiths: 'strategic penetration'. In using this phrase Griffiths was arguing the need for socialists to work for television. This was a challenge, because television was seen as being controlled either by the ideologies of state broadcasting or by the profit motives of commercial entertainment.

Nevertheless one broadcast of an exciting left-wing play could make contact with more people in one night than it would on an entire national tour: 'To work in television as a playwright will be to seek to exploit the system's basic "leakiness", so as to speak intimately and openly, with whatever seriousness and relevance one can generate, to … the many millions of cohabitants of one's society who share part of a language, part of a culture, part of a history, with oneself'. To persist in writing only for the theatre is to volunteer to be cut off from the main action – and any fame that comes from theatre writing will be 'pickled in a sort of class aspic' (Trevor Griffiths 1977: no page number).

Griffiths shared with McGrath not only a very typical 1970s sense that society is class-divided but also that it is a duty to position one's work as an artist clearly against the dominant class. His strategy has two problems, how-ever: one is to do with the effectiveness of a single play within the general flow of broadcasting and the second is that it takes us back into the difficulties around putting on work in fairly traditional theatre settings, as with Brenton's and Hare's entry to the Lyttleton and Griffiths's work for the Old Vic.

But there was another option. That was the project of taking over a whole theatre and programming it with events and activities which embrace values and forms outside the dominant. This happened at the Liverpool Everyman under Alan Dossor from 1970. Dossor was influenced by the methods of Joan Littlewood's Theatre Workshop, and had done time working at the Victoria Theatre, Stoke-on-Trent, when Peter Cheeseman was developing his series of local documentary shows. Dossor's overall aim was for 'Community involve-ment and celebration' but the community only came to the Everyman after it staged John McGrath's Liverpool musical *Soft or a Girl* (1971). Audiences doubled, to around 93 per cent, and expectations of the theatre changed. This meant that the audience came to trust the company: *Soft* was followed by Shakespeare and T. S. Eliot, which got reasonable audiences (details from Tanner 1974), though the 'Liverpool musical' formula was to return, popularly, in later shows. McGrath says the audiences were encouraged by 'the price of the tickets, by the informality, lack of middle-class bullshit about the theatre, and by the fact that you could get a decent pint before, during and after the show' (McGrath 1981: 51–2). While his account ends up making the Every-man feel like a club venue, it remains the case that the theatre – as theatre – managed to position itself as a community resource. When it took *Soft or a Girl* to the Fischer-Bendix factory during a sit-in, the Everyman displayed the potency of a theatre which was – well – not uninstitutionalised.

The Everyman story alerts us to one of the problems when the argument against institutional theatre is banalised into a simple opposition between theatre buildings and spaces outside theatres. This lumps together all theatre buildings as the same sort of thing, defined uniformly as that which is opposite to 'non-theatre' space. Yet there are differences between theatre buildings with respect to how they generate money, how people work in them, and what the relationships are between these people. Dossor and Cheeseman made their theatres into the audience's space not only in loosening up the use of the bar but in the sense also that it was here, in these physical spaces, that the audiences saw their histories and politics played out.

The Everyman was reclaimed by producing a show in a new form. This takes us to a final point about the institution argument, namely that it tends to downplay the effects of art. When Foco Novo took their show *Nine Days and Saltley Gates* to the South Wales miners, they wanted to do it – as a political show – in a miners' club. But their contact told them 'this show is culture and culture happens in theatres and it must have that stamp on it' (Rees 1992: 86). For the most politicised of trade unionists, the special theatre building had a distinct place. That's worth noting as a general point. For while a special building may be run for profit within a capitalist economy, and while the theatre event may be marketed as a commodity, there can yet be moments when the contact between audience and show has the potential to take the audience into some space elsewhere, to enable their fantasies and deep worries, their thrills and horrors, in a way that is more deeply engaging, and possibly formative, than a mere shopping trip generally allows for. And the opposite is also of course true. If it happens outside an institutional theatre, it's not guaranteed to be either meaningful art or productive politics.

Shows without theatres

Performance for specific communities

It is 1972, on a deprived housing estate at Lower Broughton, Salford. About three thousand people have gathered for the King Kong Festival. During the festival a theatre group performs a play about council rents. The festival ends with the burning of the giant King Kong made by the children.

The theatre group was called Inroads. They had begun life in York, as a community arts project aimed at children. But the group moved to Salford in 1971, consciously to 'set itself within a working-class community that was in change'. After working with children, the group was asked by the tenants' association to develop a play about rents: 'They said it would help to convince people not to pay the rent increases if we did a show.' The rent increases had been triggered by the Conservative government's Housing Finance Bill of 1972, which provoked rent strikes across the country. The show was called *The Rents Play*: 'The scenes showed how the tenants were involved and why they wouldn't pay the rent. There was an agitprop didactic element'. From here the show was taken to other estates where, in alliance with the tenants' associations, the group knocked on doors and leafleted, inviting people to a performance followed by a discussion.

The Rents Play was followed by *The Nurses Play*, created to support the nurses on strike. To widen the campaign, members of Inroads decided to try and perform in factories. From this work emerged in 1975 a new company, North West Spanner. Its outlook and values were shaped early on by the factory performances: 'We thought if we were really serious about playing to workers, we'd better find out about work' – so they stopped performing and got jobs in hospitals, with one of them leading a strike. And when Spanner reconvened as a funded company, they habitually employed 'escapees from the workplace'. For the company it was more than a matter of playing in 'non-theatre' spaces: they deliberately made porous the line between theatre work and industrial work.

Over three days in spring 1975 Spanner did 'eight performances in four factories, and one on a Trades Council demo in Liverpool for the release of the Shrewsbury pickets [a construction industry dispute]'. Their relationship with workers in the dry docks led to *Safety First or Last* – a show about health and safety – done on the back of a truck. As with Workers' Theatre of the late 1920s, it was toured to factories and picket lines. The next show was prompted by the arrival in the group of Elsie Hallsworth, a mill worker. *Winding Up* explored the textile industry, and in particular the activities of Courtaulds, whose operations were seen to have led to the loss of 12,000 jobs. The major aim was not just to inform: at a time of mill closures 'we wanted to get across that they should fight back. And we made the point that it was better to have fought and lost than never to have fought at all' (all quotations from Itzin 1979).

Thereafter other shows tackled disputes in other industries. Similarly other companies, across the country – Banner, Belt and Braces, Broadside, Open Cast, Red Ladder – were committed to similar projects, working through trades unions, local authorities, community associations, schools. Rough Theatre did *Squat Now While Stocks Last* for squatters' benefits and at demonstrations against the Criminal Trespass Bill (Williams 1978). For these companies the space they were playing in was, in effect, an ideological as much as a physical space. They viewed their work as contributing directly to workers' understandings of, and thus attitudes towards, their own conditions of work. By changing these attitudes the shows could, potentially, change the balance of power in British industrial relations.

For Spanner and similar groups theatre was a 'weapon' (see A nationalised theatre), part of a range of rhetorics for persuading people into understandings (and action) in relation to their circumstances. Their theatre was interested in people as the subjects of particular material circumstances which shape their lives and identities. For Spanner the moment of contestation of those circumstances – rent strike, factory picket – was the necessary point of engagement. For other groups the point of contest was less important than developing understandings about, and capacity for dealing with, specific rule-bound environments, such as prisons and hospitals. This work moves over time from doing shows for people in particular circumstances through to making shows with them as a part of the process of helping them to live with and in those circumstances. There is perhaps a shift from explicit contestation of rules to an emphasis on 'personal development'. This shift alerts us to the question which always becomes more apparent once theatre practice has moved outside a designated building, namely: what is the job of work being done by the theatre in that specific place?

Performances in specific places

When Spanner arrived at a factory – and others at community centres or arts centres or schools – the group set up their performing space, arranging chairs, or mics, or screens. In effect they were bringing to the location elements of theatre architecture, the relationship between spectators and performers traditionally organised by a theatre building. While the touring group battles to make the best of the conditions it has got, a different sort of performance seeks to absorb into itself, to have itself actively shaped by, the architecture and arrangements of the location. Such a performance does not therefore readily transfer from one location to another – it is 'site-specific'.

Mike Pearson, who worked with RAT Theatre, Cardiff Laboratory Theatre and Brith Gof, says 'site-specific' performances are:

> conceived for, mounted within and conditioned by the particulars
> of found spaces, existing social situations or locations, both used
> and disused: sites of work, play and worship: cattle-market, chapel,
> factory, cathedral, railway station. They rely, for their conception and
> their interpretation, upon the complex coexistence, superimposition
> and interpenetration of a number of narratives and architectures,
> historical and contemporary, of two basic orders: that which is of the
> site, its fixtures and fittings, and that which is brought to the site, the
> performance and its scenography: of that which pre-exits [sic] the work
> and that which is of the work

The 'work' here is the theatrical work, not the 'real' work, as Spanner would have defined it. And the work of performance is both responsive and partially transformative. 'Performance', says Pearson, 'recontextualises such sites: it is the latest occupation of a location at which other occupations – their material traces and histories – are still apparent: site is not just an interesting, and disinterested, backdrop' (Pearson and Shanks 2001: 23).

This is clear in Brith Gof's *Gododdin* (1998). The name of the show comes from a Welsh poem telling of the heroic, but defeated, resistance of Scottish warriors against the Anglo-Saxons. This gained in metaphoric force as soon as the show was put into 'the engine-shop of the enormous, disused Rover car factory in Cardiff, itself a potent symbol of economic decline and industrial decay'. The scenography 'brought the outside inside': 'hundreds of tons of sand, dozens of trees and wrecked cars, and thousands of gallons of water, the latter of which gradually flooded the performing area during the performance' (Pearson and Shanks 2001: 103). Six performers, becoming more exhausted, battled with these conditions. The ancient tale, placed in this site, came to image the destruction of work and lives brought about by recent right-wing governments based in London.

Brith Gof brought into the car factory the apparatus of theatre. This consisted of three elements: a way of doing the work (designing the scenography of setting and sound, scripting the performances); conscious use of rhetorical address to the audience/participant; explicit management of the contract and relationship between performer and watcher. This apparatus tends to distinguish site-specific theatre from site-specific art (for an account of which see Kaye 2000). As noted earlier, artists in the 1960s experimented with putting their own bodies into the picture, so to speak, and this developed into the form known as 'installation', where, for example, a gallery space might become an 'environment' of objects, images and the artist herself. But the sculptural use of the living human body doesn't have, nor is really interested in, the elements of the theatrical apparatus. And in the case of the room in a gallery, the installation is not much interested in the specific site either. Where the installation is set up in a very specific site, however, there begins to be more need for – and more interest in – organising the relationship with spectators and, secondly, absorbing into the performance what Pearson calls the 'narratives and architectures'.

It is in the coexistence of 'narratives and architectures', Pearson argues, that the potency of the form lies. In a disused car factory those narratives were both apparent and emotive. They were part of a set of performance practices which, in the 1980s, reflected on, and helped to make cultural sense of, a society which was beginning to be designated 'post-industrial'. While these 'narratives' imply histories, a different type of 'narrative' derives from the apparently 'everyday' rules and behaviours associated with particular environments. Take Charlie Hooker's *Mainbeam*, commissioned by Newcastle's Basement Group, for Gateshead multi-storey car-park (1983). This 'ballet for vehicles' choreographed four cars and four pedestrians with the latter pacing rhythmically on a grid marked out on the ground while the cars followed the shape of the car-park space before reversing onto the grid. It was a heightened version of the multi-storey's own conventions of rule-bound manoeuvres.

By contrast to North West Spanner on a housing estate, the instances of derelict sites with histories or rule-bound everyday spaces propose a different status for the theatre work. Here theatre draws from the place it is being done – the already existing history of the locations enriches the theatrical discourse, is absorbed into the framework of the performance. Or the already existing rules of the environment provide a text for performance, so that it is less an analysis of those rules than an extension of them. These examples either assume there are no longer people at the site or view the people as transient but behaviourally governed in some way by the site. The people imagined by this sort of event are conceived not so much as materially shaped by, but temporally caught up into, these circumstances.

Interfaces

The performance in the everyday functional site of the car-park highlights characteristic, but perhaps usually invisible, relationships and rules. An extension of this work finds performance transforming sites which are non-functional, not visited on an everyday basis. Such a site might be the area under a large motorway intersection. In September 1993 Fine Rats International made an event *Under Spaghetti Junction*, in Birmingham. They had already, in June 1991, done *Under the M5: Dreams and Desires* in Smethwick. The latter site in particular was a convergence of multiple histories, of canal, rail and road. Both sites combined the monumentalism and simultaneous evacuation produced by industrial development. *Under Spaghetti Junction* took its audience round a one-way system controlled by fencing, cameras and marshalls. Amongst various spaces they encountered Ivan Smith's 'Curl Up and Dye', a hairdressing salon in a service tunnel covered in graffiti, juxtaposing the place of beautification with the 'beautified' motorway, individual styling and signatures in paint. Similarly Francis Gomila's wire mesh cage with bathers under UV lamps was joking tensely with body, technology, entrainment and pollution – and the embrace of leisure rather than facing the facts of the environment.

In this sort of site there are neither given narratives nor agreed rules. The site is rather more of a 'non-site' – appearing to be outside of specific history or functionality, even if not actually so. The performance in a non-site has an effect less of recontextualising it, perhaps, than of transforming it ... Like cyclists suddenly encountering fairies hanging from trees or middle-aged women crawling by the roadside. These were two moments from Art on the Run's events in 1982 for 200 cyclists doing the John O'Groats–Land's End cycle ride over three weeks. Art on the Run, alias Natural Theatre from Bath, organised a range of randomly encountered sights – roadside statues holding flowers, a demonstration by the Anti-Cycling lobby – as adjuncts to the ride, momentary transformations of familiar moments on the journey.

Where the cycle ride differs from Spaghetti Junction is that it takes place not only in various different locations but in the passage from one location to another. In part this is a straightforward development of a logic which, having got beyond the building, starts to explore how expandable the frame to performance might be. It is interested in space and distance as elements of performance language and as effects on participants and spectators. A relatively early example of a performance that spread itself across several locations was Albert Hunt's collaboration with his students at the Bradford College of Art to stage the Russian Revolution in the streets of Bradford (1967) (see p. 77). This worked not as realist imitation of the revolution but as temporary transformation of the habitually lived relationships in a northern town, where what was being transformed was not simply places in the town but the rhythms of the day and the relations between spaces. Progress through the town and through the day is interrupted by unaccustomed events.

What might be called 'transition' performance takes various forms, to explore various frameworks. A contemporary of Albert Hunt's in Yorkshire, John Fox, started to develop with his company, Welfare State, performances which were processual – literally in the form of procession – and communal: 'on the first day of September 1972, the group set out on a *month's* procession-performance across the West Country, following the route from Glastonbury to St Michael's Mount'. There were 'stops on the way for a series of participatory rituals held on the sites of important religious monuments' (Ansorge 1975: 41), but these site-specific moments were gathered up into the larger thing which was the procession between places, moving on through time. In 1995 Forced Entertainment took its audiences and performers on a guided tour of Sheffield aboard a bus, reciting not the facts of the city but the different histories – 'the official historical, the personal, the mythical and the imaginary' – which all, as at the motorway junction, inhabit the same place (Etchells 1999: 80).

Where movement between one place and another sets up relationship between those places, repeated exposure to moments on the journey – or to different stages in an unfolding event – leads to layered impressions and reactions, complexifying one's initial relationship to the thing. In each sense the point of interest is not something specifically located, but is in the transitions between one local moment or place and another.

For instance, in 2005 Station House Opera did a performance in three different locations simultaneously. These locations were none of them theatres – a shop in Birmingham, an ex-church in Colchester and a warehouse in London. 'In each venue an audience watches a live performance, alongside video streamed over the internet from the two other locations projected on screens placed side by side.' The intention was to make 'three performances together creating a larger fourth performance, telling intertwined stories that are both universal and true to each venue's own localities, cultures and concerns' (Station House Opera 2008).

This has been called 'telematic' performance. Lavender defines such performance as 'an event involving two or more geographically distinct sites, linked by telecommunications technology so that the event takes place in mutual interaction between the different locations. It is also available to a virtual audience on the internet. The performance is only complete by way of the interaction in real time between the participants, so that a single hyper-event ensues' (Lavender 2006: 558). The hyper-event might be that 'fourth performance' – one which cannot be encountered from any fixed location but is felt to be there. This, clearly, is not just outside theatres and outside buildings, but at the edge of material space.

Through the late 1980s and the 1990s, as the technology had developed, numerous performance events used digital media in order to correlate two different spaces, usually where one is present to spectators and the other is live relay or virtual space. For example Stelarc, a sort of latter-day Victorian showman, had his musculature connected to electrodes which could be controlled by operators at remote sites. Their use of the keyboard could induce muscle spasms in him. The richer development of a practice that is interested in interface – as physical and virtual – has, however, been taken forward by Blast Theory. In *Uncle Roy All around You*, for example (see Audience), street and online players collaborated to reach a goal, and then to make a promise to each other. In such work we can note that we have stepped away from the concern with sites – or even non-sites – and their specificities. The interest here is in relationship between sites. Where earlier we may have said there was imaginative and emotional engagement – indeed cathexis – of site, here there is cathexis of interface.

It is not the technology alone, however, which has produced the cathexis of interface. In a very different instance Sally Mackey aims to theorise the performance of 'place', which is 'a perceived environment or geographical area with which individuals (or groups) believe they have a personal relationship' (Mackey 2007: 181). To demonstrate her argument Mackey analyses a year-long performance event curated by the London International Festival of Theatre. *Feast* comprised activities carried out by artists and members of the local community on two adjacent London allotments in 2003–4. As a result the 'taken-for-granted place was re-envisioned and seen anew by the participants', who 'spontaneously found' meaning in what was going on (Mackey 2007: 187). In particular the final event drew on people's experience and memory of previous activities on the site. This enables Mackey to suggest that, by contrast with a one-off performance on a site, the performance of something which has become 'place' is characterised by ongoing and evolving process. In this process not only do distinctions between performer and observer break down but the 'participants', as they can only be called (see Audience), develop over time a lived and felt relationship to the site, making it thus a specific 'place'.

Now although an intensified sense of specific 'place' may seem the reverse of interface between sites there is a basic similar principle. This has to do with the cumulative effect of dispersed spatial and/or temporal engagements. Whether it is a cycle ride, a Blast Theory game or a gardening project the concern is not with a discrete performance work but instead with the relationship – believed and material – between participants and project. The discovery of connectedness over spatial or temporal distances, together with the sense of accumulation, are constituent parts of the effect.

The example of *Feast* may now point us towards that which is more than technologically determined about cathexis of interface. It seems to step away from derelict, inscrutable or evacuated spaces. All that work around sites coincided with studio performances which imaged individuals caught up into the flow of heavily mediatised, urbanised, alienated lives. It was the feeling of the late 1980s amid the dismantling of state support and productive industry. So too, the capacity of this work to dwindle into a commodity version of itself – Dogs in Honey and the endless imitators of Forced Entertainment – this was also very 1990s. By contrast, the interest in relationships between sites, the interfaces between them, seems much more the space of possibility – albeit sometimes frightening or bewildering possibility. *Feast*, like a Blast Theory game, is not discovering for us an eternity of non-space but offers, instead, the conditions for psychic reinvestment. All of this performance has a late-1990s interest in networks, undiscovered connectivities – not hierarchies and layers but flow and emergence.

In these instances the dramaturgy is the machine which brings spaces into conjunction, it makes the interface visible or specified. The address is to individuals and in particular to their experiences. Some of these experiences may not be possible without theatrical mediation. It is not the site which is enhancing the performance but the performance which has opened up the space for play. In that sense, curiously, a theatre of interfaces is doing much the same job of imaginative work as the theatre which goes on inside those institutional buildings.

Useless buildings

In spite of the huge variety of activity outside theatre buildings in the second half of the twentieth century, by the end of the century those buildings were again becoming interesting.

Gloria tell how they went through the phase of thinking that theatres were the problem, belonging to their parents, and how they would get real diversity in black box studios – but found that the audience for black boxes is more homogeneous than it is for the town rep. Then they took *Lady Audley's Secret* to Hamburg: 'We were playing in a nineteenth-century vaudeville theatre and we all just went: Ohh, it's so beautiful! And suddenly no one asked us why we moved like that or why we had all that music because this was its *home*' (in Tushingham 1994: 126). Gloria, like some of their contemporaries, wanted to get into 'big theatres'.

Once inside, Station House Opera felt the urge 'to occupy every part of the theatre – if it was a proscenium, every part of that rectangle, every part of the whole space, equally'. That 'equally' has force. The intention is to avoid the hierarchical arrangement whereby the theatre is simply used as a platform for performers. By using all parts of the theatre – offstage, in the air – the new work was trying to challenge, from inside, the theatre building's conservatism. But more than that: Station House Opera were trying 'to make theatre out of the physical limitations of the form. So we don't walk off in the wings. We're always physically stuck in that space' (Julian Maynard Smith in Kaye 1996: 202).

Once you look at it through eyes accustomed to conventions of site-specific performance, the theatre building itself appears as a place of limits, of resistant materiality. But it is different from other sites of performance in that the physical specificity of a theatre often carries assumptions about its traditional performance functions. By engaging with it while resisting its functions, the attempt to 'occupy every part of the theatre' plays with – and takes apart – assumptions about how theatres work. Theatres, Julian Maynard Smith says, are 'never really very pleasant places', for the reason that 'they don't know what they are' (in Kaye 1996: 202).

Gloria's Neil Bartlett got his theatrical 'home' when he took over direction of the Lyric, Hammersmith. In a series of revivals of classical European texts he did Marivaux's *Island of Slaves* in 2002. It was played in an auditorium boarded over to the level of the dress circle and covered in sand. The audience sat splattered around the playing space while close, now, above their heads was the grand Edwardian manner of Frank Matcham's interior. The Marivaux text, from 1725, was typically playful, politically risky and occasionally nasty. Its tense relationship with its own cultural context seemed to prompt, and become part of, an event in which Marivaux's fantasy island was played on a provisional, architecturally dislocated platform – where old theatrical grandeur was both pressingly present and at the same time buried under sand.

By the mid-1990s a number of theatre companies had developed a keen interest in spaces which seemed to have lost their sense of identity or purpose, if they ever had one. As we have noted, one of the key emblematic spaces was the industrial site where production had ceased. Another was the supposed non-space, the space apparently in the interstices of other activities, the space always traversed and never occupied, such as a motorway junction, a station mall, a block of streets.

A version of such a space is the empty railway arches underneath London Bridge Station, where the company Shunt established the Shunt Vaults (2003 onwards). This is not, however, a site-specific performance. While Shunt have chosen not to work in theatres, the building's value to them is as a place where they can make work and develop an audience. It also, of course, shapes the dramaturgies for shows in that the occupation of a whole building 'allows us to explore ways of making the audience's whole experience part of the narrative of a performance'. Without demanding that they role play, the audience is invited to engage from the moment they enter the building. In *Amato Saltone* they were addressed 'as participants at a swingers' party, with no physical separation (at least, at the beginning of the show) between the audience's and the performers' space' (Twitchin 2008: 52). They are taken on a journey through the building, following the performance through a series of narrative situations, so that their experience of being in the space itself informs – while also being informed by – the sense of the show. This became even more apparent with the establishment in 2006 of the Shunt Lounge, where for the audience simply paying to enter the space is more like going to a bar-cabaret than going to a 'show'. It's a space where new work can be tried out, not only in the Vaults but also directly in the bar area: a performance might suddenly transform the 'public' space, just briefly, into an unexpected 'theatrical' setting. The audience, up to 2,000 per week, are harder to organise in these circumstances in that they develop their own ownership of the space, based on repeated attendance, much as one does in club or bar.

This experiment revisits something like the Arts Lab of 1968/9, but now with a keener sense of audience as participant that developed in the 1990s. And while it may be a refusal of theatre buildings, it is at the same time a return to a building. In this respect it is both outside the 'disciplinary system' of theatres, but inside a different disciplinary system. For the Shunt Lounge also draws on another 1990s development, the culture of clubbing. Connected into the social behaviours and values that are structured by clubbing, the Shunt Lounge hovers on the edge between assimilating performance to the range of things that happen in a club – where dance clubs already have their own range of performed activities – and extending an audience's daily experience through engagement with performance. Quite like theatre really …

Which takes us back to that strange entity, the theatre building. For, after a couple of decades when its reason for existing was questioned, it too began to enter the category of the non-space, the space without a viable identity. At this point, when the theatre building once again becomes an interesting place for performances, what is going on? It can perhaps best be explained by the concept that Raymond Williams called 'structure of feeling'.

To many in the early 1980s the institutional theatre and its building did not seem to offer itself as a viable means for articulating feelings about British society and life. It was associated with that which was established, commercialised, artistically complete – as it were, finished. So theatre workers began to look for new 'scenes', new scenographies of feeling, such as the post-industrial setting, the alienated city. But theatre buildings too can become this sort of space if what happens in them unsettles established hierarchies, is provisional, flirts with failure. At the heart of all this work, in whatever setting, is not so much post-industrial objects and textures but process, transition, provisionality. Melodrama, that early harbinger of modernity, delighted in its sudden and clever scenic transitions, but it contained them in narratives that had a pleasurably tight grip and very definite endings. A century and a half later the focus tended to get attracted to transition and transformation but now in contexts which sought to be more open-ended, fragmented, risky.

Outside those buildings the traditional industrial base of the British economy was being sold off and run down. The trades unions associated with that industry had their power conspicuously challenged, if not broken, in the 1980s. And with their decline disappeared shared ways of thinking about work, social structure and history in industrial societies. The community organised around the factory, physically and intellectually, was decentred. And instead of a united, politically conscious, movement of opposition both to government and social hierarchies, the articulate left wing of politics split into a range of arguing and more or less deracinated groups.

Into this sort of scenario comes the theatre building newly reoccupied – with shows that look as if they only half belong, uncertain if the conventions about the space still apply, always slightly unconvinced about getting away with it. Reframed within this context, the architecture itself begins to become expressive, appropriately capturing feelings about a society which has lost something traditional while never being healthily renewed, where old-fashioned structures have had their day but so have their glamour and certainty, where, in short, all is provisional and fragmented.

In 1905 the construction of the Aldwych and Waldorf theatres was part of the development of an imperial boulevard which expressed the dominant feeling of the day. A century later the theatre building has learnt to do cultural work as a site of impossibility, risk and instability. Indeed its artistic and emotional value could be said to come from the fact that it is no longer part of an imperial boulevard or a progressivist vision of urban community. It is, perhaps, precisely because it is a building without purpose that it is theatrically interesting.

Body and non-body in performed spaces: some examples of scenic objects and spaces defining and shaping bodies at specific dates, in specific modes. The particular relationship of body and object can suggest bodily potency or vulnerability, so too there is a sort of textural exchange between body and scenic object.

3. Festival Theatre, Cambridge, *Antigone*: the director Terence Gray (1931) was aware of German Expressionist scenography: here the stage is organised by scenic steps and platform.

4. Gaiety Theatre, Manchester, *Hindle Wakes* by Stanley Houghton (1912): an Edwardian realist interior scene: table, chairs and bodies.

5. Station House Opera, *Scenes From A New Jericho*, performed on a building site at the top of the Zeedijk near the Central Station in Amsterdam (the site became the Golden Tulip Hotel). The performance was part of the Amsterdam Zomerfestijn, 1986.

6. Lewisham Players, *Meerut*: a Workers' Theatre Movement sketch (1932) by Charlie Mann, as depicted on the front of *Red Stage*: the worker-players hold poles as they perform the inmates of an Indian prison (the author is standing on the right).

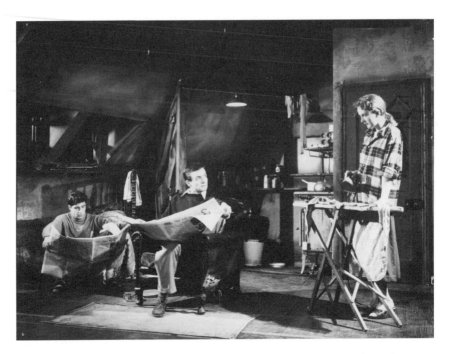

7. Royal Court Theatre, London, *Look Back in Anger* by John Osborne (1956): a 1950s realist interior scene: ironing board, bodies.

Chapter 2

Who does it

This section describes those whose labour makes a performance happen.

It begins with actors, who form the majority of theatre workers. It then looks at directors and writers, with brief mention of designers.

In the modern period there have been several experiments with the organisation of performance companies. These have a bearing on definitions of what actors, directors and writers do. So too, while the craft of acting has been traditionally learnt as apprenticeship or training, the modern period has opened up ideas about the qualifications necessary for performance. At different times both amateurism and an explicitly non-theatrical training have been important. This importance often derived from the sense of the wider work that acting does in society, its politics. That politics is expressed as – and the contract with the audience is established by – modes of performing.

After considering actors the section moves to describe the craft of directing, which becomes formally labelled in the modern period, and thereafter implicitly challenged. So too the role of the designer was formally recognised. Finally there is the writer. When the twentieth century begins there is a feeling that necessary reformation of theatre creates the need for serious writers. By the twenty-first century there was doubt as to the relevance or effectiveness of a specific role for the writer.

The organisation of actors and companies

In the 1904 plans for the National Theatre emphasis was placed upon the need to establish a company of performers employed for at least three years. The advantage of such a company was that its members could develop their potential through knowledge of each others' work and build on previous shared experience.

This sub-section considers the various ways that actors and other company members have structured their working relationships in the modern period.

Repertory

The change in theatre practice advocated by Edwardian radicals was as much to do with the methods of programming theatres as with putting on radical new plays. The proposed new national theatre would be organised along 'repertory' lines, so that no play would be given more than three or four times in succession. This organisation of the programme ran directly counter to the methods of the actor-managers. They favoured repeating the same play night after night, with themselves in the lead role, for as long as it would draw audiences. Such programming was known as the 'long run'. The long run was also favoured by entrepreneurs who had invested in the theatre as a profit-making enterprise. If a show – such as *Les Misérables* – turned out to be successful, there was no point in taking the risk of replacing it with something else that was untried. The long run guaranteed the fastest and safest profit. At the same time it contributed most to the exploitation of all actors except stars.

In the opinion of those who supported the repertory system there were two forces at work in London theatre in the early years of the twentieth century: 'There is the force which treats the theatre as a trade to be exploited to the greatest possible profit, and there is the force which treats the theatre as an art' (Howe 1910: 12). Art was encouraged by increasing the numbers of plays which were tried out and by keeping the production of them fresh and committed. A play in a long run settles into stereotyped and formalised performance; a play that changes from night to night keeps the cast more on its toes. Where the company was valued as an entity it created an artistic 'unity of effect' in shows (see Rowell and Jackson 1984).

A second impact of the repertory system was that it changed the focus of attention in the work of putting on shows. For actor-managers the play was their star vehicle. Although the play may change, their role at the centre of things, with all their individual charisma, remained constant. For entrepreneurs who controlled theatres linked into touring circuits, the acts were interchangeable from one theatre to another. Where theatres existed simply as receiving houses to touring companies there might be little obvious artistic policy governing the selection of work and, in particular, no necessary correlation between the demographic situation of the theatre and the work it shows. Glasgow people got English touring companies. Against all of this the repertory system lays heavy stress on the identity of the performing company. While plays change, the company remains largely the same, but, in order to cope with the pressure from frequent changes of play, those who take large parts in one show may well do smaller parts in another. The system thus works against the production of celebrity culture. With the eradication of a structure that tolerated 'stars', repertory was a better arrangement for actors in general.

Furthermore the company has the status of being 'resident' at the theatre. They do not pack and leave after a week. This residency creates the conditions for greater closeness to the community in which the theatre is situated, as with Annie Horniman at Manchester's Gaiety. Thus when the repertory idea made its first challenge to dominant theatre practices its power came from its facilitation – and celebration – of the productive potency and community relevance of the theatre and its company.

Built into the model, however, is a role which came to be dominant. That is the artistic director, who in their own person combines the theatre director with the manager of the company. The preparation for shows tended to follow the model of the director-led rehearsal, usually working from a pre-written script. While actors may have taken parts of different sizes in different productions, the roles of other company functions were more fixed – the set designer did not, in the main, alternate with the stage manager. This methodology became more apparent as more formally designated roles appeared. In the early days directors would arrange their own lighting and sound, but following such initiatives as the training for technical disciplines at the Old Vic Theatre School technical design emerged in its own right midway through the century.

The company thus had a specific structure which shaped its working relations and, very often, its approach to the material. As theatre practices changed, this structure itself came to seem old-fashioned. By the 1950s rep production had settled into a formula:

> The vast majority of plays were three-act, one-set plays, usually in domestic interiors of different levels of the middle class. The entrances were dictated by the kitchen, the dining room (if it was upper middle) and the outside … The similarity of the plays made it possible to rehearse them in a week, in a style of writing and acting that was constant. Design was a matter of using the same flats, cleated together in different formations and painted differently each week. The great art was 'dressing' the set – that is choosing the properties which were borrowed, on the promise of free seats, from shops in the town. (Gaskill 1988: 17)

This is the Royal Court director William Gaskill, looking back from the mid-1980s. By then the sense of rep's staleness had been compounded by its association with local authority funding, and therefore with 'civic' values, city councillors and constraints on radical art. There were exceptions: Richard Eyre's regime as artistic director at Nottingham Playhouse, 1973–8, commissioned and mounted plays by the young radical dramatists of the day – Brenton, McGrath, Griffiths. David Hare was literary manager. Fifteen major premieres were done. Audience figures went up 10 per cent in 1973–4

(Rowell and Jackson 1984: 136). And meanwhile the executive manager and his civic paymasters muttered despairingly about radicalism. By the 1980s they could relax: the permanent company was disbanded and a rash of musicals and modern classics followed like a nasty infection. Much the same had spread across the land.

Ensembles

At the heart of the ensemble is the commitment to work made with others as a group of artists. This contrasts strongly with, and offers an alternative to, the career of a jobbing actor or designer, who adapts to new ways of working and new conventions in each job. Prior to the twentieth century there had been other models of working which resisted the casualisation of actor employment. In the early seventeenth century Shakespeare could count on some form of continuity because he, and the leading actors around him, were all 'sharers' in the company. In the nineteenth century the stock company would often be centred on a family, where each member had their customary roles. The difference of the ensemble ideal, however, is that it suggests that, without actual shared ownership or blood relationship, commitment to a method of work can produce, in a group of unconnected people, a closeness similar to that of family.

In the dominant British theatre tradition of the 1920s and 1930s ensemble playing was a rare thing. For this reason the visit by the Compagnie des Quinze in 1935 had considerable impact. The force behind this 'ensemble', ironically, was a man who behaved as an *auteur*-director, Michel Saint-Denis. There are stories of him positioning actors in stage pictures calculated to the centimetre, much as Granville Barker used a floor cloth marked in foot squares for rehearsing *The Madras House*. When Saint-Denis did *The Three Sisters* in John Gielgud's season at the Queen's Theatre, London, in 1937–8, 'Every move and piece of business was prepared beforehand on paper'. The effect, says Gielgud, was that 'Many people remember that production as being of [sic] the most perfect examples of teamwork ever presented in London' (Gielgud 1963: 91).

The 'teamwork' here was more of an aesthetic effect than the work of a genuinely egalitarian team. Both elements – aesthetics and working relations – are bound up in the concept of 'ensemble'. The theory is that the ensemble's organisation and mode of work, with their stress on mutuality, can lead to a different quality of performance. The ensemble stages its togetherness, and the pleasure for the audience comes from this contrast with what many experience in their own working lives. Ensemble playing offers the sight of people working together in conditions of mutual trust and respect.

These are the principles Saint-Denis attempted to establish in London. For contemporary with the season at the Queen's, he was teaching at the London Theatre Studio, alongside George Devine, later artistic director of the Royal Court theatre. The Studio work had the following aims: 'The general idea is to unify the various elements of the theatre ... to produce a homogeneous group of people working in the theatre – a troupe that can work by itself and for itself; with writers, musicians, mechanics trained to support it' (Marius Goring in Wardle 1978: 56). As Saint-Denis put it in 1960, 'it is the company that gives the place its spirit. The public is attached to the men and women they can see in the flesh.' In ensemble work, quite apart from writing or design, one of the basic pleasures of theatre is the audience's felt connection with the players. Conceived in this way the ensemble concept potentially makes a challenge, both organisational and aesthetic, to the role of individual *auteur*. 'I come back to that human reality which is indispensable to artistic reality. To me the unity and quality of a performance ... depends mainly on a quality and unity which should exist in the company before the work on the play begins' (Saint-Denis 1960: 84, 83).

By 1960 Saint-Denis's educational base in London had been closed for over a decade. George Devine had not imported the ensemble model to the Royal Court. And it seemed to the director Tyrone Guthrie in 1961 that 'The ensemble, if it exists at all, can only be technical. There is no collective life of the company which passes like an emanation from the stage to the audience' (Guthrie 1961: 242). But yet, in the same year, another voice, always on the edges of dominant theatre culture, declared: 'I do not believe in the supremacy of the director, designer, actor or even of the writer. It is through collaboration that this knockabout art of theatre survives and kicks' (Littlewood 1970: 133). This is Joan Littlewood, and in the work of the company of which she was a founder member, Theatre Workshop, many audiences would say there was a definite sense of an 'emanation' of collective life from stage to audience.

Littlewood's principles had been developed alongside Ewan MacColl, first with his Theatre of Action – 'a small collective of would-be political actors' (MacColl 1986: xxxvi) – then with their joint Theatre Union and then, after the Second World War, with a re-formation as Theatre Workshop. Based initially in Manchester and with many years spent touring, Littlewood's and MacColl's development of an ensemble company was contemporary with Saint-Denis, operated in a space politically and demographically very different from the training schools of central London, and had more forceful results. The early work developed alongside, and in dialogue with, the activist sketches of the Workers' Theatre Movement. *John Bullion* had its origins in a WTM sketch but, while Littlewood and MacColl shared the politics, they wanted to improve the performance. Largely self-taught they embraced Europe-wide developments in theatre practice (see p. 83). While the integration of speech and movement and the rhythmic organisation of scenes were as important as the work of Saint-Denis, the model of approaching a show went very much further and influenced a whole generation.

It began with group analysis of the text and discussion of its social and political issues. Early rehearsals might be spent entirely in improvisation: famously the actors in *The Quare Fellow* (1956) did not get sight of any written text until they had exhausted themselves tramping around a makeshift 'prison' yard, had experienced – indeed 'lived' – the power relations of a prison regime. Closely parallel to the written text, the improvised material was then blended into it. In this method the actor was not just the vehicle for, but the source of, dramatic text. As such, the actors developed the capacity, and authority, to improvise sections during performance.

Immediately the Second World War ended Theatre Workshop started to tour. Britain was at peace, but, like the rest of the world, now in the shadow of a deadlier weapon than any hitherto invented. In February 1946 a new show opened in Newcastle: *Uranium 235* was about the atom bomb.

The company shared 'a common vision of the future'; together they learnt techniques and explored theatre history. Relying on this, their 'most valuable resource' (MacColl 1986: lii), the show brought a range of theatrical modes and periods into conjunction:

> It begins with Democritus of Abdera. *(He is handed a chiton by one of the actors. He puts it on.)* In the course of putting on this chiton I have ceased to be a twentieth-century physicist, gone through a transition phase of being myself playing an actor, and finally taken on the external habiliments of an old Greek gentleman.   (MacColl 1986: 82)

The process of doing the show is one of the things it stages for pleasure: 'He's got a difficult costume change. This jumping about from one character to another is bloody confusing. One of these performances I'm going to come on in the Greek scene dressed as a Manchester businessman. That'd shake 'em!' (MacColl 1986: 94) And the foregrounded changes focus attention on the local material circumstances of the company as well as creating a jokey metaphor for historical necessity. A Singer enters 'half-dressed in medieval costume':

> I must apologise for not being properly dressed, but who would have thought the glory that was Greece would have passed by so quickly. But that is the way things happen – events won't wait for the last button to be buttoned … Hence the ruins of empires. The next scene should, by rights, deal with the Romans … but you probably know

all about Rome … Therefore we'll pass on without comment. In any case we couldn't afford to put Roman soldiers on the stage. For that kind of thing you need subsidies, which we don't have. We're not a rich company, at least not rich enough to be able to afford armour and weapons.   (MacColl 1986: 87: my ellipses)

Of course it's weapons that this pacifist company can't afford. The cod transparency about process aligns the audience with recalcitrant detail against solemn epic, the poor against the warlike. In doing so it produces the ensemble – or, specifically, the aesthetic effect of the ensemble – as a form of political response to the speedy march of science and warfare.

This political potency of the ensemble is physically communicated later, in a scene in Nazi Germany. Two Gestapo officers beat up Eisler:

> *They break his neck and he falls to the ground.*
> MIC. VOICE.   This scene is called 'Strength Through Joy'.
> *The two Gestapo officers become actors again and help Eisler to his feet.*
> *All three join the semi-circle.*
> 1ST GESTAPO.   The scene ends and the actor rises to his
>   feet. But there were hundreds of thousands of real
>   actors who never rose again.
> MIC. VOICE.   And there were the refugees: the writers, doctors,
>   students, scientists.
> *A woman leaves the semi-circle and stands downstage, waiting.*
> CHORUS.   He's late! Late! Late!   (MacColl 1986: 118)

The brutal small episodes are done by actors who emerge from, and go back into, the group. They are announced and framed by other voices: from microphone and chorus. The mimetic activity, however forceful, is one of a set of techniques available to the ensemble. As the scene notes the differences between acting and real life it establishes the ensemble company as something more important than individual actors or stage mimesis. In this respect the ensemble, itself so transparent about its funding and process, claims to stand halfway between the traditional fictional work of the theatre and the exigencies of real life. Its method is with fiction, but it is never subsumed into that fiction.

From here we might say that the creation of an ensemble is a more significant performance event than any of the individual shows put on by that ensemble. What is performed is a possible way of working together in the world. Through this way of working together new understandings come. The process, and the relationship between ensemble and the show it puts on, are vividly illustrated by a company that took the principles of Theatre Workshop and moved them on a stage further.

That company was Joint Stock, founded in 1973 by Max Stafford-Clark, David Aukin and David Hare. All three had prior experience with founding companies: Aukin had managed Freehold and co-founded Foco Novo with Roland Rees; Hare, with Tony Bicat, had started Portable Theatre in 1968; Stafford-Clark had been at the Traverse in Edinburgh between 1966 and 1970. The Traverse, initiated by Jim Haynes in 1962, had hosted a visit to Britain by New York's Café La Mama (1967), which so influenced Stafford-Clark that he created the Traverse Theatre Workshop in 1969. There he experimented with using the actors creatively – generating material for a show through research and improvisation, learning to play several parts in any one show. This in turn led to a new way of working with writers, with actors challenging a writer's vision or writers developing material originated by actors: for the actor might know as much about the material of the play as the writer. The Traverse principles were then developed in Joint Stock, where, in 1974, the founding three were joined by the designer Hayden Griffin and the Royal Court director William Gaskill. But the forging of a new relationship between actors and writers was not the most significant step.

Rob Ritchie's history of the company is subtitled *The Making of a Theatre Collective*. Joint Stock transformed from an ensemble into a collective. This happened through the process of working on one show, David Hare's *Fanshen* (1974). At the heart of the process was a mode of work that is enshrined in the name of Littlewood and MacColl's company, the workshop. In the workshop there is space for discussion and experiment without the hierarchical arrangements of the normal rehearsal as it hectically tries to do little more than fix the end product and open on time. The project for *Fanshen* was to take a long book about the effects of the revolution on Chinese peasants and develop it into a show. In Ritchie's words:

> At the end of five weeks, few were convinced there was a play in it.
> Gaskill's idea to set up the workshop as an exercise in democracy,
> however, began a process of self-enquiry that was to be decisive in the
> years ahead. In studying the social existence of the Chinese peasants,
> the group equipped themselves the better to understand their own.
> Actors directed, directors acted, all were entitled to question and
> criticise: pockets were emptied, earnings revealed, status and authority
> broken down and analysed.   (Ritchie 1987: 17)

The *Fanshen* process led to three effects – first, a successful production and, second, a decision to incorporate workshops into the preparation for all subsequent shows. Typically a ten-week preparation for a show would have its first four weeks as workshops with the writer only developing the playtext at the end of that period. It was a method that ensured all actors were equally engaged in the creative activity.

The third effect was that the company began to think about organising itself on collective lines. This was not quite what one of the directors had in mind: 'Gaskill's vision of the company was of an ensemble group with a specific approach to its craft. Operating as a collective had an obvious practical value but the superior goal was fashioning a common method of work' (Ritchie 1987: 21). In Ritchie's formulation here we can see where 'ensemble' and 'collective' diverge. The ensemble always had about it the twin elements of organisation and aesthetic effect. In Gaskill's vision the importance is attached to the achievement of 'craft' and aesthetic effect, to which collective organisation is secondary. The collective, by contrast, insists on the primary – political – importance of its organisational structure and process.

Collectives

At the end of 1976 Joint Stock formally decided to become a collective. In 1979 its annual general meeting laid down some basic principles – main emphasis on those actually creating the work; equal pay for all; productions playing for at least the same length of time that they were rehearsed; touring time to be equal in length to a London run.

These principles were very much in line with other collectives. An editorial in *Platform* from 1982 describes them: 'Theatre collectives stemmed from '68, "raised consciousness", an increased interest in socialist ideas, women's politics, gay politics, and a desire to work and live in non-hierarchical structures. The performers, writers and directors who formed the companies wanted to make both the content of their work, and the *way* they worked, socialist. This was a time of ventures into communal living' (*Platform* [1982]: 1). A famous example is the Marxist company Red Ladder: 'They had weekly meetings, a whole afternoon to discuss the group, to ensure that everybody had an equal role, that all work was rotated, including the Chairman of the Day' (Hoyland in Itzin 1980: 47).

In the case of Joint Stock it seems that the company continued to be torn between political ideals and aesthetic effects. Simon Callow described the company as a 'directocracy', where the traditional position of the director was enshrined. Indeed Hare's directing methods recall Saint-Denis and his micro-direction. Actors may have constituted the largest group but the company 'stood for the taste of its directors'. And most people liked that, because it meant that the work they did was of a high standard (Callow 2004: 70–7).

Thus the tension in collectives happens when the art threatens to circumvent the ideals or when collective principles dominate at all costs. In the latter circumstance the collective model radically redefines the director as a theatrical entity. After the moment of collectivisation, companies have to choose to allocate power to a director. That authority is no longer a given.

In the 1970s and early 1980s the challenge to assumed structures was articulated and energised by theatre companies of the left, where hierarchical organisation and thinking were associated with oppressions of gender and class (see Feminist theatres). These companies stated their radicalism through their methods of work. In large part this, rather than aesthetic form, was the creative contribution made by collectives. They positioned the work of theatre-making in relation to larger community activity, and, in particular, to the self-development of political activists. The specific creation of performed work was itself often fraught with difficulties. These were especially apparent around the attempts at collective writing. On one hand this practice sought to give equal ownership to the artistic vision, on the other hand it was not very effective at ensuring coherence of the artwork. The difficulties are exemplified by *Lear's Daughters*, which was scripted for the Women's Theatre Group by Elaine Feinstein, then reworked by the company. The issue of 'ownership' of the show was played out in its advertising where, in one print-run of handbills, Feinstein's name vanishes completely (Goodman 1993: 97–9).

The various issues around collectives can be explored by looking at *The Fence*. This show was intended as 'a theatrical expression' of the 'common experiences of living and working at Greenham'. 'Greenham' here refers to Greenham Common, a United States airbase in Berkshire which, in the 1980s, housed nuclear arms. In protest at nuclear weapons and warfare women activists established a 'peace camp' outside the perimeter of the fence around the base. The company of six women that made *The Fence* called themselves Common Ground. They were primarily peace activists, with only two having had prior theatre training. The show was done in 1984 in two performances only, one in London and the other at Greenham.

Early in the process there were seven in the group, and they created for themselves production roles which they would take in turns:

1. OUTSIDE EYE (the director)
2. THE SEEKER OF TRUTH (the challenger)
3. THE STARTER/INITIATOR (the devisor of improvisations and motivator)
4. FOCUS KEEPER
5. PEACE MAKER (the facilitator)
6. REALITY CHECKPOINT (to keep communication with audience in view)

7. MORALE BOOSTER (for the days we needed encouragement and inspiration) (Common Ground 1985: 128)

But even with defined roles, the members of the group testify to the difficulties of working as a collective – the need to negotiate around individual ideas and emotions, the need to find ways of confronting and expressing rather than allowing tensions to simmer, the need to establish group discipline in order to make the work.

Although the idea for doing the show grew out of a shared political project, and was a means of taking that project further, for those in the group it also became an individual journey. The tensions of the work tested commitments to the collective ideal, and for some of those with no theatre training the idea of performing a play was frightening. Not simply a protection for missiles, the 'fence' also described personal barriers between women, and indeed barriers within oneself. The fence, in every sense, had to be broken before both new personal strength and the collectivity of women could be achieved.

The show's form, in short scenes of songs, images, dialogues, stories, realisms and fantasies, derives from its collective creation. Different women contributed different elements – Theresa Boden says of herself that she was silent apart from her poem scene. Built into the show is a lively awareness of fragility, difference, difficulty. Overcoming the interior fence is almost harder than confronting the soldier guarding the base. The penultimate scene has Sally in prison learning to accept the presence and equality of other women: 'I'm a woman. (*Pause.*) I'm a woman. (*Pause.*) Please come to me. Please … Come to me. (*She waits.*)' Then two comfort her (Common Ground 1985: 127).

In a curious way the collective method of organisation and work throws the emphasis onto the difficult, even if tender, moments of individual encounter. The power of overcoming the 'fence' is stated in Tracy's story of the Newbury witch and her poem:

> I'm trying to put the world right
> In an afternoon between the cleaning and the washing up
> But I will not be imprisoned by my guilt
> And when I find myself there will be no fences.
>
> (Common Ground 1985: 126)

The image is ambivalent: the story is of a witch who spoke as she was dying, delivered by Tracy alone, anticipating a moment not yet achieved. So too the penultimate prison scene stops with the moment of comforting Sally, not with her learning from that moment. While the finale shows togetherness in a formation dance and song, it is dislocated from what precedes it. Although motivated by the opposition to the warmongers' fence, in the show's making the most important fence to be overcome was the internal one.

We can perhaps now describe better the function and value of the collective theatre work. *The Fence* had a continuity with the activity around it. For the company it was just one part of their political work – but there is more to it than that. As a show it translated into aesthetic expression the issues and experiences of being active within the larger political campaign. Those who did it testify to being altered by the process, finding deeper collectivity with others as well as confronting their own inner 'fences'. In this sense the show takes forward the political campaign by developing its activists. It is not, then, the end-product so much as the process of making the show which does the political work. That insight requires us to change a familiar cliché. Often shows like *The Fence* are described as 'preaching to the converted'. In fact what they are, after the personal journeys of the process, is a preaching by the converted.

Collaborations

One of the stories told by the development of ensembles and collectives is of the emergence of actors as creative presences in their own right. Not simply a vehicle for realising the writer's text or the director's vision, they are capable of generating material for a show. In some processes this is then worked on by writers, in others it produces a show where there is no involvement from a writer. This second instance is usually known in the UK as devising and in the US as creative collaboration.

The establishment of processes which feature workshops and devising is the coming into being of actor as author. The tensions caused by this emergence were articulated in Harold Pinter's criticism in 1967 of the interference into a dramatist's text of the 'creative' actor. By 1994, however, Simon McBurney was pushing at a half-open door when he suggested that the only way to establish a sense of real shared understanding between actors and audience was to ensure that 'the performers on stage were in greater control of the material they were performing or had in some way had a more creative hand in it than was generally accepted'. For this reason he 'set out to work with people collectively' (in Tushingham 1994: 15) and co-founded Theatre de Complicite (later renamed Complicite) in 1982.

Max Stafford-Clark had similar aims in the late 1960s; indeed there was a tradition of experiments in company working relationships from back beyond then. But while companies of the 1990s drew on, they also reworked previous models. For instance the aspiration to work 'collectively' feels very different from the model of, say, Red Ladder. In the 1970s, characteristically, there was an explicit interest in structures and systems of organisation. In the 1990s, the interest had moved, and so too the key word had morphed from 'collective' into 'collaboration'. The emphasis was placed on the experience of generating aesthetic material, where process, once again, was important, but now conceived as artistic rather than political development. Thus at its beginning the methods of Complicite encouraged the actors to play together and thereby create material as an ongoing, continuous activity. Sometimes the show was still being developed at the point at which it was exposed to an audience. And it used audience response to develop further. The text of the show emerged organically from the actors' activities rather than being pre-set in a written text. 'If you start from the company of actors together with the script, you admit that whatever the piece is, it is a combination of things and does not come about through the exclusion of one or the other' (McBurney in Giannachi and Luckhurst 1999: 69).

McBurney, like many after him, was heavily influenced by the methods and teaching of Jacques Lecoq's school in Paris. But the Complicite method also had potent, if less widely acknowledged, precursors within British theatre culture. The shaping force on much that followed it was the practice developed by Theatre Workshop through the 1930s and 1940s (see pp. 70–1). It was given renewed artistic and political life in the late 1960s by Albert Hunt and his colleagues at the Bradford College of Art. This was one of those extraordinary cultural moments when a group of makers found themselves together in circumstances amenable to experiment, much like the more widely celebrated Black Mountain College in the United States in the 1950s. Hunt's work began in educational projects, such as the Vietnam War Game, planned in collaboration with a professor of international affairs, and developed into campus-wide 'games', events such as an American Presidential election in Bradford, happening-like shows such as *The Destruction of Dresden*, the city-wide *Russian Revolution* – 'an experiment in public drama' – and a Festival of Chance (1967–8). With him in Bradford was the poet Adrian Mitchell, and John Fox, later of Welfare State, made puppets for the *Revolution*. Other visiting artists in this period included Jeff Nuttall and the experimental composer Cornelius Cardew. All the projects brought together students from different specialisms in the arts and were framed by Hunt's analysis. He viewed the education system as a totalitarian structure in which pupils learnt that their lives were controlled by others; this system, with its mysterious knowledge and routines, functioned theatrically. Against it, to liberate education, a different theatre had to be made – not as teaching aid or tool for control but to 'put play back at the centre of experience'. In its emphasis on play, and its role as 'an alternative form of learning situation', oppositional theatre offers a different take on social processes (Hunt 1976: 120–5).

The centrality of play here was both artistic and political. Hunt's projects were collaborative in the sense that he was deliberately drawing together different disciplines and working through group activity. But they were energised at another level by a political purpose, that of replacing oppressive structures with a discovery and release of the potency found in community interactions. In a similar way, as Heddon and Milling (2006) note, early explorations in devising work in the 1950s and 1960s seemed to be not only a liberation from the hierarchical or bureaucratic structures of theatre but also a democratic break-away from the elite authority of classic 'modern'(ist) art. Happenings replaced illusionary theatre acting with more authentic-feeling, because less 'rehearsed', performance. From this point onwards devising as a mode had written into its ideology associations with cooperation, absence of hierarchy and, indeed, freedom.

By contrast with Hunt's position, however, the focus is less politically explicit. The 'freedom' argument tends to be confined either to the domain of artforms or, at best, to theatre as a profession. Over time even this degree of precision has become vaguer, so that almost any devising practice invokes a radical or liberationist function of some sort – Heddon and Milling list twenty-four claims made by the various rhetorics, all importantly earnest. They go on to note, very neatly, that in the 1990s 'devising as a profession' seems to relate less to fringe practice than to mainstream industry and that, indeed, as a practice it seems 'rather more akin to traditional theatrical production' (Heddon and Milling 2006: 6).

Something of this shift is apparent in the definition of 'collaboration'. McBurney is apt to talk about the 'piece', the artwork, being a 'combination' of things, while the director, designer and producer get on with their separate – often authoritative – jobs. Collaboration tends to imply bringing into one place different artistic elements rather than looking beyond, or indeed structuring, the company. Contrast that with this polemical position: 'Collaborations were formed with filmmakers, sculptors, dancers and politically active groups, such as the striking Miners in 1984/85, where members of the community were encouraged to participate with creative contributions.' This is Test Dept, a group of musician-performers, formed in 1981 'in the decaying docklands of South London'. Their objective was to make response to the rightward, shopping-ward, drift of British culture and to that end set about 'reinvigorating disused industrial settings, with epic scale spectacular events working collectively with other artists under the umbrella of the "Ministry of Power"' (Test Dept 2007). Here the collaboration is not just combining artistic elements but different groupings, looking outwards, and, in particular, driven by political commitment. By the end of the century, however, collaboration was firmly positioned as artistic activity alone: it was known that the Arts Council favoured collaborative projects for financial support. Collaboration slides from being an organisational issue into being a funding category.

The work of actors

In discussion of the organisation of theatre workers the focus was on how a company generated material for a show, whether through the structure of the company or by playing and devising. These methods were often valued because they could get performances out of people who were not necessarily trained performers. That distinction – between a trained and an untrained performer – was brought to the foreground in the modern period. The concept of acting as a formally teachable craft led to the founding of institutions. With that institutionalisation, however, actors might learn values that were not just artistic but also social and political.

The emergence of training

At the start actors were trained as part of existing companies or theatres: Ben Greet, Irving and Sarah Thorne all had more or less formal 'schools' in the late nineteenth century. A couple of music colleges, Guildhall and the London Academy of Music, ran acting classes. The first formal conservatoire institution for acting was founded in 1904 by the actor-manager Herbert Beerbohm Tree, with a board including the well-established playwrights Barrie and Pinero. Tree's school, the Academy of Dramatic Art, was followed in 1906 by the founding of The Central School of Speech-Training and Dramatic Art, an initiative not by an actor-manager but by a voice teacher, Elsie Fogerty.

In the contrast between Tree and Fogerty is embodied one of the tensions that characterise the concept of training for the stage. Tree, and Irving before him, were concerned with the renewal of the profession. Actors were to be properly trained in clear techniques, and thereby the business of acting would sustain its standards. For Fogerty, voice and movement training were not of relevance only to professional actors. She taught teachers too, and these teachers were expected to engage with all sections of society. Fogerty herself worked with children in areas of deprived housing. Actor training at the start, then, was both an education in a craft and an art applied to wider social uses.

Producing the English actor

Such training, furthermore, was seen to have a national importance. In Archer and Barker's plans for a National Theatre there was a training school attached to the theatre. Although based on the Royal College of Music and Guildhall, the Archer–Barker school was not conceived as a narrow engagement with a craft. Actors would receive appropriate literary and historical instruction alongside their other studies. This was to be a fully fledged Dramatic College, giving a general education. As such it closely resembled the thinking of their contemporary, Elsie Fogerty, who aspired to have her Central School associated with the University of London, awarding diplomas on completion of the course.

The concept of a 'college' which is connected into university education was shaped by the wider political and social aims of actor trainers. The formal establishment of acting schools was intended to put an end to the exploitative employment of casual labour in the theatre. So too it was intended to put paid to dilettante dallying with the artform. The approach to structured actor training comes from a serious, and typically Edwardian, commitment to the value of apprenticeship and craft vocation and the dignity of the artisan. In addition, at the proposed national theatre, the attachment of a training school would function to keep the theatre 'modern'. The acting school, in short, is not locked into the service role of a technical college but is a mechanism for institutionalising the engagement with modernity.

An acting school will keep the theatre modern ...

The danger common to all securely established bodies is that of falling behind the times. The School should be so ordered as to help the Theatre to avoid this danger, by providing for it recruits strong in the vital principles of their art, instead of assisting it mechanically to hand on an academic tradition (however worthy) from one artistic generation to another.   (Archer and Barker 1907: 100)

Like the rest of the Archer–Barker plan, their acting school never happened. Certainly by 1910 RADA and the Central School were established, but the vision of a National Theatre with a school attached to it continued to exert its power into the next generation. And it got closer to material reality – briefly – in the institution which for many years was the nearest thing to a national theatre, the Old Vic. In 1947 the Old Vic Theatre School was founded by Michel Saint-Denis, George Devine and Glen Byam Shaw as part of a project which also included the founding of an experimental centre and a youth company. Importantly, it trained technical students as well as actors, while insisting that actors learn some of the technical skills – among its products were the founders of the Manchester Royal Exchange Company. For actors it taught the interplay of technique and inspiration within conventions of a text.

Saint-Denis and Devine already had experience of running a school, having set up the London Theatre Studio (from January 1936, in various locations, until September 1939). The Studio was supported by such people as Bronson Albery, Guthrie, Olivier, Gielgud, Laughton. While the teaching drew from Stanislavsky, the major innovation introduced by Saint-Denis was the practice of his uncle Jacques Copeau. Thus the Studio was unusual in running beginners' classes in improvisation (with mask) and mime (based on animal behaviours). The performers, with a range of competencies, were treated as an ensemble, although, somewhat paradoxically, individual good looks were validated as a crucial asset. When Saint-Denis and Devine later moved to the Old Vic, they took much of this practice with them.

Several features of both projects – the Studio and the Old Vic School – are important for the history of modern theatre in Britain. First was the assumption about what was being trained. Students were to learn to become something like the French *comédien*, a neutral instrument able to turn her/his skills to various modes of performance. The work of acting was not to be straitjacketed into simple representation. To become the *comédien*, students undertook voice and movement training. This exposed them to a wider European practice. Alongside his own Copeau-influenced work, Saint-Denis recruited the Viennese movement specialist Litz Pisk. Voice was taught not by an expert in 'speech' but by an opera coach, the Hungarian Jani Strasser. Pitsk and Strasser ensured that voice and movement work interrelated. Finally, the students were subjected to often ferocious critique of their performances. Taken all together the training constituted a spiritual journey, in which the student was broken down and then rebuilt.

While the young acolytes were being pummelled into theatricality, the Old Vic as a whole was running steadily into debt. As a consequence, in 1949, its governors forced through a change of regime and a new administrator was brought in, Llewellyn Rees of the Arts Council. Rees was horrified by what he saw of Saint-Denis's training methods. He did not understand the movement work; he disapproved of a training which did not prepare the students explicitly for the commercial theatre; and, to cap it all, he found it un-English. As Saint-Denis viewed it, 'he went into a class and saw that we were improvising animals of all types. And he wrote in his report that he had been the witness of some exercises by which we were debasing human nature to the level of animals. And that he did not think that this was necessary to learn the interpretation of our great national poet Shakespeare' (in Wardle 1978: 133–4).

The former Arts Council officer was not alone in the distress which he was caused by European theatre methods. Jean-Louis Barrault and his company created a significant impact in Edinburgh in 1947 because their performing made expressive use of the body as much as the voice. But this opening up of performance possibility also met with strong resistance. While Devine had taught mask alongside Saint-Denis, another member of the English Stage Company, director of *Look Back in Anger* Tony Richardson, was adamant: 'We don't want any of that Saint-Denis rubbish in this theatre' (in Gaskill 1988: 42). The problem was not that these methods were new. The English Stage Company, consciously radical, had no problem with newness. Indeed it had as its mission not only the promotion of new writing but also new acting. The actors associated with the English Stage Company and Royal Court theatre in the late 1950s and early 1960s were characterised by working-class voices, a cultural position that was 'alternative' to the dominant, and an unsuppressed regional affiliation. They were consciously part of a so-called New Wave of theatre art and radical politics. And many of them, just as consciously, were adamantly opposed to the methods of Saint-Denis, energetically cynical about anything which is 'physical', let alone 'poetic'. In the work of the Royal Court it was the writer who was the key figure. Actors were there to realise texts provided for them by writers, doing the bidding of the new generation of 'radical' directors: 'They were doing mime and sub-Copeau jumping about, which wasn't at all the sort of acting that was required. The plays preceded the company; so we were looking for people who would fit' (Richardson in Wardle 1978: 171). Thus it was that the English Stage Company helped to define modern English acting in the early 1960s as an art subordinate to script and director, naturally vocal rather than consciously physical. And, above all, not poetic.

With its stress on the writer the English Stage Company was, however, echoing the Stage Society of fifty years before. It was, by 1955, abrasively different not perhaps because it was new in method but because it was old. The orthodoxy of acting that remained in dominance was based, with or without a working-class gloss, in Stanislavskian principles of representation. This was seen to be kept in place largely by the work of the acting schools and the agents which disseminated their products. The challenges to orthodoxy came from companies which ideologically committed themselves to discovering, or re-creating, alternatives. And, symptomatically, these were on the edge of, if not standing against, the commercial mainstream. Let us look at two rather different examples.

Producing the 'modern' actor

Over on the other side of London from Sloane Square, in a much less fashionable and privileged area, a powerful and influential innovation in actor training was being developed. Joan Littlewood and her Theatre Workshop company had, after years of touring, come to rest in a dilapidated theatre in Stratford East. What arrived with them in that theatre was a company ethos, a set of working practices and a clear articulation of theatrical values. Littlewood believed that traditional conservatoire-trained actors were 'ingrained with poise, propriety and "tricks of the trade"'. This 'poise' combined upper-class behaviour – 'cup-and-saucer, French-window stuff' – with artificiality: 'curiously affected speech and the lack of anything resembling normal activity in the movements and gestures' (in Holdsworth 2006: 45–7).

In order to produce performances which were less artificial, and indeed less 'English', Littlewood took her actors through exercises which drew on a range of European methods. Most famously she had them playing games and improvising, developing a capacity for spontaneous responses and freedom from learnt movements. Thus, while the Royal Court was reasserting the dominance of the writer over the actor, Littlewood was freeing the actor from the written text.

Theatre Workshop training methods

- Relaxation
- Laban movement techniques (via Jean Newlove)
- Meyerhold's biomechanics and Dalcroze's eurhythmics
- Stanislavsky, 'if' and authenticity
- Research, discussion and analysis of text
- Games and improvisation

Two main features of the Theatre Workshop project should be noted: it was based in a plurality of mainly European approaches and it had a deliberately democratic imperative. These features set it apart from a different, much shorter-lived, but nevertheless influential challenge to acting orthodoxy.

In 1963 Charles Marowitz joined with Peter Brook to form the Royal Shakespeare Experimental Group, an offshoot from, and funded by, the Royal Shakespeare Company. The aim was to explore acting in laboratory conditions, without needing to produce – and sell – finished product. The two directors devised exercises that would move away from the Stanislavsky fundamentals and engage with Artaud's approach to theatre. For actors brought up on 'the ideal of inner-truth, it was a major adjustment to discover there was also *surface-truth*'. Even more difficult was to realise 'that artifice and downright artistic fraud could create a plenitude of truth for an audience' (Marowitz

1967: 172). Overall, through improvisations and exercises with rhythm and sounds, a major objective was 'to try to create a discontinuous style of acting; that is, a style which corresponded to the broken and fragmentary way in which most people experience contemporary reality' (Marowitz 1967: 168).

In his reflection on actors Marowitz notes that the 'hallmark of a good actor is his attitude towards change'. Suggesting that 'those actors who have passed through the Royal Court, Theatre Workshop and the ferment of the past ten years' are more open to change than 'the academy-bred, rep-oriented actors of an older formation' (Marowitz 1967: 172), he attempted to tabulate the distinction between the traditional and modern actor.

Traditional as against Modern actors

Let's get it plotted.   Let's get it analysed.
Fix inflections and 'readings'.   Play for sense and let inflections take care of themselves.
Plot as soon as possible.   Move freely for as long as possible.
Play for laughs. Play for contact.
Final decisions as soon as possible.   Final decisions as late as possible and always open to reversal.
It was a bad house.   It was a bad performance.
I take orders.   I give suggestions.
Am I being masked?   Am I important at this moment in the play?
Can I be heard? Are my intentions clear?
I'm getting nothing from my partner.   I'm not getting what I expected, so I shall adjust.
Just as we rehearsed it.   As the immediacy of the performance dictates.

(Marowitz 1967: 175)

Alongside the presentation of work in progress, which included texts by Artaud, Genet, Arden and D'Arcy, and a collage *Hamlet*, there were impromptu debates and improvisations responding to suggestions from the audience. This, as at Theatre Workshop, was the opposite of the English Stage Company's subjection of actor to text. Here were actors performing their freedom from text, a freedom gained from a combination of their ability to analyse and their openness to different techniques. Both these qualities, a capacity for analysis and the proficiency at 'discontinuous' acting, would later be seen, in various forms, in the work of performers associated with the new dramatic movements of the 1970s.

But while the 'thinking' actor came into being easily enough, the other side of the project – the 'physical' actor – remained difficult territory. In 1965 Brook turned to Europe again, bringing over Grotowski to run workshops with RSC actors. At this period the company's image was self-consciously radical – and 'academic' – but, even so, the engagement with Grotowski remained a minority experiment until it achieved something more like canonical status at the end of the century. Perhaps more influential in changing British practices was the arrival of New York's La Mama company at the Traverse in Edinburgh in 1967. One of the new directors there, Max Stafford-Clark, followed the model and set up a workshop for creating shows on a whole-company basis. This model he then took with him to London, when he became resident in the very place that had once insisted that actors, their bodies and their poetry should be disciplined by writers, the Royal Court.

By now, however, the doors had already been more widely opened, thanks, in large part, to Littlewood. She had an influence on key figures such as Peter Cheeseman at Stoke, Alan Dossor at Liverpool and John McGrath, who founded 7:84 Scotland and England. Through these companies her practices spread further through the 1970s. Towards the end of that period Europe was embraced once again, this time more formally, as performers left Britain to explore training possibilities in Europe. With Simon McBurney one of the most famous among them, a whole generation attended Jacques Lecoq's school in Paris. Two decades later the notion of 'actor training' found itself co-existing with another term, 'performer training'. Devising, albeit sometimes without skill, became one of the dominant new forms. Grotowski entered the university syllabus; McBurney's Complicite became a benchmark for pre-university studies; 'world theatre' and 'interculturalism' penetrated the general vocabulary. At its most rigorous end, much of this work had less to do with the performing of fictions – conventional acting on stages – than with the self-exploration of the performer through the willing, even if sometimes painful, submission to regimes of practice.

Meanwhile stage acting had set about its own project which can be seen, at a time of increasingly 'visual' theatre, as an attempt to rediscover the power and autonomy of, as it were, unassisted acting. A celebrated early example is Shared Experience, founded by Mike Alfreds in 1975, as a 'story-telling' theatre. Early shows narrated, without scene or props, big books – *The Arabian Nights*, *Bleak House*. All of the work was done by the actors' vocal control, their gestural language, their grouping. It was both a return to an ancient role – storyteller – while remaking for audiences a new, undecorated, immediacy. That autonomy of the actor becomes more intense, all round, in minority experiments by dramatists who produced written texts that refused to offer the actors any secure guidance with regard to what they had to do. Noël Greig's *Plague of Innocence* (1988) was an early example, followed by Martin Crimp's *Attempts on her Life* (1997) and the work of Sarah Kane. Her *Crave* (1998) has four speakers simply marked C, M, B, A. It is up to the actors and director to make choices as to how the written lines are going to interrelate, what activity takes place and what the sense of the stage space is. The written text does not supply character but 'speaking position', from which one or more characterisations might emerge. In making its choices the company cannot think of itself as simply conveying the vision or message of another. Its choices are its own, and in making them it articulates its own various investments in the material, and, by implication, its own personal histories and outlooks. The reality of the actor as person is thus a constituent element of the show while it happens. Technique ceases to offer a safety-net in difficult fictional territories. While it had always required emotional effort and psychic investment, this new development entailed more searching exposure, in that character choices were always at the same time actor choices.

These have, so far, been minority experiments. The dominant employment of actors – in television – requires simply the deployment of a variant of the old-fashioned technique. Alongside it, in live performance, a new dominant is settling into place, collaborative devising and an embrace of consciously diverse 'physical' forms. A major impetus towards this came through the educational structure which Elsie Fogerty had seen as necessary to the teaching of drama, namely the university course. But with it perhaps came the very thing which Archer and Barker had been concerned to remove, dilettantism. On the one hand, then, there is apparently a high-level acquisition of craft underpinned by somewhat conservative values; on the other, a lower level sampling of various methodologies underpinned by a conscious desire for experiment and change.

Amateurs

One of the most powerful energies behind dramatic activity for at least half a century was the amateur movement. Far from being a bad, half-baked or unskilled imitation of professional theatre craft, amateurism often took a consciously different approach to theatre-making.

As Mick Wallis has shown, this was a wide-ranging movement, crossing classes and emerging as much in rural areas as in towns and cities. Its approach was significantly shaped, after the 1914–18 war, by an association with adult education and, in rural areas, with social regeneration. While government policy was one driver, this itself picked up on popular enthusiasm, workers' education, gentry initiatives and – for instance – the use made of drama by the Women's Institutes for the empowerment of rural women (Wallis 2006; Wallis and Kiszely forthcoming).

For some of those involved, the amateur movement was also seen as the force which would regenerate British theatre through developing a wider community of those expert in drama. Assistance was given by the British Drama League, which established a well-resourced library, produced a monthly journal and – like other agencies including the WIs – an annual drama festival, and ran classes for actors and directors alongside lectures and debates. But amateur activity also led to more formal organisation. The oldest amateur rep in the country, Newcastle People's Theatre, was founded in 1911 as too were the Norwich Players; the Scottish National Players followed in 1920. In the section on National Theatre we see how the Scottish company had an explicit aim to change the repertoire of work. So too the Norwich company intended to expand the repertoire of what was available in their city. When they opened their theatre, in the upper room of an old pub, in 1914, it was with a group of nativity plays. Thereafter, post-war, the company under their director Nugent Monck gained a reputation for Shakespeare productions. But the impact of amateurism was not only on repertoire: it also experimented with funding arrangements, revisiting the tactics used by the Edwardian Independent Theatres and Sunday Societies. The Norwich company was supported by guarantors giving a guinea (£1.05) each, and on that basis eventually built their Maddermarket theatre. So too at the Leeds Civic Playhouse, founded in 1925, Charles Smith, a manufacturer, promoted the policy of a 'free' theatre where the audience simply made a contribution to a collection. The Leeds theatre in turn spawned a break-away group in 1932, which eventually opened the Bradford Civic Playhouse in 1937.

Bradford drew its casts from the surrounding towns. Although the shows were under the professional direction of Esmé Church, the 'whole organisation', as J. B. Priestley celebrated, 'is run on democratic and amateur lines' (Priestley 1947: 49–50). Note those two adjectives: 'amateur' can be 'democratic' because it is not caught up into the wealth-based hierarchies of the professional theatre. Alongside the experiments with funding noted above, it was also, on a much larger scale, tied into schemes of public support. A number of Rural Community Councils coordinated the work of other agencies in drama provision. Local Authority Education Departments provided funding, infrastructure and advice, and the National Council for Social Service, above the RCCs, monitored and advised. In 1926 the Adult Education Committee of the Board of Education noted there were 'good grounds for hoping that the drama is sufficiently deep-rooted in the instincts of the people to ensure that the recent dramatic revival … will substantially enrich our national life' (in Wallis 2006).

While the amateur movement did not eventually supply the overall increase in educated audiences and did not change how theatre was done, it did very powerfully suggest how theatre could function differently in society. Whether it was the modelling, as at Bradford, of a democratic organisation or the links into schemes for social regeneration a defining feature of amateurism in the first half of the modern period is the necessary relationship between theatre and non-theatrical activity. A very clear example of this is Unity Theatre, founded in 1936. Its origins lay in one of the most active groups connected with the Workers' Theatre Movement (see Movements and manifestos), the Hackney-based Rebel Players founded in 1932. Its significant difference from those groups, and the point at which Rebel Players became Unity, was that it was based in a permanent building, in Britannia Street, King's Cross, London. 'Unity Theatre Club' had a committee/rehearsal room downstairs and a theatre upstairs. The investment in this building by amateurs was an attempt both to build a wider audience for working-class and left-wing theatre and, at the same time, to give as much emphasis to the art as to the politics. The building of the audience was in tune with the political imperative of the day, in that the older Communist Party line of 'class against class', which had informed much WTM work, had shifted to the creation of a Popular Front, drawing together almost all classes, liberals and communists, against fascism. From its base in King's Cross Unity encouraged and supported the formation of leftist theatre groups across the country. Its main mechanism for doing this was through an alliance with Victor Gollancz's Left Book Club: in April 1937 the Left Book Club Theatre Guild was born. Its role is summarised in the aims of John Allen's booklet *Some Notes on the Formation of Left-Wing Amateur Theatre Groups*. The two major needs, according to Allen, were the organisation of an audience and the access to suitable plays. Plays which were no longer suitable, in his opinion, were those of simple political agitation (Chambers 1989). The problem for Unity, as for the rest, was finding the right plays.

A very early Unity success (1936) was a staging of the American *Waiting for Lefty*, a rousing strike play in realist mode. This they took out to bus garages in 1937, where bus crews were on strike. But, after *Lefty*, new plays tended to be compared to it, often negatively. It did, however, encourage two amateurs to write a play – Robert Buckland and Herbert Hodge, both taxi drivers. Their play, *Where's that Bomb?* (1936), tells of how a worker poet is persuaded by the British Patriots' Propaganda Association to write a story that will 'instil in the mind of the worker his duty to his employer, his duty to his country and above all, the dreadful danger of attempting to think for himself' (in Chambers 1989: 70). The stories are to be written on lavatory paper and distributed free. But the writer has a nightmare in which his stereotypical characters appear, led on by the devil Money-Power. It ends with the characters revolting against Money-Power and the writer waking up to find himself confronted by debt collectors – but he refuses to sell his script. It was a huge success and marked Unity's capacity to develop new forms.

At the centre of Unity was a professional engaged with experimental work – John Allen was a founder member of Group Theatre, which did the verse plays of Auden and Isherwood, and worked with Michel Saint-Denis at the London Theatre Studio. But coming in from outside, encouraged by Allen, was new work by amateurs. Herbert Hodge followed up with *Cannibal Carnival* (1937), a 'vulgar spectacle' as he called it, which manages to evacuate all cherished positions: it works, as Mick Wallis says, as 'a wild cartoon that both attacks class society and offers a comic pastiche of the Marxist grand narrative' (Wallis 2004: 181). *Carnival* split its audiences, not unsurprisingly, but a more complete success – of legendary status – came from another amateur, a Post Office civil servant, Robert Mitchell. And it came from classic amateur territory. Mitchell suggested they do the sort of thing that he had done before with a local group, the Tavistock Players – a pantomime. The script he produced, *Babes in the Wood*, was pantomime pastiche turned to satiric political ends. Running from winter 1938 until early summer 1939, on the eve of war, it was a ferocious attack on the policy of appeasement of fascism. With savage accuracy a living Prime Minister, Neville Chamberlain, was represented on stage. Amateurism at Unity was not an earnest subservience to, but a knowing exploitation of, traditional theatre forms.

Running through everything, as in the WTM, was a commitment, as Allen put it, to theatre as 'a practical means of furthering the cause' (in Chambers 1989: 95). The link between those making theatre and those struggling by other means was crucial. One of the threats to the viability of this link was theatre training. By Joan Littlewood's account of RADA in the 1930s, training involved learning to inhabit upper-class lifestyles and values. Trained performers would seem inherently different, in both body and mind, from their political associates. Thus in the Prologue to Montagu Slater's *Easter: 1916* the audience are told they will get 'No high-falutin inventions more or less convincing, but a plain narrative of things that you know happened and – well – things you make happen. We want a few of you to come on the stage to act … We don't want people who have been trained in the Royal Academy of Dramatic Art.' Instead they want a 'tram-driver', 'a conductor', 'an engine-driver'. Apparent – but planted – volunteers come up from the audience (Slater 1936: 9). The show, from 1935, was done by Left Theatre under the professional direction of André van Gyseghem in association with the North London Area Committee of the Amalgamated Engineering Union. This Prologue with its claim to plainness precedes a play which was dramaturgically experimental and performed by a company of whom at least two were RADA trained. It is a rhetorical ruse designed to cement the bond between actors and audience on the basis of a shared disavowal of professional theatre values and unity in socialism.

Thirty years later, when Broadside Mobile Workers Theatre made their first show, *The Lump*, about non-unionised construction workers 'we decided we actually wanted to make the play with workers' (in Itzin 1980: 238). Their second play, about Lucas Aero-Space, again used workers to supply information and help shape the play. Making the play 'with' workers involves a higher level of involvement than union sponsorship, even if much of the involvement amounts to advice about industry processes. But the authenticity of the amateurism here is less important than the rhetorical reaffirmation of the values associated with the amateur movement. Broadside, as much as Left Theatre or Unity before them, were invoking a model of theatre that is validated by its links into non-theatrical interests and, hence, by its capacity to speak to people about the realities of their lives. The very fact of its distance from professionalism thus becomes, for amateur theatre, the guarantee of its value and significance.

Actors as activists

When Left Theatre worked with a trade union, when, indeed, it called itself Left Theatre, its members were declaring a commitment to, and then campaigning for, a political position. Acting as a servant of illusion gives way to activism, an engagement with the avowedly real. This shift redefines the role and function of theatre workers in society.

The earliest obvious case of the relationship between acting and activism in the twentieth century is that of the performers associated with the suffragette movement (see Feminist theatres). This campaigned for rights for women and, in particular, women's right to vote. Converted to the cause of Votes for Women, the actress Elizabeth Robins wrote a play – of that name – which she called a 'dramatic tract'. It was staged in 1907 at the Court Theatre. But Robins did not simply become a politically inspired author. She was a committee member of the Women's Social and Political Union, spoke publicly for the cause and was the first president of the Women Writers Suffrage League.

The same year saw the founding of the Actresses' Franchise League. Many leading writers and performers were associated with these two organisations, from the activists such as Edith Craig, Cicely Hamilton and Robins through to stars such as Lena Ashwell, Lillie Langtry and Ellen Terry. They wrote, produced and performed in plays and sketches in order to campaign and raise funds for the suffrage cause. And they marched in public demonstrations. These events suggest the curious status of the actor as activist.

Their political demonstrations were organised so that women of similar status or occupation marched together in separate sections. The Actresses' Franchise League were famous for their clothing, decorated with the pink and green colours of their organisation. In the march of 1910 the AFL section followed behind the sweated workers. Thus, immediately after the women physically broken by their work at making shoes and clothes, came Decima Moore in 'a grey and white striped dress, with a tight-fitting skirt of the latest fashion that forced her to take tiny steps' (quoted, and described, in Stowell 1992: 41). Lena Ashwell was similarly dressed up, carrying a bunch of pink and white flowers. These actresses were, in a sense, in costume, dressed to insist on their celebrity and charisma alongside their political commitment. But it's a strangely ambiguous image. On the one hand they are showing that the suffrage cause is supported by all sections of female society, including its stars and entertainers. On the other, they are confirming that the world, even within female society, is clearly divided along lines of wealth and privilege.

This ambiguity tends to hover around later instances of celebrities espousing causes. The more clear-cut cases of actor activism, however, are those which defined themselves against celebrity, and with it theatre hierarchy and, indeed, charisma itself.

One of the most unsettling propositions to emerge from the movements for sexual liberation of the early 1970s was that 'the personal is political'. Against an assumption that politics was done in activities, usually by men, outside the home, feminists argued that the internal arrangements of the home themselves reinforced divisions of power, and became thereby a site of political activity. The male activist who assumes that he is serviced by the woman at home himself perpetuates an arrangement whereby women are confined to particular spaces, activities and roles.

The belief that the personal is political had its effect on company organisation and on relationships between companies and their audiences. For women in sexually mixed companies their potential as theatre makers was often felt to be delimited by the interpersonal conduct of men. The creative as well as political issue for women and black theatre workers in the early 1970s was to develop a theatrical voice of their own, one that was not shaped and underpinned by masculine and white assumptions. They needed to work therefore towards a restructuring of the theatre company itself. This was most obviously the case in the separation of female performers from mixed companies. But there was also a celebrated instance of a gay socialist performer refusing to continue to work within the humiliating framework of assumed heterosexual, albeit socialist, norms. Noël Greig went on strike, on stage, in the middle of a show.

Activists at this period took the view that they were not simply making political theatre but that theatre activity was itself a mechanism for doing politics. Thus they became closely engaged with the structure and economics of theatre as an industry, developing new models of collective (see pp. 73–6) and non-hierarchical organisation. This view of theatre in turn shaped ideas about the responsibilities of the performer with regard to audiences. As John McGrath defined it, there was a class solidarity experienced by the performers. Their relationship with their audience was a contract. One of the 'unifying principles' of 7:84 was 'to keep faith' with the working-class audience 'by going back time after time'. The effect was that they 'appropriated us: we belonged to them' (McGrath 1981: 77). Back in the late 1920s socialist groups within the Workers' Theatre Movement discussed their work with fellow activists, so performances thus took their place within a larger political framework. The absorption of the show into such a context led to the 'post-show discussion', a device which had been used earlier by Unity Theatre but became almost compulsory in the 1970s. When such discussions took place the founding assumption was that the performers were answerable for the political positions in their work, and that consequently they would be able to explain and if necessary defend them. So where theatre is a method of doing politics the discussion is virtually as important as the show in that it's here that the performers perform their real commitment.

> I genuinely believe that heterosexual women cannot play lesbians convincingly. And also, if you're going to do anything that's to do with sexual politics, you've got to be able to justify it to the audience, because we're not simply in the theatre business, we're in the business of sexual politics in theatre. I realized that if afterwards the actresses couldn't totally support what they had said in the play, then it was a mistake.   (Jill Posener in Wandor 1986: 102)

Where the answerability for the message became most crucial was in the case of lesbian and gay theatre. A particular issue faced by lesbians and gays as a marginalised group was invisibility. They existed in a world which assumed they were heterosexual. Such an assumption denies the homosexual person their identity. So the early campaigns of lesbian and gay activists put much emphasis on coming out: announcing in public one's identity as a homosexual. This gesture, in abrasively condensed form, ended the first show by Gay Sweatshop, *Mr X* (1975), written by Drew Griffiths and Roger Baker. Mr X is subjected to a sequence of oppressive regimes, of school, work, church, and the 'discreet' gay club. For gay members of the audience the thrill of the show had two elements. In hearing the stereotyped discriminatory phrases, they could recognise that others had shared the experience. As with early feminist work, there was a powerful effect in the realisation that the suffering was not confined to oneself. But further, these discriminatory phrases were now being quoted and played back by those against whom they were directed. Gay, like feminist, performance worked to take control of the discourse. The play's climax comes when Mr X, seated in the audience, interrupts the Entertainer's racist and sexist patter. He refuses to laugh and refuses to shut up. He is mockingly invited to take the stage himself: '*Mr X walks to centre stage and faces the audience.* My name is Mister ... My name is (*Actor gives his own name*) and I live at (*His address*) and I'm gay.' In the first performance this was the actor Alan Pope. He goes on to state that he likes men sexually and declares a refusal to continue with the hidden 'twilight' life. The show ends with these two sentences: 'It's taken me twenty-five years to say this. The next twenty-five can only be better' (Baker and Griffiths 1997: 30). The audience now must witness this as coming from Alan Pope himself, the 'out' actor in front of them. Mr X has vanished, a theatrical fiction.

This is more than a moment at which the actor takes responsibility for the role and its message. It is, likewise, more than a moment in which the actor comes out from behind the role. Alan Pope replaces Mr X, standing centre stage in his stead. The actor is thus staging himself. And he shows himself to be in control of that process of self-staging. What this produces, in the culture of the still repressive mid-1970s, is an image of bravery held there as a moment of theatrical fullness, both a result of the rhetoric of the play and an authentic presence in its own right. It is not an activism alongside, or indeed despite, theatre. It is activism which takes its power from the working of theatre.

When the actor is activist there may be different relationships with, and values attached to, the performed play. But almost always the concept of actor as activist relegates the play to an element within a larger performance, namely the performance – the manifestation and furtherance – of the actor's commitment to a cause.

Non-acting

Where someone acts for political reasons, then the emphasis might be on the political cause rather than the quality of the acting. Furthermore the actor, trained or otherwise, who has views on the uses to which acting is put demonstrates that the actor is something more than a biddable functionary. In electing to perform outside of traditional structures and working relations of theatre, the activist/actor takes performing into new cultural and social spaces.

Nevertheless, activists often seek to do the thing which is conventionally recognisable as 'acting' – playing a part, imitating, pretending. A later development in the twentieth century saw the cultivated attempt to produce a mode of performing which is not imitating or pretending.

A notion of performing which isn't acting was developed in the rather intellectual climate that surrounded the American avant-garde form of the happening, from the 1950s. This entered British performance culture formally in an event organised by John Calder at the Edinburgh Festival in 1963 and thereafter in the work of The People Show, who first performed in 1966. Initially working from experimental scripts by the poet Jeff Nuttall, The People Show increasingly began to improvise in front of the audience. The group quarrelled and divided over the degree to which it wanted to be anarchic. When Nuttall said he was 'interested in the overall accidental form that occurs when the self-determined actions of a number of individuals are set together' (Nuttall 1979: 46), the key word is 'form'. Roland Miller, by Nuttall's (stridently personal) account, was more interested in anarchic release of individuality than in scripted form. In whichever mode there was space for performers to play out their own fixations and obsessions and to respond to what came back from the audience.

Such work remained, however, largely a theoretical and minority interest until the 1980s. During the late 1960s and the 1970s there had been a return to performance which is not-quite-acting in the work of the political activists. The mode from which so much explicitly political theatre derived was agit-prop – agitation towards political action combined with propaganda to disseminate political understanding. This was used by the Workers' Theatre Movement groups in the late 1920s/early 1930s, and then rediscovered in the early 1970s. It makes its effects by developing stage images that promote a clear and easily graspable typification of a social or political situation. In *Strike While the Iron Is Hot* (1974) Red Ladder used their ladder to display workplace hierarchy. A 'management figure', with an umbrella which says 'Profit' on it, climbs the ladder and has a conversation with his director, who is offstage. Later two union representatives come halfway up the ladder for discussions. The simplified picture does its work without much need for participants to 'act' as such.

The main quality that was needed was disciplined attention to the job in hand, an emphasis less on creation than efficiency. For the activists of the WTM this discipline itself constituted a powerful performance rhetoric. To see its mode of operation, take *Meerut*, a sketch from 1932 about British repression in India. Up to six performers held poles to make an image of a prison cell from which they addressed the audience. In his notes on *Meerut* the author,

Charlie Mann, insisted the poles be kept rigorously still, but not, primarily, on grounds of realism. They are not 'portraying a jail, but symbolizing imprisonment'. When the actors get to a mass-spoken line the poles need to tremble, but they must not be deliberately shaken: 'Grip them hard and the very intensity of your feelings will do the trick.' Similarly the ending, when the bars are thrown down, must not be anticipated. The sense of 'strain' will emerge from the tenseness of the performers. They must, he says, both feel the sketch and mean it (Mann 1985: 106–8). When Ewan MacColl did the piece with the Red Megaphones they 'drilled' themselves as if for 'an athletic event'. It is not an invitation to do mimetic acting. They must instead act out of conviction. This conviction, combined with a display of their physical discipline, will create the effects. Here the drilled efficiency of the political vanguard is also the source of the stirring emotion.

As with most theatrical forms agit-prop was practised with different degrees of understanding and ability. Its general relevance here, however, comes from its endeavour to show clearly rather than to imitate accurately. The activist performers spoke a message in which they believed. Where one of them might, for example, show the role of a capitalist, the image had two elements to it: a demonstration of the capitalist's function within the diagram; a calculatedly brutal simplification that marks the performer's political distance from the role that they demonstrate.

Thus agit-prop requires two main techniques. First is a conspicuous discipline governing voice and body of the performer which articulates intensity of conviction: this must not have any trace of pretence. Second is the making of a quotation effect, a refusal fully to inhabit the image, where pretending is undertaken in order to position the performer and spectators at a distance from what is shown: in other words, a deliberately limited acting. The two techniques come together in a form which was also driven, very often, by political commitment, but which aimed to explore an issue in more detail than agit-prop. Abjuring explicitly emphatic rhetoric, it foregrounded its commitment to the discovery and sharing of information. Its effects may have been both agitational and propagandist but it did not always conceive of itself as immediately ancillary to a political action. This form was the documentary (see Deferring to the real).

Many documentaries require high levels of traditional acting, but we need to note here the version of the form developed by Banner Theatre of Actuality. Banner made issue-based shows. *Dr Healey's Casebook* (1977) was commissioned by the trade union representing workers in the public sector, the National Union of Public Employees. The show was designed to reveal the conditions of work and levels of pay of these workers. Banner's technique in making the show, here and elsewhere, was based on interviewing, and taking verbatim accounts from, the subjects of their show. The verbatim text would be spoken on stage in front of projected images of the real speakers. The performers were both speaking words to which they were sympathetic and at the same time marking these words as those of others, a mode of delivery that required an absence of anything which smacked of conspicuous acting. Such delivery has its own discipline and technique, but these, once again, amount to a performed distance from the thing understood as 'acting'.

The turn away from the 1970s political culture had two influences, I think, on new theatre makers. As is regularly noted they faced a tougher financial climate, but economics alone do not necessarily determine form – agit-prop is extremely, so to speak, cheap. But agit-prop was 1970s. There was no longer the same political imperative driving the work. Where groups were politically conscious, they had to develop a different vocabulary. The turn away from politics as a driver was a turn towards foregrounded exploration of new stage languages (see Other than words). This was helped by the influx of people with art trainings (although in the 1970s such people as Welfare State made explicitly political work). The 1970s groups had revealed both the sterility of the dominant theatre culture and the opportunities for working in new spaces. That distance from dominant, traditional theatre was deeply inscribed, so the turn towards new stage languages was predicated on not being conventionally 'theatrical'. This led towards explorations of two different sorts.

First there is non-acting as aesthetic effect. In Forced Entertainment's *Emanuelle Enchanted* (1992) a curtain was used to punctuate the scenes. It was a device that was carefully used inefficiently: it might open when the performers seemed unprepared, 'waiting nervously', or setting the stage for a forthcoming scene'. Seemingly the performers had 'obvious disagreements … about what should be shown and when'. The apparent non-acting and awkwardness about being on stage were part of a general figuring of difficulty with 'theatrical representation' (Etchells 1999: 142). This worked metaphorically to show alienation from learnt mechanisms of communication. Where the techniques of theatre presentation are imaged as burdens and problems, the show is not rejecting theatre. It is making an aesthetic – and possibly ethical – effect out of failing to do theatre.

The second sort of non-acting is organised behaviour. In his The Ting: Theatre of Mistakes (founded 1974) Anthony Howell was under the influence of minimalism. He constructed shows that were based on simple exercises, rules and repetitions. In *Going* (1977) 'four performers watched the actions of one performer and then at staggered intervals attempted to imitate the actions that they saw as near-perfectly as they could.' This structure 'came from the philosophical point that we were performers not actors: we were involved in conditions of being rather than conditions of acting' (in Kaye 1996: 132–3). Rather than being an aesthetic statement of 'non-acting', here there is nothing to act. And rather than being a rhetorical display of discipline, as with the WTM, these 'exercises' are studiedly mundane. All that is required is a submission to rules. It is a model developed by Howell's former associate, Julian Maynard Smith, who explains that he started performing once he realised it was not about 'being someone else' and that you did not have to be good at it in order to do it. Thus Station House Opera's shows are also created from systems of rules, now not necessarily figured as abstract exercises but deriving from the nature of the materials employed. In a performance based on a pulley-system or handling breeze blocks, the rule-bound element derives initially from the law of gravity. In such circumstances the performers' choices are largely set for them by the conditions they are in.

Looking back over the various non-actings, it is worth noting that when you take away the acting you don't always have the same thing left. The People Show stripped down to an anarchic individualism; the WTM had as its raw material commitment to political party; the 'being' of Theatre of Mistakes was a disciplined presence that challenged both representation and libertarianism. In short, underneath acting you don't find nature. You find sets of values usually determined by the cultural moment. In the same way, acting itself is a performance of, a bringing into being of, values of one sort or another.

The politics of performing modes

Agitational acting wants to produce an audience that shares a political outlook; confessional acting publicly disclaims the capacity to interfere with the public. And, while this latter enjoys generating a level of undecideability about its tone, both may be said to make the actor's person rhetorically central to the show. Much of the traditional business of acting, however, has been focused on the work of engaging an audience with an acknowledged fiction. This engagement may range between an acceptance of the fiction as a credible articulation of a world that can be recognised as really existing through to a sense that the fiction is satiric, ironic, offered up for analysis. To produce the different sorts of audience engagement acting will efface or foreground, as necessary, the work of the actor. Sometimes that foregrounding will seem to reveal the real performer 'behind' the role, but such a revelation is usually an acted effect.

These general uses of acting are not new to the modern period. What is perhaps new is the idea that the particular form of an audience's engagement with a show carries within it ideological assumptions, if not explicit political values. A company's choice of performance mode may then be read as a statement of that company's values. Thus when, for example, the feminist company Monstrous Regiment did *Time Gentlemen Please* in Leeds in 1978 it was barracked by feminists and gay activists in the audience. The company had departed from the agitational-cum-realist aesthetic of feminist theatre by cultivating a cabaret mode: 'It's often very reactionary in content, so the challenge was to use that form in a way that challenged the audience's preconceptions about the relation of women to stand-up comedy' (Susan Todd in Itzin 1980: 277). To some this was not challenge but excuse: 'Far from creating a Dietrich image in order to subvert it, Monstrous Regiment appears to indulge itself in the creation, to revel in the fantasy' (Sandra Hunt in Wandor 1986: 72). The politics of oppressed groups in the 1970s put mode of representation high on the agenda.

And the 1970s had also discovered the major twentieth-century theorisation of the relationship between theatre aesthetics and political value in the work of Bertolt Brecht. In his tabulated comparison between the Aristotelian theatre and the Epic theatre and in his attack on 'culinary' theatre, Brecht had polemically argued for a new kind of theatre production appropriate to a new age. He modelled a form of performance in which actors, and the design, demonstrate the action and interactions of the play as something to be looked at critically, holding them up for inspection. For Brecht's company, especially in the circumstances of Germany in the late 1920s/early 1930s, this was something more than a formal device. The fiction was constructed by the agency of performers who themselves embodied a political intelligence, being seen to view the material – and audience – through this intelligence, and in doing so to work towards socialist revolution.

On stage, classical Brechtian method never properly established itself in the British theatre. It came closest in the 1970s with the Brecht productions at Whitechapel's Half Moon theatre (from 1972), which included Steve Gooch's translation of *The Mother*, later to influence a range of 'learning' shows with women at their centre, including 7:84's *Little Red Hen* and *Yobbo Nowt* and Red Ladder's *Strike while the Iron Is Hot*. So too it apparently influenced stage design, where the 'bare stage' aesthetic popularised by the Royal Court was given a political inflection by the Brecht-influenced director William Gaskill. But mainly the effort to locate a Brechtian tradition in British theatre has focused on writers, with the problem that, if you approach with a sufficient level of generalisation, almost anything, even if pre-Brecht, can be identified as estranging, historicising or gestic. 'Brechtian' became a label pinned to any work that was political, anti-commercial and showed the lighting rig. The more profound general effect was a sensitivity to the function and values of form. At the high theoretical level this was worked through, often in painful detail, by analysts in the emergent academic discipline of film studies. But among the political theatre groups, form was also a key consideration. Red Ladder changed from the heroics of agit-prop to a more realist mode in response to the 'downturn' in political climate after 1974 (Itzin 1980: 48).

The re/turn to Brechtian theory came about in the highly politicised 'counter-culture' of the 1970s. This not only created new urgency around form and performance mode, but it also brought Marxism to bear on aesthetics. These were not entirely new concerns, however. Minority voices in the British tradition had already made critiques of form and mode. Most famously, the Edwardian scenographer Edward Gordon Craig had launched an attack on stage realism and its main vehicle, the actor. He argued in 1907 that the stage could only be 'free' once it broke the connection between 'actuality and art': 'Do away with the actor and you do away with the means by which a debased stage-realism is produced and flourishes' (Craig 1980: 81). For Craig realist acting was incapable of showing something greater, which he defined as the life of the spirit. Twenty-five years later that greater thing was defined by activists of the Workers' Theatre Movement as the class struggle. While naturalism showed the surface, a form was needed to disclose 'the reality which lies beneath' (in Samuel *et al.* 1985: 101). Amongst its treatments of explicitly political issues, such as militarism, exploitation of labour and colonialism, the WTM did a sketch called *Their Theatre and Ours* (1932). The issue of stage representation was that important.

The WTM's division of 'them' and 'us' is based in social class. But the developments of efficiency in travel and communications in the early twentieth century had facilitated a different sense of them and us, based in region and in conscious difference from a cultural centre. Marie Lloyd apparently couldn't get much of an audience in the East End of London. And when Vesta Tilley sang 'Burlington Bertie – the Boy with the Hyde Park Drawl' up West, Ella Shields made a success out of her satirically distanced 'Burlington Bertie from Bow'. Further afield, Scottish theatre-makers resented touring English companies and developed an explicitly Scottish repertoire. Similarly, the Gaiety theatre in Manchester cultivated a 'Manchester school' of playwrights. In their separate ways these examples all suggest an awareness that form comes from somewhere and speaks for someone, that is to say, that it carries value and affiliation.

It is more in its function of defining them and us than in its Brechtian invitation to analysis that performance mode was deployed in the 1970s. One of the clearest examples of it at work is in the 7:84 company's *The Cheviot, the Stag, and the Black, Black Oil* (1973). The show's author, John McGrath, was clear about the links between form and class: a working-class audience, he says, likes directness, comedy, music, emotion, variety, effect, immediacy, localism, and, lastly, sense of identity with the performer (McGrath 1981: 54–8). In *Cheviot* the effort was also to stage local Scottishness. The show's form was based on a ceilidh and the company played as ceilidh entertainers, using their real names. From here they stepped into the roles of the narrative: these might be conceived as cartoon-style caricatures or as more explicitly realist creations. The mode of performance worked to produce a series of related effects. As with Brecht's company, the 7:84 actors had a personal authority deriving from their reputation as a politically committed company, with their commitment evidenced, in part, by the conspicuous hard labour which touring involves. When one of the company stepped into a caricature role, as with Liz MacLennan playing Lady Phosphate of Runcorn, the audience was invited to share with the performers the pleasure that comes from an imitation that is willfully exaggerated. The target of that imitation is positioned as a shared enemy, and the audience is brought onside.

At another moment, Alex Norton comes forward to sing as 'himself'. When he played at Lord Selkirk in top hat it was shared fun with the cartoon but the delivery as himself has greater seriousness. That seriousness is marked throughout by a range of devices – the use of Gaelic, folk song, poetry, documentary facts. These moments give weight to the political message which the performers embody, because in these moments they are not, so to speak, playing.

Contemporary with John McGrath's work with 7:84, and similarly of its period, there is Albert Hunt's work with, mainly, students at the Bradford College of Art. Hunt, like McGrath, had explicitly political aims. But the mode of performing he developed was more conspicuously playful, and more intensely political precisely because of that. Take his description of Chris Vine as Nixon, as Marilyn Monroe, as Tony Curtis: 'Throughout all these switches, Chris Vine remains himself, playing with a Yorkshire accent. But the megalomaniac look in his eyes, and the thrust-out chin is Nixon's. And the wiggle of the hips is Monroe's' (Hunt 1976: 101). This is a rather more searching exploration of the relationship of performer and role than was required in McGrath's show. The 7:84 actors moved in and out of role sequentially. Hunt, by contrast, layered the roles one over another, having them played simultaneously (see too Marowitz's experiments pp. 83–4). This mode of performance thus sets in motion something very much more complex. A 7:84 performance was anchored in the real presence of the politically committed company. No such confident basic reality anchors Hunt's performers.

For a start, they were students rather than members of an established touring company. Secondly, the mode of performing refused to confirm where the real actually lies, as it were. When Chris Vine does Nixon, who is the primary presence, the most really real identity? This mode of performing is based in play and, above all, in contradiction, 'between what people saw, and what they were told they were seeing, between the real performer physically *there*, and the parts he said he was playing' (Hunt 1976: 103). Personas are obviously fictional but, at the same time, as fictions have a powerful impact.

A good example of this doubleness, and an illustration of how this mode of performance can refunction a text scripted for another mode, is the production of *Belle Reprieve* done by Split Britches and BLOOLIPS in 1991. The show was based on the film version of Tennessee Williams's *A Streetcar Named Desire*. Split Britches is the lesbian company comprising, mainly, Lois Weaver and Peggy Shaw; BLOOLIPS a gay company comprising, here, Bette Bourne and Precious Pearl. Throughout, the familiar personas of the performers were in evidence, with Bette in particular specialising in the production of an ironic, reflexive quality to what he did. After a scene of tap-dancing Chinese lanterns, Bette as Blanche protests that he wants to be in a real play, with real scenery, and a 'theme and plot we can all follow'. Lois Weaver's Stella replies that they talked about it 'and we decided realism works against us'. Bette continues, saying his mother wants him to be 'playing a real person with a real job, like on television'. As Lois says, 'You want realism, you can have it,' Peggy, as Brando as Stanley, begins to play the role for real (Bourne *et al.* 1996: 178–9). These remain 'cross-dressed' actors, but the stage becomes violent and difficult. His ironic aura evaporating, Bette as Vivien Leigh as Blanche as Bette becomes vulnerable. Peggy produces from within herself an emotional violence that is Brando, Stanley and Peggy. These are multiple fictions but their violent presence is not illusory. The realism works 'against' them because it pins them down to single characters, gives them no doubleness that can ironise and defuse that violence.

This realism also limits the pleasure. At one moment Lois Weaver, playing Stella, talks direct to the audience. Presenting as feminine and blonde, she describes Cassandra, the prophetess of ancient Troy who was destined never to be believed; and then she imagines herself as one of the soldiers in the wooden horse, in love with the 'blonde' Cassandra. Speaking as this soldier, feeling Cassandra's hands on her breasts, she is both male and female: 'Somebody stole my woman ... filched her from history, and I'm here to get her back. I am a powerful warrior.' As she speaks she reveals a tight, strapless dress and begins to pose like Marilyn Monroe: 'I'm in here. Can't you see me? I'm having sex with the fortune teller that men don't believe' (Bourne *et al.* 1996: 168).

Stella, the lesbian performer, the mythic Cassandra, a Greek warrior in a horse and the 'sex object' Marilyn Monroe are all fused together. Characterisation is replaced by multiple identity. That multiple identity is both a celebration of lesbian desire and an act of political reclamation. Marilyn Monroe is reinhabited but is no less sexy. The politics of the performing are in the pleasure, and the pleasure is as much theatrical as sexual.

Directors

The emergence of the director

The concept of the theatre director was only just beginning to emerge at the start of the twentieth century. Writing in 1938, Somerset Maugham said 'director' was an American word, whereas the English word was 'producer' (Maugham 1961: 103).

In his 1910 book on the new concept of the 'repertory' movement, P. P. Howe links the emergence of the producer to the contemporary revitalisation of theatre:

> The art of producing is a part of the art of the theatre which, if it is not altogether the outcome of the new spirit abroad, has developed contemporaneously. The function of the producer is to give artistic unity to the representation upon the stage. The artistic conscience of the theatre is in his keeping. As this artistic conscience has developed, the function of the producer has been realised to be increasingly indispensable. (Howe 1910: 182–3)

This new artistic conscience is contrasted with the commercial conscience of a dramatist such as Tom Robertson working in the1860s. His work is at a level that doesn't need a producer:

> But with the production of plays more elusive in their spirit than the comedies of Robertson – which might well, indeed, be produced by the stage-manager, since they are as well within his understanding as that of the author – the stage-manager has seen the rise of the producer. It was not a case this time of supersession. The stage-manager retains control of all the mechanical work of the stage. The producer is the new supplementary authority who assumes responsibility for the artistic unity of the whole. It is a simple matter of allotment of function. The dramatist supplies both letter and spirit. The stage-manager is competent to deal with the letter, and the producer's business is to interpret the spirit. (Howe 1910: 185)

As the new repertory movement develops, so, says Howe, 'the producer might be expected to come into his own' (Howe 1910: 186).

Howe might have had in mind one of the people most closely associated with the new repertory movement, Harley Granville Barker. Barker was himself an actor, a playwright and a producer. While his plays, with their radical edge, were clearly inhabited by the 'modern' spirit it was in his productions of Shakespeare's work that he became most famous as a director. These productions drew from the antiquarian experiments of William Poel, who had returned to a version of the Elizabethan platform and simple setting. But Barker was not being antiquarian. His *Twelfth Night* was played in front of six backdrops with only one full set. Rather than an empty stage, the drops marked specific place. At the same time they remained militantly flat and decorative, with Orsino's court in front of a yellow and black patterned cloth. The result was neither traditional picture-book nor scholarly antiquarian. Its individuality foregrounded the concept of the production, where the concept was a creative intervention by the director which stood alongside, and worked with, the creative input of the dramatist. At this point the twentieth-century idea of the director comes into view.

And then it fades again. In the years after Barker the roles remained ill-defined although there was incipient tension between director and author. In places the old model of the actor-managers persisted, with star actors or actor-authors, such as Noël Coward, arranging the production around themselves. As an author Somerset Maugham still believed in 1938 that the director should be little more than Howe's stage-manager, dealing with the 'mechanics' of the play. This was a reaction to the increased interference from directors by contrast with his early career. The author's text, he complained, was being used as a vehicle for the director's ideas. Not content merely to 'interpret', the director saw it as 'an opportunity for an original creation of his own' (Maugham 1961: 146). Where authors were dead things were easier. The art of directing came into its own as an authorship in staging classical texts which had a history of being done in various different ways. This was and is most obviously the case with Shakespeare.

Shakespeare's work was pre-eminently the vehicle which enabled development of directorial experiment because it was neither obviously commercial theatre nor issues-based contemporary experiment. Here, as Poel and Barker had shown, the director's creativity becomes obvious in its own right. Here, too, lines of influence developed. Poel's work influenced Nugent Monck, who did Shakespeare and classical productions at the Maddermarket theatre in Norwich in the 1920s. Monck, in his turn, influenced Tyrone Guthrie. But Guthrie also knew directly the work done by Poel and Barker, the latter of whom

Guthrie regarded as the 'the only great British director' (Guthrie 1961: 78). Much on the model of Barker, in 1936 Guthrie thought of doing Shakespeare in a scenography with no concessions to realism, with actors organised in choreographic patterns.

From Barker, though, there was another line, which went through his disciple Harcourt Williams, who worked at the Old Vic 'to carry Barker's stylistic reforms into the stronghold of popular Shakespeare. This meant a purge on Bardic rhetoric, continuity of action, and the principle of designed production' (Wardle 1979: 21). Williams's approach to Shakespeare influenced John Gielgud, whose 1932 production of *Romeo and Juliet* for the Oxford University Dramatic Society was regarded as innovatory. In Gielgud's later Shakespeare work another influence became clear: Guthrie suggested his 'exquisite production' of *Merchant of Venice* at the Vic in 1932 was influenced by Michel Saint-Denis and his Compagnie des Quinze, who in their turn were adapting the principles of Copeau. In his interaction with both Saint-Denis and Theodore Komisarjevsky Gielgud was a key figure in strengthening the role of the director in the 1930s.

The emergence of these lines of influence suggests two things. First they begin to establish something like a textual history of directing, where concepts can be passed on. Second, insofar as directors such as Guthrie were conscious of these lines, they claim an autonomous and self-knowing art of directing. That art was recognised in its own right when in the mid-1950s the English Stage Company launched its Associate Director scheme.

Methods of direction

The ESC did much to promote 'writer's theatre'. By also encouraging new directors it was implying that it is the director as much as the author, and both rather than the actor, who is the creative force. Indeed at this time of new writing defined teams of directors and writers established themselves: through the Associate scheme came Lindsay Anderson, who worked with David Storey, and John Dexter, with Arnold Wesker; elsewhere Peter Hall and Harold Pinter developed a working relationship. But what had already become apparent earlier in the century with the great directors – Barker, Monck, Guthrie, for example – was that directing was itself a mode of writing. Guthrie was famous for his ability to organise the rhythm of a production, a flow of movement across the stage and through scenic units, often carried visually in his trademark banners and swirling fabrics. Of directorial method he said that it was out of 'suggestions [glances, small movements, tentative tones exchanged between actors], out of ideas only half formed in the consciousness of any single individual, that a good director builds up a scene, instinctively feeling, rather than consciously knowing, which of these half-formed suggestions to accept, which to reject' (Guthrie 1961: 57). Guthrie's younger contemporary, Joan Littlewood, insisted that the production never got to a stage where it settled into a fixed, stable state. To keep the actors always inventing she cast them against type and discouraged any reliance on established structures of technique. She forced them away from the physical script imposed by their training, as director rewriting the actors' bodies.

These methods contrasted stridently with the somewhat older method of Michel Saint-Denis, who arrived for rehearsals of Obey's *Noah* with all the positions and moves worked out. Saint-Denis had an interest in wordless moments of activity (getting Alec Guinness really to listen to his character's squeaky boots), but his method of arriving there did not share the work of creation with the actor. In a similar way his colleague, George Devine, who managed the English Stage Company from the mid-1950s, prepared 'an annotated prompt copy' before rehearsals. Here too the actor was expected to serve a pre-written text, both that of the author and that of the director.

This contrast leads into two lines of development. First, the Guthrie method was taken up and extended by later twentieth-century directors, many of whom have nothing explicitly planned before they enter the rehearsal room. The work of rehearsal is to enable the actors to explore, to test, to create. This process of exploration can be continued into the performance through readiness to improvise and respond spontaneously to stimuli. It is an approach that altered both the practice of rehearsal and the director's role. As Simon McBurney of Complicite describes it, 'We would sort of construct a playground in the rehearsal room and then out of that playground things would emerge and the pleasure of it was a crucial element, the pleasure of that creation' (in Tushingham 1994: 17–18). Almost unbidden by the director 'things' emerge organically from, not the play, but the playground.

The second development concerns the director's attitude to the dramatist's text. When she did seventeenth-century plays Littlewood dug out neglected works and came at them afresh, working with their action and verse. A director such as Robert David Macdonald, on the other hand, felt free to remove or change such text, famously cutting away one-third of Ford's Stuart tragedy *'Tis Pity She's a Whore*.

Macdonald's *Whore* was done with the Glasgow Citizens' Theatre. Under the triumvirate of Giles Havergal, Philip Prowse and Robert David MacDonald, the 'Citz' became famous for its production style through the 1970s and 1980s, with practices that extended the range of what might be considered theatrical authorship. The Citz style was characterised by a foregrounding of the relationship between the director, dramaturg and designer – at the expense, some thought, of the author. Thus the show about Diaghilev, *Chinchilla* (1977), was directed by Prowse, who was principally a designer: 'Everything about *Chinchilla* stemmed from Prowse – the idea, the setting, the events – and his conception resulted in MacDonald avowedly writing for the company, almost to order' (Coveney 1990: 92). When four years later Prowse did Marlowe's *Massacre at Paris* it was the design and conception – rather than Marlowe's notoriously fragmented and 'incomplete' text – which gave coherence to the show. The design

> rose by steps from the auditorium into the semblance of a Gothic altar prepared for a funeral, the edifice draped in black and dotted with bunches of candles. The actors arrived like Jacobean conspirators through the stalls, gargling and coughing and arranging their properties. They were to perform before the Virgin Queen, who particularly appreciated the downfall of the Duke of Guise and, by implication, all Papist infiltration sponsored by Philip of Spain. Prowse thus sharpened the proceedings with a keen sectarian edge, and achieved a turbulent farce enacted in a whirl of black and gold for the slaking of Protestant righteousness.   (Coveney 1990: 166)

In shaping the sprawl with a found sectarian significance the designer works as dramaturg. The written text is little more than the thing that provokes or tempts meditation on, and fantasy about, the interactions, emotions and illusions suggested by the play.

For the Citz's historian Michael Coveney this relationship between the status of writing as against that of directing and designing became characteristic of its period: 'finally breaking the shackles of the new social and theatrical realism of the 1950s and 1960s, theatre returned to a sense of its own "theatre-ness"'. New writing was 'removed from the agenda' in favour of 'new theatre': 'There was a concerted upsurge of interest in new physical forms of design, dance, musical and narrative aesthetics' (Coveney 1990: 151, 154). Perhaps more clearly than at any other time in the century the 1980s saw directors and designers gain creative prominence as important as that of playwrights. This return to 'theatre-ness' was caused partly, Coveney suggests, by economics – realism requires expensive settings. But in part it also grew out of challenges, through different company organisations, to the status of script and the method of generating material. In the late 1960s / early 1970s people not trained as performers formed companies – in particular, art and design students were embracing performance. Collaborative creation came to refer not simply to the work of actors devising material, but to conversations and explorations across disciplines.

For historians of written plays the 1980s looks like a theatrically arid time. This oft-repeated critical position always feels rather satisfactory, because it demonstrates how bad things were under Margaret Thatcher's government. But historians of 'theatre' have a merry time with the 1980s, which saw the emergence of all sorts of new work – generated, however, by collaborations and companies. The writer was far from being the primary author. The new ways of 'writing' released theatrical energy not simply because they provided new means of generating material in economically straitened times, but also because they opened up a new range of material. This was the era of the 'refunctioning' of classic texts, of adaptations of historical material, as seen at the Citz or in the work of Red Shift. And for those who want to find in 1980s theatre a response to Thatcherism, it is here in two senses. First, under a government which invoked a crudely jingoistic sense of history those refunctioned texts offered new, complicated relationships to historical material. Second, under the governmental by-words of 'realism' and 'responsibility' the director-designer stages shimmered with sensual fabrics and fantasy spaces, fluidly interrelating pictures and shapes, perspectives inviting to a new sort of pleasure … as the early Gloria show put it, *A Vision of Love Revealed in Sleep*.

Characteristically for the time it took its impulse from historical material, the life of the artist Simeon Solomon. Also characteristically, this opened the door into a riskily sensual domain. The show began at London's Drill Hall theatre in 1989 with a smoke-filled space, a large red velvet curtain concealing the stage, a piano playing. When the lights went down, the curtain slowly opened to reveal a wall of black fabric on which captions were projected: 'Vision: A person seen in a dream or trance'. After the last caption, to a phrase of music, the black curtain falls to reveal a dimly seen, gold-painted back wall, in front of which are four posing platforms and a grand piano. It has 'the effect of a grand artist's studio'. The pianist then pauses, hands suspended in the air. With him on stage is 'a semi-naked man, posed like an artist's model, partially draped in a length of dull red silk'. A single light bulb is snapped on, revealing the powdered white body and red hair of the semi-naked man. He speaks as if woken from sleep, moving between everyday vocabulary and a semi-biblical register. Later he breaks from this gentle, 'elevated' tone, and talks directly to the men in the audience in a way which is 'chatty, sexy' (Bartlett 1990: 87–8).

The speaker is Neil Bartlett, director and author as well as performer. With him at the piano is Nicolas Bloomfield, his collaborator in the company Gloria. Both are present for the audience as, apparently, themselves, yet they are also performing. The performance is not, however, an imitation. It evokes the world of its subject, Simeon Solomon, but it slides between that and the present. And, while Bartlett talks directly to the audience, the performance textures – the smoke, the velvet, the powder, the sleepy voice – are carefully thickened, beyond the everyday. This is theatre not as mimesis but as dressing up, not so much pretence as pose. The effect emphasises the presentness of the show, in all its thick texture, then and there in front of the audience. It refuses any division between illusory theatricality and direct address. Here the theatrical apparatus is part of direct address. The eventually naked body is shaved and powdered, not simply a naked body but one cosmetically foregrounded. Exceeding what would be required by mimetic accuracy, it deals in the unnecessary and the overdone.

Bartlett's spoken text depends heavily on use of the personal pronoun, in whatever register he speaks: 'Of all the lives I could cry for, tonight it is him I choose to mourn'; 'I don't know why I do it. It's just something I do. I follow strange men sometimes' (Bartlett 1990: 88). The 'I' that speaks is identifiable as Bartlett, an openly gay man whose work specialises in the 'personal' narrative. The reference to 'tonight', and later to 'this theatre', combines with flirting with the men in the audience. The Drill Hall was famous for its lesbian and sometimes gay repertory. The time was the year after the passing into law of the infamous Section 28, a legal restraint on 'promotion' of homosexuality. Bartlett's studied flirtation with his audience is knotted up with Solomon's history of discrimination. The pleasurable here-and-now not separable from a still-present there-and-then. The sensuality has a political edge.

It's given force by the fact that Bartlett stands there not just as actor but also director: 'this is his book,' he says, showing a book. 'And everything I say tonight is true' (Bartlett 1990: 88). When an actor claims truth, it is dubious. So too the book is not necessarily a guarantee. This, though, is not a theatre of signs, of standing in for something else. It is a theatre of presence – not simply because of its sensual textures but because Bartlett the vulnerable actor is doing what is required of him by Bartlett the director. Closing the gap between actor, author and director, the show gets its power from the presence in front of us of the director.

Company style

The style of *Vision* was to become identified with the company that made the show. So too in the work of the Citz the house-style not only made coherent a fragmented text such as Marlowe's *Massacre* but also produced a continuity linking the different shows together. In effect the individual shows were subsumed into a larger performance which was the performance of the Citizens' Theatre. Robert David MacDonald knew this: 'The essence of a company will take over the essence of a play and all plays will, sooner or later, tend to become plays about theatrical companies' (in Coveney 1990: 145). The company comes to be both author and subject of the performance. This is one development of late twentieth-century approaches to directing.

A second, and later, development comes when directors apparently step away from individual authorship and submit themselves to a shared process. One obvious sign of it is the practice of 'co-directing', where there is no single voice of authority. More complex is the work of the 'collaborative' companies. For instance Forced Entertainment begin by building 'some crude environment in which to work, using materials from old sets or whatever else is to hand. The building of this environment is important to us.' The 'director', Tim Etchells, also places himself in this environment and the company improvises for long periods. Etchells is clear of the distance between this and a scripting approach: 'over the years we've come to rely less and less on preconceived ideas and more and more on these complex accidents or discoveries made in the rehearsal studio'. The most important element is: 'The idea of process, to go into a room and "see what happens"; the fact that when you enter the room you have no idea whatsoever about what will happen.' Similarly Declan Donnellan, of Cheek by Jowl, says: 'I don't "see" the play in my head before I enter the rehearsal room, or indeed during the rehearsal process.' Working mainly on pre-scripted material, and especially Shakespeare, Donnellan opens up space for the unplanned: 'I never have any preconceived idea of how I will rehearse. That idea emerges once I have begun the process. The important thing is to know that you don't know how you will proceed.' And problems get solved when nobody is trying to solve them, when in a break a gesture is accidentally spotted, a line overheard (Etchells and Donnellan in Giannachi and Luckhurst 1999: 25, 24, 26, 27, 20).

Note the word that both Etchells and Donnellan use at the point where they declare their distance from that which is planned and pre-scripted: 'process'. Growing out of the emergence of workshopping and devising, 'process' has become a key word in theatre-making vocabularies over the last decade or so. It's a word that signals a position in relation to creation. It can suggest a valuing of the collaborative and ensemble. As Etchells and Donnellan use it, it sits on the opposite side from planning and pre-scripting. And for some, such as Simon McBurney of Complicite, it is more important than finished outcome; the work is always being made and is to be seen as such. 'Process', then, might be the opposite of that which is stratified, prescriptive and closed.

But process notwithstanding, Donnellan has his name on the Cheek by Jowl shows, Etchells writes the published essays, McBurney is the company master. They may not enter the room with an author's vision, but each facilitates – and owns – what happens. There may be a shift in the definition of directing, but the director-figure remains firmly in place. Process is important, then, not necessarily for its organisational effects but for what it means. In a way thoroughly in tune with 1990s philosophy, process is flow and open-endedness or – rather – the fetishisation of those. As such it becomes not just a way of making the show but the thing that is shown. Forced Entertainment's rehearsal method of building spaces became 'a part of what is presented onstage, so the characters in *Emanuelle Enchanted* (1992) and those in *Hidden J* are all involved in building spaces, in manipulating the world they exist in' (Etchells in Giannachi and Luckhurst 1999: 26).

To embrace process is to embrace that which seems to be the feeling of the 1990s. Process thus has the facility to become an image for contemporary experience. In a way that Howe would have recognised in 1910, the director remains the guardian of, if not the artistic 'conscience', then the artistic relevance. The new 'spirit' is process. And in, as it were, interpreting this spirit directors have shown their independence from scripts and writers.

Writers

The modern period has experimented with the writer's role. It has seen the playwright as solitary producer submitting texts to theatre companies, through regular partnerships between writers and directors (see above) or writers and companies (Shaw and Stage Society, Churchill and Joint Stock), to the absorption not only of the writer but the act of writing itself into the company, on the model of company research, collective writing or creation by group devising. It has perhaps become more easy in the modern period to make a secure living by being a playwright. This has to do in part with laws of copyright but also with the development of publishing, which has realised the economic value of the playtext as book. That value has been underpinned by the study of plays in formal education.

For many now the key creative figure in theatre is assumed to be the writer. 'Twas not always thus, as they say. Writing for the stage was once regarded as a lesser form of literature, all too vulnerable to interventions from others during the production process. Theatre writers, subjected to the piracy and plagiarism of the commercial market, had the roles of hacks. When the backlash against melodrama and spectacle began in the late nineteenth century, the elevation of respect for the written text was seen as the way to renew the seriousness of theatre. The radical new Stage Society of the Edwardians set itself against both commercialism and triviality by promoting the playwright.

Fifty years later, in the same home theatre – the (Royal) Court – the English Stage Company launched a similar campaign to renew theatre through the cultivation of writers. By way of supporting new writers in their craft – and giving them an institutional place – the Royal Court established its Writers' Group. Its repertoire also drew on modern European work – by Sartre, Ionesco, Beckett – which in effect demonstrated that it is the playtext on its own which can cross borders. And the enemy, once again, was seen as commercial spectacle in the form, specifically, of the H. M. Tennent producing company. Tennents (see Managers) had a reputation for doing lavishly costumed, celebrity-studded shows. With a stranglehold on London's West End they captured a mass audience. To the crusaders for new theatre the sure marker of success was, therefore, an inversion of the Tennents model: the director of the ESC, George Devine, expressed a gleeful contempt for the audience (Rebellato 1999: 112). In its support for writers, especially those who are demonstrably free of the commercial marketplace, the ESC brought to a culmination the fifty-year endeavour to position the writer, as opposed to any other theatre-maker, as a kind of barometer which indicated whether theatre is serious or not.

This seriousness had particular defining features which can be suggested by looking at the views of someone whom Devine and his Courtly crew regarded as the enemy playwright *par excellence*. He was, naturally, associated with the glutinous Tennents, though less as a client than as another theatre homosexual. Terence Rattigan – it was he – had acquired notoriety for himself among the 'serious' theatre people on the basis of two essays on the playwright's role. The earliest one, 'Concerning the Play of Ideas', appeared in the *New Statesman* in March 1950. This attacked the sort of drama associated with Shaw. The problem with 'theatre today' is not, says Rattigan, that 'so few writers refuse to look the facts of the present world in the face but that so many refuse to look at anything else' (in Wansell 1995: 249). As a description of the work of one of the leading dramatists of the 1940s, J. B. Priestley, this was not really accurate. But accurate critique was perhaps less important than the polemical restating of a position that had at an earlier date also been articulated by Somerset Maugham. In *The Summing Up* (1938) Maugham warns against the problem of ideas and argues that the demand for ideas will lead to the decadence of theatre. Again the problem is the real: 'the drama took a wrong turning when the demand for realism led it to abandon the ornament of verse' (Maugham 1961: 138). Realism, for Maugham, had an anti-dramatic effect.

To the eyes of earnest Courtiers of the late 1950s, such statements are an abrogation of the serious writer's duty to engage with ideas and real-world facts. In addition Rattigan committed the cardinal sin of ceding his right to be abrasively authoritative. In the preface to the second volume of his *Collected*

Plays (1953) his effort to characterise the writer's relationship with the audience led to the invention of a notorious image for that audience, and its power: 'a nice, respectable, middle-class, middle-aged, maiden lady, with time on her hands' – Aunt Edna (Rattigan 1977: xi–xii). While great novelists and composers can ignore her, the dramatist cannot, for she will tell the world if she has wasted an afternoon in the theatre. And the world will listen – as Joe Orton knew when he used 'Edna' to author scandalised letters to the press about his own plays. This, however, was much more covert, and indeed playful, than the ESC would wish to be. They were the ones, not Orton, who, by insistently disseminating banned scripts, led the charge against theatre censorship.

For them serious theatre faced facts and maintained its abrasive authority, by means, principally, of the agency of the writer. Thus, as the issues around theatre changed in the later 1960s and the 1970s, the arguments continued to focus on the position of the writer as the barometer for the state of theatre. So when David Edgar spoke of the difficulty of doing a 'committed show' with repertory actors, this revealed the bankruptcy of the repertory system (even though Richard Eyre's repertory company in Nottingham had just done a series of 'committed' pieces) (Edgar 1979: 13). Nevertheless writers still needed a company of some sort – while they may well be visionary they are also dependent. It's the nature of that dependency which symptomises the times.

For Edgar in the same piece argues that plays about public subjects can't take place in rooms but must have at their disposal large stages. His own play *Destiny* achieved its effect, he says, by being done by the Royal Shakespeare Company at the Aldwych. This argument coincides in date with Brenton's and Hare's argument as to why it was necessary for them to get into the National Theatre, and Trevor Griffiths's line about strategically 'penetrating' television (up its tube presumably). In the late 1950s it was enough for the serious playwright to be on the small Royal Court stage – indeed anything larger might be unserious. In the mid-1970s there is the notion that the serious place to be is in the National or Aldwych. But against that viewpoint John McGrath argued that the real engagement was to be found on the touring circuit (see pp. 46, 100). Shortly after, Noël Greig showed, in *Plague of Innocence* (1988), that you could produce a play of huge scope in the form of a narrative that might be done, if economically necessary, by the dramatist himself. In other words for some people serious public space was the subsidised theatre of the biggest companies, while for others the public was a dispersed entity. As much as for Maugham or Rattigan the negotiation around the correct audience, and the correct way of treating that audience, tells us not about abstract seriousness but about the positioning of dramatists within changing economic environments.

Definition of that positioning is one of the key activities of the modern period. There are two aspects to it. First, the role of the independent playwright emerges as the key serious creative. Take two moments about ten years apart. Christopher Fry became famous after Tennents cast celebrity actors, including Laurence Olivier, in his plays; John Osborne, by contrast, enabled Olivier to breathe new life into a fading career by providing as vehicle *The Entertainer* (1957). The dependency of star actor and author shifts. So, schematically, there is Noël Coward in the 1930s in the role of actor and socialite-cum-author, as characterised by himself in *Present Laughter* (1939); Rattigan a decade or so later was author rather than actor, but still a socialite. Osborne dropped easily enough into an available stereotype, 'angry young man', participating in events around Royal Court causes such as nuclear disarmament. Hare, who begins as infiltrator with Brenton, discovers the celebrity potency of being not socialite but socialist. From Coward as society artist to Hare as state artist, the modern period discovers what a serious public dramatist is.

Second, it shapes the way people now approach the study of theatre. Playwrights, being used to writing, are well positioned to produce commentary of their own on theatre. Publishing has become alert to the value of playtexts and hence playwrights. And within this world of print – and especially the print produced for the academic market – a particular story is told relentlessly. This story has at its heart the ESC and its heroic effort to make authors the serious creatives. So when 'new writing' was rediscovered, yet again, at the Royal Court in the 1990s – Kane, Ravenhill, Neilson – the press coverage knew precisely the discourse whereby new writing comes with outrage, just as it did with, say, Edward Bond. Thus most narratives of post-war British theatre circle around '1956' and, indeed, a proper book on modern theatre might be expected to have at its heart accounts of the works of playwrights.

And to those we turn. But not quite yet. Two more small observations need making.

First, when Rattigan said 'the only theatre that has ever mattered is the theatre of character and narrative' (Wansell 1995: 249) it could be argued that, as his work shows, he was trying to open up space for something usually tidied away. Call it perhaps desire, passion, sexuality – the stuff that all too often couldn't be said. Maugham makes that explicit when he speaks of 'the emotional power of rhythmical speech', when he encourages dramatists to use verse, dancing, music, pageantry. Indeed for both of them writing is richest when it is something more than writing. But this something more all too often belongs in that domain with which, as we know quite well, British theatre has problems – the sensual.

Second, let's look at how we might think again about that great moment when the Courtly folk saved British drama from trivia, music and gorgeousness. We have noted that, fifty years after the Stage Society, the ESC replayed the promotion of writers' theatre. When it was first done it could be described as a classic modernist gesture. A small avant-garde group leads the way by priding itself both on its authority and its exclusiveness. The ESC seems to repeat, after the event, the modernist gesture, in circumstances very different, where 'progress' had been made in arts and society by, often, state-driven initiatives. If we borrow Raymond Williams's terms we can suggest that the radical new company, in order to define itself against the dominant, actually adopted a position that was culturally residual rather than emergent. For the emergent work was asking deep questions about the relevance of writing to performance. That it took time for those questions to be heard may be explained by the repeated return to one particular version of the place of the writer in British theatre.

The Look of the Stage: some examples of a stage clearly designed to be looked at, as if flattened out, arranged in a way which is rhetorically 'visual', offered for visual consumption. But also a stage that looks back, watching us watching it, sometimes flirting.

8. Savoy Theatre, London, *Twelfth Night*: the director, Harley Granville Barker (1912), rejected the lavishly pictorial Shakespeare but so too he moved away from the antiquarian platform. This, the only set scene in the show, was coloured in bright pink, white and acid green.

9. Citizens' Theatre, Glasgow, *Troilus and Cressida*, directed and designed by Philip Prowse (1973).

10. BLOOLIPS, *Slungback and Strapless or the Life of Mme Mao*, Shaw Theatre 1985/6: Bette Bourne and Precious Pearl with Lavinia Co-op (top), Phil Harmonia (left) and Diva Dan (right).

11. Forced Entertainment, *Emanuelle Enchanted (or a Description of the World as if It Were a Beautiful Place)*, 1992.

Chapter 3

What they make

This section of the book is concerned with describing the artworks of the modern theatre. It begins with very 'written' written texts and ends with shows in which the written and indeed the word are of lesser importance.

The readable tradition

This is a name I have given to work which feels consciously 'written'. It often invokes, as an effect, previous dramatic modes and its pleasures have to do with cultural competence – the ability to recognise, and know the provenance of, earlier forms – and with enjoyment of the sounds and shapes of well-crafted verbal text. The tradition in the twentieth century began with Shaw and the movement to restore status to the writer in reaction against a theatre practice that had become dominated by spectacle and machinery.

In calling this tradition 'readable' I am using Roland Barthes's definition of '*lisible*' and '*scriptible*' texts. These are often translated as 'readerly' and 'writerly', though 'readable', as Culler renders it (1986: 190), is a more strict translation. The 'readable' text locks the reader into a well-established and mechanical relationship between signifier and signified; the signifiers refer unambiguously to signifieds, and create pleasure in the security of that reference. In the writable text by contrast the signifiers do not make any automatic or secure reference to signifieds and are thus playfully mobile. The act of reading feels participatory and creative. There is, then, a political contrast, between the readable text which subscribes to an established system of values and the writable text which assumes the fiction/world can be created anew. This political contrast is underpinned by different pleasures: the readable offers pleasure in linguistic order and shape while the writable offers 'jouissance' – ecstasy that comes from a break in, a transcendence of, the rhythm of normal order. Readable pleasure offers comfort, writable ecstasy unsettles.

In taking Barthes's model across from prose fiction to plays we need to note the particular use to which the readable dramatic text puts the signifier–signified relationship. It does not offer a sense of a directly accessible 'expressive' action. It is often cynical about theatre's capacity to generate emotions through imitative acting and makes audiences sceptical about identifying with emotionalism and expressivity. Laughter is not playful but ironic and knowing. All this works to deny the signifier's capacity to deceive, and to secure the audience into knowledgeability.

Ambiguity is not favoured by written texts. They insist, for example, on fixing their effects very precisely. The long directions of Shaw and his contemporaries are notorious; to these can be added the precise arrangements for stage activity specified by Travers or Stoppard. In doing this through the verbal text the plays seem to be almost as effective read in silence as watched on the stage. Thus they do, indeed, make theatre thoroughly readable.

Shaw

The impact of Shaw can be illustrated from one of his early successes with the Stage Society at the Court theatre, *Major Barbara* (1905). This impact has two elements: the first has to do with Shaw's positioning of his dramaturgy as against previous plays; the second has to do with the popularity he achieved in the theatre. This coming-together of declared newness with audience enjoyment secured the basis for his ensuing huge reputation.

That declared newness is a tactical masterpiece. For the writing in no way looks 'experimental', with numerous elements in *Major Barbara* deriving from the older form of 'Society' drama. The speeches of the armaments manufacturer Andrew Undershaft have a poise of syntax and epigrammatic rhythm reminiscent of Wilde: 'Come, Biddy! these tricks of the governing class are of no use with me. I am one of the governing class myself; and it is waste of time giving tracts to a missionary' (Shaw 1967: 120). The texture of a sort of quotedness, referencing earlier drama, is emphasised when Undershaft discusses possible careers with his son Stephen. Having dismissed all the eligible professions, he concludes: 'Rather a difficult case, Stephen. Hardly anything left but the stage, is there? (*Stephen makes an impatient movement*)' (Shaw 1967: 122). The potential laugh is triggered by the recognition that they are on a stage. The bigger Stephen's movement, the more stagey it looks. And from what we know of Shaw's attitude to acting, he would have encouraged size of gesture here. The actor would then have a difficult transition to Stephen's next line: '(*rising and looking at him steadily*) I know the difference between right and wrong' (Shaw 1967: 122). Large stagey impatience shifts to moral steadiness. Understatement throughout would make it easier. But if acted as Shaw wanted, with big gestures and sharp changes, the whole thing could feel like debased melodrama – with the father's cynical response as the proper one. For this quotedness comes in a context which was doing things differently. As a result the bodily enactment of emotion loses its authority; the physical work of acting becomes something of an embarrassment.

This problem around acting has already been mapped out in a sequence of conversations at the Salvation Army hostel, where Undershaft's daughter Barbara is a Major. First, Barbara talks with Bill, a working-class bully who is on the point of religious conversion:

> BILL   (*almost crying*) Ow, will you lea me alown? Ev Aw ever offered to meddle with you, that you cam neggin and provowkin me lawk this? (*He writhes convulsively from his eyes to his toes.*)
>
> BARBARA   (*with a steady soothing hand on his arm and a gentle voice that never lets him go*) It's your soul that's hurting you, Bill, and not me. (Shaw 1967: 90–91)

This is watched on stage by Undershaft. He is watched by an audience that knows his cynicism. A hierarchy is set up: at one end Bill, almost crying, 'writhing' – physically mobile and emotionally expressive; then Barbara: effective, calculated, hypnotic, not expressing her own emotion, physically and verbally disciplined; then the watching inscrutable Undershaft, not, as it were, acting at all, and most powerful.

Similarly, in conversation with the classical scholar Adolphus Cusins, Undershaft pastiches Cusins's quotation from Euripides, and then shifts to his own measured prose, syntactically balancing money and power. Cusins is associated with classic poetic grandeur, locally recognisable to the audience as a version of Gilbert Murray's Euripides translations from 1904 onwards at the Court. Undershaft, made up to look like Shaw, specialises in that which can be read as 'anti-expressive', restraint and prose.

The pleasure in the Undershaft speeches comes from the representation of effortless control over speech, which sits in tension with his cynical reversals of assumed values and politics. As he hands over a cheque to the Salvation Army he notes how the horrors of war make him richer. And his donation seals the despair of his daughter, who wants to refuse all funds from manufacturers of social evils. But her admirer Cusins is delighted with Undershaft's reasoning and to celebrate the moment gets a flag and trombone, so that Undershaft may play while the Army march. With trombone in hand, and his daughter in despair, the armaments manufacturer is christened 'Dionysos Undershaft' (Shaw 1967: 109).

This moment is a neat image of capitalism's capacity to absorb all argument and opposition by spawning a relativising rhetoric even while the world remains materially divided by class and wealth. Simultaneously it manages to make gleeful high emotion out of this cynicism and relativism. Masquerading as understatement and cynical self-control, the dramatic pleasure actually offers a fantasy of thrilling articulateness coupled with unashamed directness.

We are told that the audience who gathered at the Court for *Major Barbara*, as for others of Shaw's Court plays, was self-consciously radical. They rejected the dominant theatrical culture and embraced progressive philosophies and politics. They applauded the play's argument at every turn. For they were getting a fantasy staging of competence and clear-headedness, under the guise of tough cynical thought. The theatrical effects work to undercut emotionalism and expressivity. Undershaft himself is a fictional ideal of verbal competence and philosophical dexterity. Even made up to look like Shaw, he is a fiction. Indeed, thus made up, he helped to construct that articulate entity which was the public image of the writer known as Bernard Shaw.

Travers and Coward

If Shaw was recycling Society drama, Ben Travers rediscovered farce for the twentieth century. He did it most famously in the 'Aldwych Farces' done between 1925 and 1933. *Rookery Nook* opened at the end of June 1926. At the centre of the play is a pair of young men, one of them married. The other men tend to be both older and conspicuously eccentric – a 'hen-pecked' husband, a 'weather-beaten' veteran Admiral, a German: setting at a distance the war years. Add to this the women: apart from the innocent attractive young woman trying to escape from her stepfather, the others are domineering and moralising, gossips, parochially leery – in short they are machines for entrapment. The contrast is stated when Gertrude enters to a stage which has been covered by the contents of Gerald's case, unpacked while he and Clive drink whisky. She 'surveys the disorder of the hall with severity'. They meanwhile 'interchange glances of protest and helplessness' (Travers 1979: 129). She catches them at it. The young men's untidiness is combined with vulnerability. Their 'disorder' is offered as innocent and endearing.

In positioning the young men in this way the play contributes to the construction of the post-war gender culture of the 1920s. Maugham's *Home and Beauty* (1919) has similar exploited young men, both husbands to the same hard-edged selfish young woman. It was this attitude to young men that Orton seized on, exposing its homoeroticism in *Loot* (1965). So too he exploited, for political ends, Travers's basic mechanism, that the farce specialises in subduing real-world norms to its own necessary logic. With a stage set up to look like an imitation of the real world, it proceeds to give its objects and furnishings the aura of theatrical properties. Further, Travers invents an 'imaginary' cat in order, it seems, to deliver a single pun in the final act. The cat lives in the kitchen, is never seen, but is shooed away when the kitchen door is opened. Early on it makes a noise when Clive apparently treads on it. It is clearly not real but its appearances are the source of business in which it is treated as if real – or, rather, where actors show their capacity to represent something as real. Orton replayed this in Truscott's line in *Loot* about 'these three walls'. When it declares its realism is provisional, the signifier is offered for pleasure on the basis that it doesn't signify.

Thus the new farce situates its audience somewhere very similar to where Shaw has them. By way of a parallel, look at the moment when Gertrude tells Gerald that his wife will not be arriving. He 'Assumes very saddened expression'. When Gertrude says she herself has to be away, he looks even sadder: 'Clive signals to him not to overdo it' (Travers 1979: 152–3). Here the representation of expressive emotion itself becomes the joke, where the value, just as with Andrew Undershaft, is placed on restraint and planning. The Shaw tradition allows its audiences to be sceptical about – or indeed unmoved by – expressivity. For such audiences the uncomfortable feature of theatre is mimesis, theatre's technique for taking spectators into different or challenging emotional spaces. Where the business of doing mimesis is turned into provisionality and play, life becomes altogether more comfortable.

That comfort is arranged with iron discipline. Shaw's lengthy directions are precise about responses required. So too, although at less length, Travers organises the stage. In planning the revelation of Rhoda to Twine silent or still elements are as important for the effect as noise and activity. Travers carefully places Twine for the unfolding of the sequence: 'at back of stage, looking over L. shoulder at Clive and Gertrude'. He has his back to the audience, looking up at the balcony, then sits near the kitchen door. He hears a noise and thinks it is the cat. With the words 'Poor pussy' he opens the door, and the pussy – Rhoda – appears (Travers 1979: 129–31). The effect requires, rather than expression from the actors, a precise and controlled submission to the mechanisms of the scene. The silent Twine, sometimes with that expressive medium, the face, turned away from the audience, is the key to making the whole thing happen.

This sort of writing insists on a certain way of being on stage. Acting has to be more concerned with 'technique' than with expressivity. This is a point Noël Coward made very clearly when he warned amateurs off *Hay Fever*: 'it has no plot at all, and remarkably little action. Its general effectiveness therefore depends on expert technique' (Coward 1979: xvi), which, at the first performance, in the Ambassadors Theatre 1925, Coward as director oversaw.

Hay Fever circles remorselessly around theatre's untrustworthiness in the business of representation. In Act 1 the actress Judith tells her son that she is beautiful and sad. He tells her she was never beautiful: 'Never mind; I made thousands think I was.' And as for sad: 'If I say I'm sad, I *am* sad' (Coward 1979: 18). That of course is how acting works. And from here the audience is taken on a dizzying ride in and out of staginess. Having flirted with Richard until he gently kisses her, Judith announces '*enjoying herself*' that her husband must be told: 'There come moments in life when it is necessary to be honest – absolutely honest' (Coward 1979: 57). 'Honesty' of emotion is by now very difficult to define. For not only Judith's behaviour but also that of others seems continually to quote staged responses. The dialogue and its emotions regularly dip into pastiche. This is marked brutally when the young ingénue Jackie says that she doesn't want to play a parlour game in which people do actions in the manner of particular adverbs: '(*speaking winsomely*): It's all my fault – I know I am awfully silly, but it embarrasses me so terribly doing anything in front of people' (Coward 1979: 51). Just moments before Judith has done an action to illustrate 'winsomely', to the hilarity of her viewers. Now Jackie, apparently sincerely, speaks 'winsomely'. And as that irony detonates we see the actress who specialises in ingénue parts acting embarrassment at doing things 'in front of people'.

The pastiche and quotedness, and the evacuation of 'honesty', seem to run counter to the quality of 'readability' proposed at the top of this sub-section. But where the relationship between signifier and signified becomes troubled, this works to refix it in a more radical way. Shaw and Travers encouraged the audience into a scepticism about the signifiers of expressivity by securing identification with cynical, 'clever' characters. Travers's remodelled farce establishes an adherence to theatre logic that moves independently of real-world logics. Coward, eschewing Travers's retrograde values around gender, penetrates further, as it were, into scepticism and theatre logic. There are no clever identification points, only the machine of theatre itself.

Early on Judith announces: 'I'm much more dignified on the stage than in the country – it's my *milieu*. I've tried very hard to be "landed gentry," but without any real success.' She then evokes the thrill of a first night, picturing the critics 'all leaning forward ... emitting queer little inarticulate noises as some witty line tickles their fancy' (Coward 1979: 20). The rebarbatively dismissive image of critics underlines the confidence of this proposition of theatre's autonomy. The character, an actress in a country house, is delivered by an actress on a London stage. Theatre glamour offers, in that moment, to efface the traditional status of country gentry. It shows it can imitate the milieu of the country while simultaneously evacuating it of significance. 'We none of us ever mean *anything*,' says Judith's daughter (Coward 1979: 61). While it has an endless capacity for imitation – quoting learnt lines and behaviours – the more it imitates the less it can honestly mean. There is continual production of mimetic signifiers, but what they signify is the business of mimesis.

The readable play insists on attending to theatre as medium. It disallows not merely expressivity but any assumptions about transparent communication of the 'real'. Subsequent readable plays will pick up on, and find their places in relation to, Travers's witty conservatism and Coward's evacuating technique. The heir to both is Joe Orton, whose *What the Butler Saw* uses farce to unsettle farce expectations about gender while at the same time replicating performance modes that were decades old. But the argument needs to go further.

Stoppard and Ayckbourn

Like Orton, Tom Stoppard had read his Travers ... *Travesties* is set in Zurich in 1917, for at this moment present in the city together were Joyce, Tristan Tzara and Lenin. The coincidence of their being in the city allows the play to imagine the crossing of the paths of these artists and/or revolutionaries. The theatrical fantasy of their intertwining is then framed by a device that emphasises that much of the theatrical activity might indeed be fantasy. The events in that year are recalled by the character Henry Carr, himself based on a real original attached to the British consulate. Old Carr's memory is not always now accurate, however. So at a number of places the same conversation may take different directions, break off, repeat. Stoppard suggests that these 'time slips' be marked 'more heavily by using an extraneous sound or a light effect, or both' (Stoppard 1976: 27). He wants there to be no confusion on the audience's part with regard to the erratic logic of misremembering which controls what they watch on stage.

The younger Carr performed in a production of Wilde's *The Importance of Being Earnest*. This gives the play its cue to slide in and out of Wildean utterances. But the play's literary promiscuity by no means stops there. Each of the main characters brings their own particular discourse – of, say, Marx-Leninism or Dada – into the world of Carr's memories. The exchanges in one scene all take the form of limericks and in another the historical account of the socialist revolution in Russia is done by Carr's butler as a set piece.

Late in the play there is a discussion between Carr and Cecily, the Leninist librarian – although she thinks she is talking to Tzara. Cecily argues that art should have a purpose, Carr denies it:

CECILY: Art *is* society! It is one part of many parts all touching each
          other, everything from poetry to politics. And until the

whole is reformed, artistic decadence, whether in the form of the perfectly phrased epigram or a hatful of words flung in the public's face, is a luxury that only artists can afford.

CARR: Kindly do not confuse a Dada raffle with Victorian high comedy –   (Stoppard 1976: 74)

Stoppard's play has itself produced both the epigram and the hatful of words (one of Tzara's devices for creating poems, turned into farce when he mistakenly uses Joyce's hat, which is then donned by its owner). The play is provocatively volunteering itself as decadent, an artistic luxury, but safe in the knowledge, perhaps, that its audience at the Aldwych Theatre, London, watching a production by the Royal Shakespeare Company, will instead be assured of its own cultural competence, its own ability to discriminate Victorian high comedy from Dada.

It might also be inclined to assent to a possible philosophical take on this supposed decadence – namely, that the play proposes that people can get trapped into language forms and registers, which come with their own logics and values. When Carr slides into a pastiche of Wilde, we may understand him to be driven by the vanity of his younger self, playing the lead in the comedy. When he and others get caught up into an exchange in the form of limericks, it is a more arbitrary logic which takes them over. So too the Marxist phrases and analyses acquire the status of free-standing linguistic entities that entrap people's brains, allowing them to make utterances without – and this will not surprise critics of 'left-wing jargon' – thinking about what they utter. All the pastiches come to acquire similar value, as pastiche, whether they are limericks or analyses of social divisions of wealth. In sliding effortlessly from one to another, all framed within memory slips, the play demonstrates that eventually everything is relative.

Or, to put it rather differently, the play performs its capacity to make everything relative – to turn everything into pastiche, to be sceptical about the relationship between language and truth, to embrace all values. Though not quite all. A little later from where we left them, Cecily talks about Marxist revolution and common ownership of a country and its resources. But in Carr's memory he is focusing on something else: 'Coloured lights begin to play over her body' says Stoppard's stage direction; faintly there is 'the sound of the big band playing "The Stripper"' (Stoppard 1976: 78). Cecily may, suggests Stoppard, climb on her desk. Meanwhile she describes how Marx and Lenin oppose 'liberal quasi-communist opportunism, economist quasi-internationalist imperialism' etc. This spectacle in front of us is, we know, at the Aldwych. The date, more significantly, is 1974. Four years into the life of the Women's Liberation Movement and coinciding rather precisely with the year in which the political organisation of the National Union of Mineworkers brought an end to the Conservative government under Edward Heath, at this happy juncture *Travesties*, proceeding with its sceptical relativising, produces an image of political woman as comic spectacle.

This is merely Carr's memory playing him tricks, we might say, another moment of quoted theatrical tackiness. But Shavian anti-expressivity gives way to Travers's dextrous conservatism. The play requires that this moment be constructed as spectacle in its fullness. It thus allows for enjoyment not perhaps of the destruction of over-stated theatre, but for the destruction by theatre of over-loud woman.

While Stoppard was having his giggle at the Aldwych, and Orton was delighted to get into London's Haymarket Theatre, Alan Ayckbourn's *Absurd Person Singular* opened in Scarborough, at the Library Theatre, in June 1972. Thereafter it moved to London.

This apparently 'provincial' milieu is intensified by the farce action. Ayckbourn has a precise eye for the jagged nuances of status within the middle class as demonstrated through behaviour and furniture. Each of the acts is set in that spatial barometer of taste and aspiration, the middle-class kitchen, and Ayckbourn is exact in his instructions for the sets. In Act 1 Marion, wife of the bank manager, is intrigued by the design of Sidney and Jane's kitchen: 'How on earth did you squeeze that machine so perfectly under the shelf? Did you try them for size or were you terribly lucky?' (Ayckbourn 1979: 26). The kitchen has a full range of 'gadgetry', 'surrounded by smart formica-topped working surfaces' (Ayckbourn 1979: 13). Everything fits because Sidney made the shelf himself. In 1972, 'Do-It-Yourself' was more class-specific as an activity than it became three decades later. D-I-Y was the means by which those who wanted 'modern' homes could afford them. Sidney and Jane are modern, aspirant and poorer than the bank manager.

In his Introduction to *Absurd Person* Ayckbourn notes that 'Its last scene darkens considerably.' In an attempt to allow the characters 'to dictate how a play should run', a 'natty' dénouement is not 'superimposed'. This dramaturgic approach comes from Ayckbourn's belief that comedy can be both funny and serious. An artificial resolution has no place in something which needs to be 'truthful' (Ayckbourn 1979: 8). Now, if this aspiration to be truthful looks odd alongside the preceding texts, what is the play being 'truthful' about?

Take the moment when Ronald gets an electric shock. He is brought down from the table where he was standing and put on a chair. They decide he needs to be kept warm. The only supply of clothes in the kitchen, where they are trapped, is the washing basket. So he is progressively covered 'in an assortment of laundry, both male and female. He finishes up more or less encased in it but still quivering' (Ayckbourn 1979: 71). There are two sequences running together here – the inspection of someone else's laundry, the wrapping and attempted 'resurrection' of a quivering man. This man is also the bank manager, but now, encased, male and female, quivering, is a different entity. Two different ways of viewing the stage are in juxtaposition: the forensic attention to nuances of taste and decorum in picking through the laundry, a less assured witnessing to a transformation that is potentially 'mythic' in its vocabulary. That mythic potential develops more strongly as the act ends. The five of them trapped in the kitchen are a miserable bunch – Ronald quivering slightly, Sidney shivering in his vest, Marion drunk, Eva lying inert. Then Eva begins to sing –'dreamily' – the 'Twelve Days of Christmas'. The others gradually join in. The 'bedraggled quintet' begins to sing more boldly; offstage the dog begins to howl. Geoffrey bursts through the door, announcing the doctor, and turns to survey the image; his jaw drops; the singing continues. This in its mess, disorderliness and exuberance is a domesticated Dionysiac celebration. Yet it remains always just explicable as a typical scene of farce embarrassment. The signifiers dance around promiscuously, never agreeing to lock the audience into one way of reading.

And in that sense the farce works rather more cruelly than anything Orton produced, and is rather more teasingly imponderable than much of Stoppard. Ayckbourn's text does not refer – or indeed defer – to a 'master' text, to in-jokes, learned references, 'philosophy'. The electric shock gives the audience something tonally unsettled. By the end of the play Ayckbourn resolves it less equivocally. A party game – called 'Musical Dancing' – is organised by Jane and Sidney. It turns wilder as, under Sidney's 'increasingly strident demands, the dancers whirl faster and faster whilst accumulating bizarre appendages' (Ayckbourn 1979: 101). While Shaw's 'Dionysos Undershaft' was a cynical irony and Orton's Sergeant Match in his leopard skin a knowing pastiche, Ayckbourn's 'party game' rejects these containments. In part Dionysiac – the religious frenzy and whirling – this is also a middle-class dance of death. And it doesn't conclude.

If Coward's play functioned to make systems of signification implode, it nevertheless allowed to remain in place protocols governing the attractive display of technique. Ayckbourn also requires technique, but his farce pushes towards an effect of greater bodily stress. In doing this it is moving the 'readable' tradition somewhere different. In 1972, as companies discovered the possibilities of creating work by devising, with actors subsuming the writers, Ayckbourn shows the benefits of a mode that can perhaps best, here, be described as 'writerly'.

Poetic drama

In the so-called 'golden age' of British theatre, at the turn into the seventeenth century, plays written in verse tended to be the norm. By the time of the second 'golden age', in the Edwardian period, serious plays were in prose. Plays in verse had become associated, during the nineteenth century, either with the somewhat antiquarian gravitas of poets' plays (such as Tennyson's *Becket*) or the satire and burlesque of wits such as W. S. Gilbert.

Then in 1904 a play in verse was done at the home theatre of the newest, most progressive realist drama. This was Gilbert Murray's version of Euripides' *Hippolytus*. It was followed by *The Trojan Women* (1905) and *Electra* (1906). In a verse style drawn from Swinburne and Morris, these versions of ancient Greek drama offered a different way of inhabiting the Edwardian stage. They did not take their reference point from contemporary life but dealt instead in mythic stories. The spoken text did not carry the features that locate it in recognisable conversational interaction, nor did it operate as a vehicle for argument. It was governed by rhythms that derived from poetic meter rather than epigrammatic or expository prose syntax. These rhythms were particularly obvious in the activity of the Chorus.

The reappearance of the Chorus

It is in the Chorus that the return to the Greeks produced its most radical departure from the norms of contemporary stage conventions. For the Chorus does not belong in a world of fictional characters. It inhabits a specifically theatrical space which is unavailable in daily life. It engages the protagonists yet also comments on their actions directly to the audience. Its presence anchors the play in the activity of a multiple entity. This entity may remind the audience of the theatre's roots in communal dancing and singing but it also presents a being which is articulate without being framed by the parameters of individual character.

For performers the Chorus presented technical problems connected with the difficulties of group speaking and for a producer/director there was the problem of dealing with the bodies of the seemingly static Chorus. Contemporary with Murray's translations, the voice training pioneered by Elsie Fogerty specifically addressed group speaking. Early on her productions of Greek plays with her pupils aimed 'to recover what I should call the Dionysiac spirit in Greek Drama'. In this respect Fogerty saw her project as differing from what was being done at the Court Theatre: 'we had advanced a little beyond these ideas of classical frigidity: we had thought and felt in terms of the Dionysiac

Ecstasy' (Cole 1967: 34, 40). That aspiration to Dionysiac quality aligns Fogerty with some of the European experiments in theatre and dance, and makes a clear challenge to realist modes.

Fogerty knew that it was not a matter merely of speaking. The Greek Chorus danced as they spoke, and in association with her colleagues Ruby Ginner and Irene Mawer she developed an entity that spoke and moved in unison to music. The break came in 1911, when she rehearsed her Chorus without music, 'speaking in the rhythm in which they had sung before – for the music had been kept strictly to the metric beat – and suddenly we realised we had done the thing we wanted: modern Choral speaking had been born. We achieved a cadence to which it was possible to move – a veritable dance of words' (Cole 1967: 42). This technical work gave a material underpinning to the multiple choric subject. It modelled a relationship between body and voice unlike anything that had been seen in theatre, not only giving the performer a new way of inhabiting the stage, but in this intimately harmonised group also creating a new physical entity, an ensemble.

Fogerty's preparation for *Murder in the Cathedral* (1935)

'The one impossible thing with a chorus is to take a group of people who have had no common technical training together, who are strangers to each other and are unused to an accepted type of movement with speech, and hope to make of them a united whole.' 'Where unison action exists, it comes from a marked united impulse on the part of the whole group, and it will be harmonious – yet they remain individuals, not acting under a uniform command.' 'The great peculiarity of Eliot's choric work was the way individual threads of character ran through the whole of the choruses. ... very soon we realised that we were doing not strictly choral work – but orchestral work: each speaker had to be like an instrument, in harmony with the other voices during the ensemble passages, but repeating a recurring phrase in an individual tone.'   (Cole 1967: 164–5)

Although Murray's Greek Chorus spoke verse, a Chorus can also speak prose. The key point is less the metrical rhythm than the sense of rhythmic interrelationship within a group of voices. Whether they speak in unison or separately these voices are organised by an overall formal shape, the function of which is to deliver a speech act which is collective. This gives their speaking a quality which is very different from, say, the formalised individual brilliance of epigrams. The Chorus enact their united interdependence. In doing so, through the material organisation of bodies and voices, they make physically present a utopian ideal of unity (see also Sidnell 1984: 98). This effect was used by the politically activist writers of the Workers' Theatre Movement. In Tom

Thomas's *The First of May* (1932) groups speaking, then beating their feet, in rhythm gradually build to a climax when they come together with flags raised. Disciplined collectivity comes to a point of fullness which embraces the audience. In doing so it embodies the guarantee of workers' potency.

There is one further distinctive element to Chorus. As I noted above, it occupies a space that can only exist in theatre. Its presence on stage does not derive from imitation of daily life but from conventions that aim to do something other than reproduce dailiness. Thus when the Chorus appears it creates a change of gear from the recognisably real into a space which is somehow beyond. For example, late into their stay-down strike at the bottom of the mine, in Montagu Slater's *New Way Wins* (1937), young Dai, fevered, lies with his head on his uncle's knees – a secular *pietà*. Then on each side of the stage stands 'a dimly-lighted figure, a man and a woman'. They speak of the work of mining as a metaphor for human potency struggling with the weight of history: 'turn away from lights and trams and whitewash / Into the critical *Present* where workings narrow'. From here they develop a heroic call:

> Have you got new men (otherwise we are lost)
> Have you got new men, themselves shaping
> Time in the shape of their knowledge of necessity, shaping
> Time according to the seam, according to geology
> Time for man, not man for Time   (Slater 1937: 55, 57)

Howel enters, tells the others to listen: from the shaft they hear singing: 'Cwm Rhondda'. They have won.

The 'poetic' text often occupies a theatrical space impossible in reality yet nevertheless physically present in the organisation of bodies and voices. 'Poetry' is a theatre effect and not merely the arrangement of words on a page. Poetry need not be verse.

Verse and poetry

One way of distinguishing stage verse and poetry was proposed by E. Martin Browne in an essay called 'Poets on the Stage'. It was written for a feature on 'Poetry in the Theatre' in the first edition of *Theatre Today*, in 1946. The pride of place at that date is significant, for the decade or so up to then is perhaps the high point for theatre poetry in the modern period.

Browne suggests links between theatre poets and music-hall revue and radio. The link to music hall is a 'frankly unrealistic' convention. This I take to be the displayed verbal surface to the scene, the rhymes and rhythmic coherence. A scene written in verse is not transparent communication – its metric ornamentation to itself calling attention. Verse has the effect of framing and quoting. It operates like a turn in a revue, which employs direct address to an audience. As W. H. Auden noted, it could be 'something which is no imitation' (in Sidnell 1984: 65), breaking with mimesis to make a new stage language.

The link to radio is through a different effect. It is that capacity, almost unique to the sound medium at that date, to open up new, even impossible, perspectives on a scene. It's an effect Browne called the 'intimately profound' (Browne 1946: 21). In finding his parallel in radio Browne was both modernising and making more materially explicable a rather older model for poetry's profundity. This had been articulated by the poet-dramatist whom Browne did so much to promote, T. S. Eliot. In his 'Dialogue on Dramatic Poetry' from 1928 Eliot proposed that poetry on stage has its consummation in the ceremony of Catholic High Mass. Drama 'springs from religious liturgy' and, after contemporary experiments, should return there (Eliot 1999: 47).

Eliot first experimented with poetic drama in *The Rock*, which Browne directed in 1934 and *The Times* labelled 'Ecclesiastical Revue'. In his subsequent work, *Murder in the Cathedral* (1935), also directed by Browne, Eliot stripped away much of the materiality of the theatrical event. The Chorus of women of Canterbury were not to move; the scene was unspecific and unchanging, the actual Chapter House of the Cathedral standing in, without scenographic embellishment as the Cathedral itself. This stripping down is then dramaturgically foregrounded. Chorus and Messenger refer to busy but offstage activity; the various independent speakers are differentiated from one another not by 'character' but by schematic attributes, appearing in series as optimistic or worried Priests, as contrasted Tempters. There are, nonetheless, some sharply theatrical effects. These are largely based in the organisation and content of written text. One famous example is the jarring tonal change when the Knights enter: 'We rode hard, / Took ship yesterday, landed last night' (Eliot 1962: 37).

More substantial is the overall fetishisation of the individuality of Becket as central figure. In contrast to the group voices of the Chorus and the Priests and Tempters sorted into illustrative series, he stands alone. This solitary status is underlined in the mid-way 'Interlude', which consists of Becket's sermon. The longest solo speech in the play, this is also in prose. It is prose, however, which has as much intensity as the poetry, if not more. For while the surrounding poetry may be said to belong to a theatrical genre, the prose at the centre, with its antecedents in the church sermon, evokes the spiritual authority of the priestly utterance. At the heart of this most famous of modern poetic plays there is a display, as it were, of the limits of profundity of theatre poetry.

That religious view of theatre poetry was challenged by the poets associated with one of the contemporary experimental theatre groups. The Group Theatre was founded in 1932 by John Ormerod Greenwood, led by Rupert Doone, and included W. H. Auden and Tyrone Guthrie as early members. Operating within a circle of young, politically aware, intellectuals, Auden and Christopher Isherwood knew of the experiments in European theatre which barely surfaced in Britain, apart from in isolated ventures by their own contemporaries such as Terence Gray at the Festival Theatre in Cambridge and Peter Godfrey at the Gate in Covent Garden. Their play *Dog Beneath the Skin* (1936) combines some of these European experiments with their own Marxist-based political outlook. It is a mocking and cynical account of descent into fascism on mainland Europe and in the classically pastoral English village, here called Pressan Ambo.

The journey through Europe is motivated by the search for the missing village aristocrat, Sir Francis Crewe. Alan Norman is selected from the village to make yet another attempt to find Francis. A dog accompanies him. Their journey takes them to the royal palace of Ostnia with its murderous artistic monarch and its Red Light district selling many varieties of sexual pleasure, to a lunatic asylum in Westland where people are addressed by a nationalist leader through a loudspeaker, to the Nineveh Hotel's female star who destroys men, and back to the village. These settings produce a series of images of human lives that are degraded and alienated, where fact and news are controlled by profit, where sex is sold as commodity, where romance, nationalism, art and entertainment variously obscure and distort human relations.

The tone is often wildly, blisteringly, parodic. A Chorus of waiters recites an epithalamium over eighteenth-century music while Alan embraces a dummy woman. It is, too, a display of poetry as virtuosity, with Alan and his Dummy speaking triplets or the chorus of vulgar voices in the hotel restaurant chattering vacuously, Bahamas rhyming with pyjamas. Very different is the Chorus telling us directly 'We show you man caught in the trap of his terror.' It is an urgent radicalism targeted at its intellectual audience:

> You cannot avoid the issue by becoming simply a community digger
> O you who prattle about the wonderful Middle Ages:
> You who expect the millenium after a few trifling adjustments.
> (Auden and Isherwood 1986: 155)

While Eliot's next steps after *Murder* were towards poetic plays that lost the feel of poetry, Auden and Isherwood moved in *The Ascent of F6* (1937) towards more prose, but a prose that was as weighty, as poetic, as the verse. Mr and Mrs A are a suburban chorus who listen to the radio, read the papers and enjoy entertainment. When they go off on sudden holiday the lighting cuts to Michael Ransom's mother talking to herself 'in a hoarse and penetrating whisper', promising she will always be with him, and then his voice, coming from far off, frightened: 'It's the Demon, mother' (Auden and Isherwood 1972: 43). In a culture of romance and adventure stories, of surrogate mediatised emotion, of nationalisms and easy heroism, Auden and Isherwood shaped the poetic play so that it offered something more 'intimately profound' than the brittle surface yet at the same time, through its brutal shifts of tone, it made both intimacy and profundity problematic. It thus set poetry against both revue and realism.

Marginalising the poetic

The decline of modern theatre poetry from its high point may be said to be part of a process initiated by the poet-dramatist Eliot. It came from a distrust as to what theatre poetry could do, an unwillingness to allow those effects which are both secular and universalising.

In the same 1946 edition of *Theatre Today* as published Browne's essay, Harold Nicholson's 'Poetry and Realism in the Drama' noted how poets can approach a sense of realism by adopting verse patterns that are so flexible as to suggest everyday speech, which was Eliot's trajectory. The everyday was then lucratively tarted up into stylish urbanity and surface polish by the plays of Christopher Fry, much prized by smart theatregoers. Verse glamour is not necessarily poetic profundity, however.

In a literal sense the profundity of effect – the sense of underlying depths – was reintroduced by means of the prose play. John Arden intended that his *Live Like Pigs* (1958) be heard on two levels – first, the apparently familiar realist interaction between a travelling family and the other residents on a council estate; second, a register of speech derived from the music hall, which belongs with what Arden calls the 'poetic' structure of the play (see Hunt 1974: 50). Arden's experiment here was characteristic both of his own restless exploration of theatre forms and of his contemporary moment. In general, however, in the later twentieth century poetic drama came to seem an anachronism.

And the tradition gradually dwindled. It has its formal point of dismissal in a play from 1990, Tony Harrison's *The Trackers of Oxyrhynchus*. Its ruse is the archaeological discovery of a fragment of a Greek satyr play. This is the way in to a parable about the politics of 'high art', which is predicated on suppression of the obscene, the popular, the shared and the vital. The satyrs dance in clogs, have phalloi, organise audience chants. By contrast, the character Kyllene speaks in the manner of Victorian verse delivery, with a pediment on her head.

This feels like a parodic demolition, which Fogerty might have recognised, of the frigid classicism of Murray's translations at the Court. Harrison's very brilliant verse text is being used, it seems, to kill off the tradition of poetic drama, a killing made particularly effective because it took place in the National Theatre. For while Harrison's popular verse was allowed to stamp on high poetry, to the delight of audiences, the National is not a regular forum for exposition of genuinely popular arts. *Trackers* was not bringing to the National a lively new stream of popular verse drama.

This, and the inheritors of the tradition, were somewhere else. In a set of minority practices poetry was being revisited as a vehicle that gave access to new ways of saying things, new voices, new profundities even. Two cases might exemplify these practices.

Benjamin Zephaniah's *Job Rocking* (1987) is a series of poems about a fantasy project for the unemployed, a 'job club', written before he knew anything of the black oral tradition. The poems structure the piece as a set of turns for solo and multiple voices, and the job club ruse allows for the exhibition of black stereotypes, fantasies and social critique. The job centre setting is on levels and gleams with the new technology of the time, the computer. Unlike other 1980s plays depicting alienated modernity, however, the stage has a very different feel, because of the verse speaking, the movement to the rhythm, the alternations between individual and chorus. As with other choric texts this produces both the sense of a unified, skilful group, able to resist job clubs, and also a feeling of pleasure in that unity. The text alternates between knowing jokes about social types and, on the other hand, a formal poetic structure, with repeated lines, delivered for the enjoyment of the verse patterns. It knows its real context but enacts its distance from realism. It thereby makes the space for a resistance founded in dexterity and pleasure.

A similar sort of access to, if not pleasure, then sensuality was enabled by a perhaps more intimate profundity. After the heyday of sexual liberation culture and in response to cuts on touring, Noël Greig developed a mode of theatre writing that was in a new poetic register. By the mid-1980s, the big 'public' history plays – the 'state-of-the-nation' plays – had found their way onto the big stages and had become the tired formulaic utterances of a liberal dominant. They told, too, the histories of that dominant. Greig's 1988 *Plague of Innocence* uses the panic around HIV to envisage a new political order which represses desires and certifies its opposition as plague. The play's form allows it to be done by any number of performers. When Greig worked on it he invited performers to deliver the lines they want to deliver … in other words, to speak their desire in relation to the text. So the writing – in a way which may seem the opposite of verse's tight organisation – allows space to the performers, space in which they take choices. This process mirrors the fictional narrative, which, in the face of new authoritarian power, discovers connectedness and resistance:

> a thousand, thousand bodies, walking
> together
> naked
> holding each other
> advancing
> towards the guns.   (Greig 1994: 141)

This sort of work is registering both the need to speak of large things and the marginalisation of doing so. It still seeks to express transcendence but now without the confidence of the faithful. Even more than it had once been, the poetic is a minority form. Maybe, as Somerset Maugham thought in 1938, the damage had been done long ago, when drama had taken its 'wrong turning' and abandoned verse under pressure to do realism.

Realisms

One early twentieth-century commentator said that realism was invented in the modern period and that the first realist play was Elizabeth Baker's *Chains* from 1909 (Howe 1910: 146). Certainly realism has been dominant. But it's also slippery. For as soon as you get hold of it you find it described, both then and now, as 'naturalism'.

Naturalisms

Of the terms realism and naturalism it is the second which is perhaps the easier to pin down. This has been done best by Raymond Williams (1980) in his essay 'Social Environment and Theatrical Environment: The Case of English Naturalism'.

Williams identifies three senses of naturalism. The most common denotes 'lifelike' reproduction. The second has to do with a philosophical position allied to natural history and science. The third is familiar from the literary movement which began in France in the 1860s and surfaced in Britain about twenty years later. Works produced by this literary movement are concerned with rather more than reproduction presented as 'lifelike' and conceived in scientific and social terms. They aim to show character and action in a very particular relationship with environment. Williams thus defines the distinguishing feature of theatre naturalism in this way:

The novelty of the naturalist emphasis was its demonstration of the *production* of character or action by a powerful natural or social environment. This is radically distinct from exemplifications of 'permanent' human characteristics in an accurately reproduced natural or social 'setting'.   (Williams 1980: 127)

An accurate setting on its own may, in the loosest sense, be called 'naturalism', but it is simply a technique of scenography, 'a particular staging effect among other varieties of spectacle'. By contrast 'naturalism' as a specific theatre movement is the name for 'a dramatic form', the distinguishing feature of which is that

In high naturalism the lives of the characters have soaked into their environment ... Moreover, the environment has soaked into the lives. The relations between men and things are at a deep level interactive, because what is there physically, as a space or a means for living, is a whole shaped and shaping social history.   (Williams 1980: 140–1)

While naturalism was a forceful movement in France, Russia and Scandinavia, it was, as Williams notes, 'relatively weak' in England. It becomes apparent in the English theatre on only two occasions. The first is contemporary with the later phase of the European naturalist movement, namely the period from about 1904 until 1914. This, as I note earlier, coincided with the activity of self-consciously independent theatre-makers who were separating themselves from their own class and its theatrical affirmations. Thus, most famously, the members of the Stage Society at the Court Theatre repudiated the commercial West End and did a number of plays which can be defined as 'naturalist'. Galsworthy's plays, says Williams, 'are specifically naturalist both in the technical sense and in the sense of a conscious correlation between character and environment' (Williams 1980: 145). But the wider emergence of naturalism was hindered by the presence of a persisting Society drama mode. This is best seen in the work of Shaw who, although he was familiar with naturalism as a philosophy and was a polemical defender of Ibsen, chose to use Society drama and problem-play forms. Ironically the most clear and polemical examples of English naturalism came from outside the theatre avant-garde and did not get contemporary production, the plays of D. H. Lawrence.

The other moment of emergence of 'high' naturalism, suggests Williams, occurred in the mid to late 1950s. One of the distinctive features of the period between 1955 and 1965, however, is the range of formal experiment in dramatic writing. Alongside the innovations there were some explicit returns to earlier modes. But it is not possible to describe all of this work as naturalist. Given the general weakness of the tradition, then, I propose that we treat naturalism as a minority form which makes only a very limited appearance, and that, hence, we drop the word from the general vocabulary we use when talking about these plays.

Of course we shall still bump into things called 'naturalist' and, indeed, the blurring of naturalism with realism. One instance of this is in Stephen Lacey's account of the 1950s and 1960s. By way of building on Williams's argument he links together 'both high naturalism and post-war social realism' on the basis that they share a theme of 'the way that social forces determine and shape the possibilities for change and growth' (Lacey 1995: 69). While this has become a fairly common summary of 'naturalism', it's not quite what Williams specifies as the distinctive feature of the form. Nor does it give full weight to the discrimination between the terms made, as Lacey himself notes, by writers of the 1950s. In his essay 'Beyond Naturalism Pure' (1961) Stuart Hall argued 'naturalism in any pure sense has never been an adequate form' (Hall 1970: 214).

Besides being seen as old-fashioned, naturalism was felt to downplay the importance of artistic form. The argument is stated, amongst other places, in Barry Reckford's preface to *Skyvers*: 'naturalism … is the capturing of social reality … Naturalistic speech is ordinary speech which is commonplace. Realistic speech sounds like ordinary speech but it has to be invented to convey an area of experience which is not on the surface' (Reckford 1966: 101). This claim is suggestive on two counts: the first has to do with the interest in artistic form and experiment in the 1950s. There was a sense that the culture of post-war progressivist developments, with the new 'welfare state', had not delivered; that the public platitudes were hollow. The public and 'ordinary' language needed challenging. A deeper sense of society needed to be expressed. And, secondly, more specifically, this is not a working-through of naturalism in Williams's sense but is instead one generation of practice trying to discover a meaningful realism as against the practices of a previous generation.

The need to readjust realism so that it feels appropriate to the contemporary moment can be seen as an endemic characteristic, for a meaningful connection to that which is 'real' is realism's defining promise. Such a readjustment had taken place in the first decade of the century. Of Elizabeth Baker's 'realist' *Chains*, Howe says: 'It presents a group of ordinary people quite truthfully; that is to say, without idealisation or caricature or other deference to the conventions of the theatre' (Howe 1910: 146). In each culture, then, there are differing perceptions as to what constitutes reality. So, as reality is reconceived at different moments, an art that specialises in a recognisable connection to the real also has to adjust itself. This is a consciously literary matter.

The problems don't, however, stop here. In that experimental decade, 1955–65, if the term 'realist' is applied to all the work which offers a recognisable connection to the real, then it starts to get a bit stretched. John Arden's *Live Like Pigs*, as I note above, has familiar council tenants speaking in the rhythms of music hall. In 1958 Harold Pinter's *The Birthday Party*, set, again, in a familiar location, a seaside boarding-house, had characters speaking a language which is both recognisably colloquial and yet, at the same time, a bit too self-consciously everyday, a bit as it were quoted, somewhat noticeably organised. And in 1965 Edward Bond's *Saved*, set in the deprived urban sprawl of London, had characters who, again, speak recognisable everyday phrases but in a way which is insistently stripped down, constrained, heard as if it is caught up into and framed by something larger.

All three of these plays met with consternation from audiences and theatre critics. While the persons and places depicted might have been familiar, there was something about the manner of the drama that made these things difficult, obscure. By contrast, John Osborne's play from 1956, *Look Back in Anger*, was relatively unproblematic. It may have been saying new things but it was saying them in a recognisable way.

Given the variations bundled together under the loose heading of 'realism', and at the risk of adding yet more terms, I propose specifying it as two sub-categories. These are, in large schematic terms, two basically different ways of doing modern stage realism, which I call 'expressive' realism and 'abstracting' realism.

Expressive realism

To introduce expressive realism I shall contrast it with the other sub-category of realism. In exploring how it works we can then also begin to think about the relationship between dramatic form and society.

Let's take Terence Rattigan's *The Deep Blue Sea* from 1952. For many in the mid to late 1950s Rattigan's work would be about as far as serious drama could get from society. The New Wave radicals regarded his plays as apolitical and formulaic money-spinners designed for a commercial theatre. In *The Deep Blue Sea* you will find no direct references to the Cold War, life on rationing, panics about homosexuality. Instead there is the story of an unhappy woman who has left her husband and lives with a lover who has grown tired of her. But audiences in the late forties queued up to watch Rattigan. While contemporary intellectuals may have regarded him as lightweight, our problem, looking back, is to understand how it was that Rattigan caught the interest of a mass audience – how, indeed, this sort of expressive realism connects with society.

Contrast with this an earlier play, from 1943, J. B. Priestley's *They Came to a City*. The play shows various different sorts of people arriving at the walls and gate of an unknown city, entering it, and re-emerging. Like *Sea*, this doesn't seem to have a one-to-one correspondence with contemporary society (it was mid-war, Jews were being rounded up across Europe and the killings were well underway). But *City* nevertheless has the feel of being about something larger than what it shows on stage. The characters who get excited by the city, and find joy there, are the working-class old lady, the upper-class daughter, the hen-pecked bank-clerk husband, the young working-class woman and man (the latter being an explicit proselytiser for socialist values). In 1943 this can be read as being about a new future. The City is a vision of a utopian society freed from capitalism, alienation and repression. While the play doesn't make mention of the contemporary war it does engage with a dream of a future state.

Keep in mind Priestley's characters responding to the City as we look at *Sea*. At the centre of the play is Hester, ex-wife of a judge, an upper middle-class woman driven by a need to find sexual satisfaction. The object of her attention is Freddie Page, a young airman, different in class and age, a war hero with no real place in civilian society. Hester, after unsuccessfully attempting suicide at the start of the play, is nursed by Mr Miller, a doctor who, for undisclosed reasons, has been struck off the register. He is protected by the landlady of the block, Mrs Elton.

At the heart of the play, in the post-war period, is a group of people who have been dislocated from given and recognised social places. The main action is modelled as the operation of impossible desire. When Hester's husband appears he is charming, secure, and still loves her. But this rational solution to her unhappiness is made to feel non-viable within the deeper rhythm of desire and frustration which governs her behaviour.

This way of modelling dramatic action has its effect by stripping out, rather than including, specific contemporary references. We are dealing here with something which is, in its own way, as parable-like as Priestley's City. The difference between the plays is that Priestley produces an analytical response to what's going on. The staging arrangements have us watch people on the steps outside the city, walking around its walls into darkness or passing through the lit space of the open gate. The dramaturgy requires that, in delivering different parts of the conversation and in their various confrontations, the characters move up and down the levels of the steps. Constantly adjusting heights with regard to each other, constantly rearranging proximity to the City, the play manipulates a device whereby the realist discourse is placed in a larger framework which measures and calibrates the status of what is spoken as it is spoken.

Rattigan's faded room allows for none of that critical framework. But the choice of such a room is nevertheless important. By 1952 staged rooms, particularly within the commercial theatre, tended still to be the opulent, or at least well-padded, rooms of upper- and middle-class England. Hester's flat is rented and she spends most of the play in it. It is the others who move through the building – the only time she returns from outside she overhears Freddie betraying her confidence. Indeed she starts the play almost as part of the room, lying on the floor, covered by a rug. We gradually encounter her presence in the opening darkness.

Commentaries on *Look Back in Anger* see its setting, a rented flat in a large Victorian house, as symptomatic of its age, 1956. Comfortable Victorian Britain had corroded, its prosperous houses now chopped up for occupation by less-wealthy tenants. But what holds true in 1956 also holds true in 1952. Hester's room, dingy, enclosing, is as much an image for a washed-up society, catching that sense of post-war austerity, of great hopes gone sour in difficult times, of frustrated drives for fulfilment, of nagging melancholy over what had to be lost.

Famously Rattigan refused to end the play by killing off Hester. Instead he created one of his favoured moments of irresolution. At the end she puts the gas back on, then lights the fire, turns away and folds one of Freddie's scarves. Rather than leave the audience with a sense of clarity, albeit sorrowful, the play insists that something else will yet happen. The image in front of us is of stasis but not closure; an expectation that there will be more to come, but without hope or certainty in relation to it. Curiously this feeling anticipates a much more polemically stated dramatic moment three years later: ' "Well? Shall we go?" "Yes, let's go." *They do not move*' (Beckett 1965: 94).

The 1950s stasis has its roots in two sorts of wartime ending. Priestley's *City* ends with Joe and Alice going back into the world: 'we've got to go back – because we're the ones who've been – and seen it all … And then we'll hope.' It's a long utopian speech (Priestley 2004: 94). A couple of years later, David Lean's film *Brief Encounter* (1945) ends with the heroine, after her sad extra-marital fling, back in her chair facing her always-caring, always-present, never quite satisfactory husband. She too has seen something different, and has come back, defeated. Hester folding the scarf is similarly fragile, but not quite defeated. The tone of those wartime endings returns in a peacetime public world where progressivist social plans were starting to turn sour. Without explicit analysis of that world, the stage works, I think, to image its feeling.

I am calling this sort of realism 'expressive', then, because it creates the conditions in which an audience has the sense of recognising something as the characteristic experience of its own time. The form works with a stage image which is familiar, generating emotions which are transparently communicated, and from here, in the best work, moves to the articulation of a larger feeling about 'society' and 'people' in general. It constructs the audience into a position where they agree to share this feeling and recognise its expressive truth.

Deep Blue Sea comes out of a mode of writing that developed during the twentieth century and lasted for much of it. Let's move back and look at an early formation of it.

Somerset Maugham's penultimate serious play, *For Services Rendered* (1932), is set in a large house in a small country town in Kent. It centres on relationships between the Ardsley family, with its disabled son and three daughters, and their friends. The father is a family lawyer; the setting suggests the class and culture, with its French windows and opening tennis game. Over this hangs the shadow of the First World War, seen most obviously in Stephen Ardsley, blinded in the fighting. But it's there too in the collapsed hopes and optimism gone bleak. The first appearance of Howard, husband to one of the Ardsley daughters, has condensed into it a whole history of feeling: 'He is a big, fine man of forty, somewhat on the stout side, but with the dashing good looks that had attracted Ethel during the war. He wears rather shabby plus-fours and a golf coat of rather too loud a pattern. He is altogether a little showy. He does not drop his aiches often, but his accent is slightly common. At the moment he is not quite sober' (Maugham 1999: 22–3). The good looks that might have triumphed in a Travers farce are slightly dislocated in class terms. Howard is a farmer and farming has fallen on hard times. 'Are we the backbone of the country or not?' (Maugham 1999: 26) asks a drunken, inappropriate farmer. The image is a difficult one.

By the end of Act 1 Howard is asleep. Remaining with him on stage are the three Ardsley daughters. Eva has just volunteered, as usual, to play chess with her blind brother: she hates chess. She and Lois go off separately; Ethel, alone with her husband, weeps as he snores. Eva's sacrifice of herself to Sydney's obvious needs, Lois's worry about ever being partnered, Ethel's stoical claim to satisfaction: all are desperate and unhappy positions. At the end of the act, even though it shows how men's work and heroism are supported by women, the picture is of middle-class life as empty and without prospects: 'the chances are that it'll go on like this till we're all weary old women' (Maugham 1999: 28–9). Three desperate women and one snoring man together turn sour the comfortable familiarity of Britain's drawing-room drama.

This image of middle England in 1932, socially empty and cynical, is echoed in the atmosphere of Rodney Ackland's play of the same year, *Strange Orchestra*, set in a shared house where a young woman falls in love with a con man and a two newly-weds attempt suicide. But Maugham winds it up more angrily. His character of a demobbed military man, the ex-Royal Navy commander turned garage owner, kills himself. Then for the ending he produces his wildest disruption of comfortable familial Englishness. Inspired by the stereotypical picture of family teatime, Mr Ardsley attempts closure: 'I think the world is turning the corner and we can all look forward to better times in future. This old England of ours isn't done yet.' Suddenly the now unbalanced Eva, to everyone's horror, begins to sing the National Anthem (Maugham 1999: 83).

The response of critics was lukewarm, if not actually vituperative. They condemned the piling-on of emotion. It was, they conceded, theatre, but little else. But clearly there was something else. In the piled-up effects the emotionalism seemed also to express attitude and values. 'It is,' said one, 'a play of virulent propaganda.'

Like *Deep Blue Sea*, *Services* expresses not so much the emotional lives of its characters, although it certainly does that, but, rather more urgently, the feeling of a historical moment. While each play looks back – often in anger – at the previous war, a different version of the type tells a chronicle leading up to a grim threshold.

Noël Coward's *This Happy Breed* reflects on the twenty years between 1919 and 1939 through the activities of one family, their immediate neighbours, and one stage setting. The use of a single small group of people and, often, a single setting is characteristic of the form at this stage. Here the setting is the new home of the Gibbons family. They are lower middle-class, with a live-in servant, a son who is a clerk and a daughter who works in a shop.

As a vehicle aiming to express the sense of a historical period the play's selection of people and setting foregrounds the matter of social class. When Queenie is presented with the clothes she must wear as a bridesmaid at her brother's wedding, she is furious: 'Thank heavens none of the girls at the shop can see me looking such a sight.' After a few exchanges she adds 'I just don't like looking common.' When her father says that 'according to some people's standards I suppose you are common', his wife expostulates: 'She's nothing of the sort' (Coward 1979: 312–13). This energetic attention to minute but earnest discriminations of class has a comic effect. It derives from the sense that this behaviour is being quoted by those who are above it in class terms. *Happy Breed* was written as one of a pair to be done by the same actors, the other being *Present Laughter*, a comedy about theatrical and celebrity people.

At the same time there is also sentiment around the Gibbons's status as the 'ordinary' people of Britain. At the end of the play the father, Frank, speaks to his baby grandson about the imminent war. He looks to a time when the attempts to appease foreign aggressors will stop: 'the people themselves, the ordinary people like you and me, know something better than all the fussy old politicians put together – we know what we belong to, where we come from, and where we're going. We may not know it with our brains, but we know it with our roots' (Coward 1979: 372). The effect of this is not ironic. When the play was filmed by David Lean in 1943 it chimed with a national mood, looking forward – rather than back – like Hester, in trepidation. The play's mode of expressive realism became necessary to, and then symptomatic of, a particular moment in cultural history.

That mode was responsive to, and shaped by, changes in society and culture. To see this more clearly let's go back to the period following the end of the First World War. This saw the appearance of dramatic works that specialised in cynicism. Somerset Maugham crystallised the attitude in *Home and Beauty* (1919) where a selfish young woman marries the friend of her husband, supposedly killed in war, but then sets her eyes on a richer catch. A feature of this realism is that it generates character that seems to articulate social mood. It is very like a domesticated version of the socially representative, if not 'world historical', characters which Georg Lukács found in, for example, *King Lear*, where the conflict in one family enacts a historical tension. Thus the character type of the hard young woman became a shorthand figure for a mood of post-war cynicism.

As a modern young man with a feel for his times Noël Coward also produced a vehicle for these brittle characters. Using an eccentric family and their weekend guests, *Hay Fever* (1925) (see pp. 123–5) makes the mode very witty but even more hollow. Tone is more important than plot. High emotion functions as pastiche, narrative is replaced by stasis, dialogue is all too frequently quotation of attitude. The effect, we must note, is not simply that of generalised cynicism. Coward knew the tradition he was working in, placing himself in a line from Pinero and Maugham. His contribution to that line works to evacuate of significance the class that was central to pre-war drawing-room comedy, and to characterise that comedy as equally vacuous. A similar evacuation is staged in Miles Malleson's *The Fanatics* (1924) where a group of young people in a 'sumptuous' middle-class house earnestly talk. The women, not cynically seen, talk about men and sex, and sexual pleasure. A young man talks about the cynicism of the post-war world. It's the same feeling, but not comic.

With a class position dislodged from the dramatic centre, and a theatre mode largely delimited to self-quotation and irony, a new theatre class, and a new class of realism, had to be found. They were not found out of the blue. While the structures of wealth and class changed little after 1918, a new class was foregrounded by dramatists. This class became interesting because they were vulnerable to the social crises around financial slump and unemployment, and to the pressures of a class-divided society. Frank has been moved from his desk at work because he can't pronounce the foreign names and is replaced by 'a couple of Ladida young chaps with Oxford accents' (Coward 1979: 303).

Their situation establishes the mode of their drama. In *Happy Breed*, Queenie attacks her parents for their stasis, but it's that which provides certainty through the Gibbons's family life. Stasis is, in short, achievement as much as entrapment. It is understatement, now, in 1942, which carries the dramatic weight, not large gestures; restraint not exuberance; fullness not vacuity. Act 2 ends with the news that the son Reg and his new bride have been killed in a car accident. The news is brought by his sister Vi. Only the silly aunt Silvia and her mother Mrs Flint are on stage: 'Don't cry, Auntie Silvia – they'll hear you – don't let them hear you.' After they exit, 'The room is empty for a minute or two, and there is no sound except the radio playing softly and the mowing machine next door.' Then the parents enter silent, sit, hold hands (Coward 1979: 343).

The dramatic trick is to generate a huge emotional response by staging understatement. It was to become a characteristic feature of this sort of realism for the next decade or so, to Rattigan and beyond. This realism seemed to have an appeal because it dealt in, that's to say dramatically constructed, 'ordinariness'. And in seeking to express the feeling of 'ordinary' life at a moment in time it also began – in such plays as *Happy Breed* – to deal with the history leading up to that moment. The chronicles of the ordinary become vehicles for expressing 'England'.

Then in 1956 that version of Britain was given a sharp shove which – once again – caught a mood. The picture of contemporary life offered by *Look Back in Anger* was of three young people living together in a cramped flat in a converted house in a provincial city. The opening has the two men reading Sunday newspapers; one complains of boredom, and the woman irons. This belongs generically with images of a society where people 'do nothing', where they are caught up into meaningless and low-level activity – alienated. It links back perhaps to those moments in *Deep Blue Sea* or *Services*, where Hester seems caught in her room, or where the women are stuck serving the men around them. In this setting Jimmy rages about the absence of any great causes to espouse. He laments that after his heroics in the Spanish war, his father dies more or less alone and unregarded in England. As he says later, 'There aren't any good, brave causes left. If the big bang does come, and we all get killed off, it won't be in aid of the old-fashoned, grand design. It'll just be for the Brave New-nothing-very-much-thank-you' (Osborne 1976: 84–5). Updated to the landscape of the atomic bomb, this feeling is consistent with other plays that express post-war let-down – the demobbed naval officer who becomes a failed garage owner, the unemployed fighter pilot. Jimmy's rage is, however, more explicitly a mourning for the old in the face of a nondescript new.

While the feelings about entrapment and loss of causes imply a society that has become unrewardingly static, this is often combined with an awareness of social division, and explicitly social class, presented as never quite secure, never quite fixed ... the potency and difficulty of the farmer in *Services*; the judge's wife Hester in a flat next door to other class migrants. Jimmy Porter tells stories of his aggressive behaviour against his wife's posh family and circle, and he laments the neglect of his friend Hugh's mother – a woman that, as Alison says, is of the sort that 'Jimmy insists on calling working class. A Charwoman who married an actor' (Osborne 1976: 64). This slipperiness is carefully foregrounded, as often happens when plays make remarks about actors. For although, as Cliff tells us, Jimmy is from 'working people', 'some of his mother's relatives are pretty posh' (Osborne 1976: 30). Without clear causes or classes, the post-war world has no shape.

Where Osborne's play departs from previous expressive realism is in its handling of that crucial setting. It seems to be almost absorbed into the lives of the characters. The repeated routine of reading Sunday newspapers delineates postures, gestures, images of bodily potential or lack of it; it is also the means through which Jimmy and Cliff interrelate. The ironing board constrains Alison's range of activity, and the iron does the damage to her body from which Jimmy refrains. All of this could be seen as a throwback to the operation of classic naturalism as Raymond Williams described it.

But it is naturalism with a heightened emotional focus, into which Osborne carefully locks the audience. At the crudest extreme there are the classic curtain lines. More subtly he has us follow the steps of Jimmy's emotional climaxes, which stage directions describe as moves in a fight: 'He's saving his strength for the knock-out' (Osborne 1976: 53). This emotional choreography leads us into what is most strikingly different about *Anger* – its remorseless focus on the central male. Jimmy's voice has a great deal of stage time, with the others as audience. Alison illustrates the various gradations in tension through her gradual approach each time towards 'breaking point'. While Jimmy has his ariatic outbursts, Alison's suffering is characterised as passive if not silent. In this she is like other 'expressive' women, another case of understatement as aesthetic effect. But now, as it were in counter-balance, there is the suffering man, who stands apart in his loudness. This is what makes the break from the past.

Furthermore, the man is not simply expressive. Jimmy invokes a whole scheme of values based in maleness. While he sentimentally mourns his father's heroism and death, he pours scorn on his mother. His best friend Hugh is positioned in parallel to his wife and given almost as much emotional weight. While the friend, never seen, remains idealised, the wife is interchangeable with her friend Helena. Even Alison's father is given space to criticise his absent wife.

This focus on males works to discriminate them from women. Women's bodies are hated as bodies. The only woman, certainly the only mother, who is positively regarded is the mother of Jimmy's friend Hugh. Jimmy, mourning her illness and death, stands in for Hugh, the friend who is absent, becoming, in that substitution, as it were his own best friend. This difference between male and female gains more value when it facilitates the ending, where Jimmy and Alison characterise themselves as bear and squirrel, driven forward on a surge of dramaturgic sentimentality that has become legendary in the annals of British drama.

Jimmy, hero of this striking 'modern' play of 1956, is said to be born out of his time. The superficial meaning here is that Jimmy is alienated from 1950s society. But he is at a deeper level out of his time, not so much because he is alienated but because, as a characterisation, he inhabits a quite old naturalism. For Edwin Morgan, writing two years later, *Anger* was 'essentially a play of pathos'. Its dramatist, he reports, 'is not afraid of being charged with sentimentality, and says that if this desire to crack open the British Way of Feeling is sentimental, he'll "go on working towards a sentimental theatre" for the rest of his life.' Osborne's next play, *The Entertainer*, 'succeeds as a play of feeling, but fails as a play of ideas' (Morgan 1970: 53–4), and in that respect, we might note, conforms with the model of drama written by a dramatist whom Osborne learnt not to say he admired, Terence Rattigan. Within this shared territory, however, *Anger*'s distinctive move was to recuperate the values of masculinity. After several decades of female centredness, the novelty – and perhaps popularity – of *Anger* may be connected to this placing of the male, once again, at the centre.

That emphasis was shifted back, however, in a contemporary play that was not initially presented at the London spearhead of new writing. Done first in Coventry, Arnold Wesker's *Chicken Soup with Barley* (1958) tells the story of an East End Jewish family from 1936 up to 1956. The political events of those years – always offstage – are viewed through the personal relationships between the characters. The politics of the streets are subsumed into the larger history of a family, a notion underlined when the East End itself is spoken of as a big mother (Wesker 1971: 63).

Chicken Soup shares with the plays by Osborne, Rattigan and Maugham a rage against contemporary society's destruction of personal relationships. Based on her experiences of office work, and her boyfriend's experience of the Spanish war, Ada, the daughter of the family, attacks her parents' notions of the 'heroic' working class and political correctnesses: 'The only rotten society is an industrial society.' It does its damage because it prevents people living a fulfilled life. The climax to Ada's set-piece clarifies the shift in political focus: 'How can we care for a world outside ourselves when the world inside is in disorder?' (Wesker 1971: 42–3) Towards the end of the play this sentiment is echoed by her mother when she explains her socialist commitment to her son: 'Socialism is my light ... A way of life ... I'm a simple person, Ronnie, and I've got to have light and love' (Wesker 1971: 74).

That alliterative gathering up – light, life, love – gives emotional solidity to the political rebalancing that is going on. The 1930s political insistence on personal discipline and group organisation is replaced, in a backlash against post-war dreams of a remodelled society, by cynicism about 'Progress', affirmation of that polemical term of the 1950s 'life', emphasis on the inner person. In these respects *Chicken Soup* is as much a product of its time as *Look Back in Anger*. But it differs from Osborne's play in two main respects.

First its ending refuses to resolve the disagreement of mother and son: 'Ronnie, if you don't care you'll die. (*He turns slowly to face her*)' (Wesker 1971: 76). The irresolution reaches back to Maugham's mad Eva singing the National Anthem, to Rattigan's Hester folding the scarf. With no squirrels and bears the play looks forward in trepidation.

Second, and more profoundly, the woman is back at the centre of the play. Sarah's husband Harry is treated as a child by his son, and the play has him become ill and incapable. Ronnie, the son, loses the political faith of his youth. His mother responds by affirming that she is still a communist, while the world around her has forgotten its past and become satisfied with the mere possession of a television (Wesker 1971: 73). Consistency, right or wrong, and a politics that is emotionally certain: these are the features of the woman at the centre.

Into this set of contrasts between men and the central woman we need to drop one other figure. Monty, a neighbour and political ally from the early East End days, has moved up north, moved class – 'I've got a little shop' – and moved from his previous political values. He distrusts all politicians and will be fulfilled when he pays for his son's education. The person who has moved from political faith to cynicism and simultaneously become wealthy and 'successful': this figure will return in later chronicles. The other figure that returns in later chronicles is the emotional woman, the engine which articulates the world in terms of feelings.

The shape that characterised Coward's pre-war *Happy Breed* is given more sharply political focus by Wesker. What is happening is that the expressive realist text, in articulating the feeling of a moment in time, feels a need to account for the process leading up to this moment. In doing so it spawns the expressive chronicle play, the story of the feeling of our times. A decade or so after *Chicken Soup*, with a new political generation and a 'counter-culture' that was sceptical of old-fashioned leftism, the chronicle play gained a sharper edge and a new name – the 'state-of-the-nation' play.

One such is *Brassneck*, written for Nottingham Playhouse by Howard Brenton and David Hare in 1973. Beginning immediately post-war, on VE day in 1945, it tells the story of a family's rise to wealth and power through the hierarchy of British society and capitalist corruption. With its use of documentary photographs the dramaturgy feels very different from the expressive realist play. For *Happy Breed* or *Chicken Soup* the big events were outside the house whereas here the archetypal British situations are staged: the large family wedding, the hunt, the Masonic Lodge. So too, many of its interactions produce mocking laughter. But some characteristic features remain. It does its looking back in anger, at the failed hopes for socialist change figured in Harry Edmunds, who goes from Labour MP, through involvement with the corrupt Bagleys, to being a Lord. Browne, who was a communist in his youth, now wants 'revenge'. It does its looking forward, not so much perhaps in trepidation but with cynicism: threatened with loss of their traditional wealth base, the family embrace the source of a new income, heroin. This final scene centres on the figure of a female stripper, the exploited woman's body imaging the sense of ruthless hard-edged entrepreneurship figured by the play. It ends with a toast to the 'last days of capitalism' as the company descend through the floor.

The domestic tone of the expressive chronicle has gone, to be replaced by recognisable images of public life and institutions. But through these thread stories of private interconnections, of families and friendships, registering the feeling of the historical moment. It reached its most extravagant form in the trilogy of expensive plays that Brenton's co-author David Hare produced for the National Theatre between 1990 and 1993. They dealt with the church, the judiciary, Parliamentary politics, and required big scenes – the Cenotaph, the lobby of the House of Commons, the Royal Opera House, a full court of law. But at their heart they had that stock-in-trade of the expressive play: personal relationships and the woman of conscience. They looked back less in anger than in wistfulness, wondering where socialism had gone. The state-of-the-nation play had facilitated a move from the private to the public, the suburbs to the centre, the 'ordinary' people to the powerful. But it remained essentially expressive – if now expensive – realism.

Abstracting realism

This mode also does images of a real world, but they can feel hard to get hold of. It is realism that has had something done to it, and it produces a troubled range of critical terms for what is going on. It begins at the start of the period.

Granville Barker's *The Madras House* was done in 1910 for an experimental season at the Duke of York's Theatre. Barker was associated, both as director and author, with the 'new' writing of the Edwardian period. This constructed plays that imitated everyday life with narratives that addressed problems acknowledged to be contemporary and difficult. Compared to a previous generation of plays, these works seemed understated. They were without spectacular events, often without suspense, usually without strongly stereotyped characters. They seemed, in short, to be plays – as contemporaries said – 'without incident'. Further, Howe (1910) says, the works of New Drama were often regarded by critics as 'not plays'. *The Madras House* is a developed example of a realism that was felt to be difficult, without incident, not quite proper drama.

The general situation worked through over the four acts is that a family business – a shop – is to be sold in circumstances where the family that owns the shop has been split apart by past marital infidelity. Much of the play is a figuring of social relations – interactions between sexes and across classes, in leisure and work situations. The inherited protocols, learnt behaviours, ideological fixations and social illusions employed in the interactions of people are minutely noted and displayed.

It did not go down well with audiences. This may have been because the texture feels difficult, an effect derived from the dismantling of previous dramatic languages. Stage 'incidents' are forcefully trivialised: Mrs Huxtable is talking about her father:

> I was at school at the time in Brighton. And he educated me above my
>   station in life.
> *At this moment Clara breaks out of the conservatory. Something has*
>   *happened.*
> CLARA: Jane, the Agapanthus is out at last.
> JANE: Oh!
> *They crowd in to see it.*   (Granville Barker 1977: 18)

Characterisation seems predicated not on coherence and 'depth' but on social environment: 'Miss Yates, by the presence of Jessica, is now brought to her best costume department manner. She can assume at will, it seems, a new face, a new voice; can become, indeed, a black-silk being of another species' (Granville Barker 1977: 58). Act 2 is set in an office where an incident of inappropriate sexual behaviour is being investigated. Apart from Philip Madras the other characters are unknown to the audience, yet the writing launches into a very detailed exploration of the interpersonal tensions. The itemisation of physical and emotional attitudes takes precedence over the development of a relationship between audience and 'deep' characters.

These wobblings of dramaturgic convention are spiked with self-aware references: to Sunday performances, to a play by Shaw, to suffragism. Each would have an avant-garde edge. The whole play is like a journey through the interconnecting spaces of middle-class shop-owning England, with our guide, Philip, slightly dislocated from it. He is 'not wholly English', of 'Eastern origin perhaps', as Barker's notes tell us.

All this is brought to a head in the extraordinary third act where the business is sold. Visually the scene is rich: a room with walls of black marble and 'darkest red', a ceiling of 'cerulean blue', a golden sun skylight, drapes, divans and a Persian carpet. Much time is spent with exhibiting young women in the latest fashions, introduced by Mr Windlesham, 'a tailor-made man' with 'hair and complexion far from human', a 'functionary' (Granville Barker 1977: 71–3). The 'man-milliner', both charming and too polished, presides over the staging of 'loveliness', which is, very literally, a staging. In ordinary light a model seems separated from her dress, seems 'half naked', until Mr Windlesham 'turns on the frame of lights which bear upon the velvet platform. The vision of loveliness is now complete' (Granville Barker 1977: 86). Barker's dialectics are worked hard here: the beauties of costume, textile, body are at the same time dependent on the exploitation of young women; the exhibition of theatrics – the staging of the bodies, the gorgeousness of colour and lighting effect – stands in the foreground while the commercial deal is done. The moment the deal is sealed takes ten lines of dialogue. The lushness of theatre is paid for by, but obscures the operation of, money. The act, we may say, is exploring the ideological functions of theatrical aesthetics.

But its major difficulty centres on the person of Constantine Madras: 'It is a handsome face, Eastern in type' (Granville Barker 1977: 80). He later announces he has become a 'Mohammedan'. Charming and clever, the owner of the business is, apparently, a Middle Eastern businessman, who derives his views from Nietzsche. He locates 'slave morality' in the moral influence of women. 'The whole of our upper class life, which everyone with a say in the government of the country tries to lead … is now run as a ballroom is run'. 'Every great public question' he later adds '… all politics, all religion, all economy is being brought down to the level of women's emotion' (Granville Barker 1977: 97–8). And he points out that the firm's customers are all 'kept' women, and its employees – some of whom we have seen beautifully modelling clothes – are 'an industrial seraglio' (Granville Barker 1977: 101). This is both highly observant about the economic position of women, and highly cynical in its view of 'slave' morality. It is the world of Edwardian England seen through the eyes of a subject of its Empire, a Muslim businessman. The dramaturgic tricks coupled now with a philosophical analysis produce for the audience an unsettled relationship to the reality they think they know.

It is this effect of disturbance and necessary reflection, rather than expression of a cultural moment, which characterises abstracting realism. Three decades after Barker the approach was programmatically followed through by J. B. Priestley. In order to avoid speaking explicitly of politics, while still addressing politics, he conceived of 'symbolic action'. It worked by producing apparently realistic exchanges which are then put into a larger, more metaphorical, frame, such as the visit of a strange inspector or the gateway to an ideal city. The resulting effect is that the same dialogue is heard in different ways, both as imitation of familiar conversation and as part of the larger metaphor.

The device is most famously used in *An Inspector Calls* (1946), where a typical middle-class family is investigated by a mysterious Inspector with regard to their individual responsibilities for the death of a young woman. After the exit of the Inspector they recover their composure by arguing that he was not 'real'.

This twist has the effect that, even though the dialogue continues to observe the stage conventions which pertain to accurate imitation, the status of the 'real' becomes problematic. If the nasty middle-class family can establish that the Inspector was fake, then they can disavow their guilt. When the father triumphantly discovers there has been no death, he describes the story as 'a lot of moonshine' (Priestley 1981: 219). Similarly his wife had dismissed the girl's story, when she came to her for help, as 'ridiculous'. The resistance to the narrative put together by the Inspector characterises itself as an insistence on real facts. In disavowing their guilt, the family questions the artifice with which the Inspector developed his investigation and the mechanism which compelled them to own up to their involvement.

Yet by now they have shown that their disbelief in moonshine is itself a symptom of arrogance and complacence. The Inspector, in all his improbability, is attractive. What makes him so is the sense of logical inevitability, the rhythmically predictable mechanism, by which the family members are going to discover themselves implicated. It is the pleasure of the ravelling-up of a detective fiction, where all the interconnections are finally found. The Inspector, as a device, operates like theatre itself, making sense of things, organising a story.

Although the detective role is a mechanism of theatre, the Inspector is simultaneously characterised as plain-speaking: 'what business is it of yours?' asks the mother. 'Do you want me to tell you – in plain words?' responds the Inspector, '*severely*' (Priestley 1981: 196). And, yes, the audience wants him to be very very plain with the arrogant mother. Priestley's theatre puts plain-speaking to work as a form of moral violence against complacent people. But it is something more than a vengeful accusation. And that something more has to do with theatrical 'realism'.

The Birling family, or at least the parents, think they can escape guilt by establishing that the specific facts of the girl's death are untrue. But they remain guilty on a different level: as types of the middle class they are answerable for social inequity, whatever local details are proven or unproven. The insistence on localised accuracy is a distraction from the typification established by theatre. Priestley distills this necessary function of theatre, to be typical rather than specific, in a brief exchange. Eric, the son, realising that he is implicated, says: 'You haven't made it any easier for us, have you Mother?' To which she replies: 'But I didn't know it was *you* – I never dreamt. Besides, you're not that type –' (Priestley 1981: 202). Mrs Birling's world, divided up into class-specific categories, is broken in on by the specificity of her son's involvement. A naturalist drama would be following this shape, showing how the inherited sin comes to rest very precisely in the family and circumstances that have generated it. But Priestley's drama is dealing in types. Mrs Birling may be shocked about the involvement of her son, who to her is unique. For the audience, however, it's completely expected. Mrs Birling's problem is that she cannot see her son as himself a type. Her conviction as to their individuality is what blinds her to the fact that her family is deeply connected, and has responsibility, to wider society. The inspecting theatre insists not on illusory uniqueness but on typified reality. It's this which gives it its political power.

A decade after Priestley the relationships within realism had become rather more tense. Writing in 1958 Irving Wardle noted that 'The past three years have witnessed the arrival of several playwrights who have been tentatively lumped together as the "non-naturalists" or "abstractionists"'' (Wardle 1970a: 86). One of these was Harold Pinter. Two years later Wardle observed that by refining away social background Pinter had given *The Caretaker* 'universality – attaining this without any reliance on the localized social framework currently regarded as indispensable' (Wardle 1970b: 132). But it was more than the social framework which was under assault; it was expressivity itself: Pinter attacked the writer 'who declares that his heart is in the right place, and ensures that it can be seen, in full view, a pulsating mass where his characters ought to be' (Pinter 1976: 9). Thus he preferred *The Homecoming* (1965) to *The Caretaker* on the basis that there was less talking in it.

This, on the surface, sounds an odd comment, given that the play opens with Max talking continuously while his son Lenny tries to read the paper. But then, considering the texture of the speech, we have to ask what sort of function it has. Rather than giving information or expressing feelings, it appears to be not wholly in the control of the speaker. The voice seems locked into learnt phrases themselves broken by patterns of pauses with a structure of their own. Later in the play these patterns of pauses establish a presence more pronounced than the dialogue. Thus Max's speech here seems to work as a response to, almost brought into being by, Lenny's silence. This is not really speech as communicative talk.

Of course it does communicate, but not the messages that the words claim to be delivering. It is instead the apparatus and framework for the power games which structure the play. These are established early as interactions within a male community consisting of Max, Lenny, his younger brother Joey and uncle Sam. When a woman is brought into this homosocial territory the classic familial positions become sharpened. Initially Max, the 'old man', appears to be the problem as he alternates between violence and 'love', swinging between good father and bad father. But it is more insistently the woman, Ruth, that is difficult. She is the object of the men's sexual consumption and abuse and yet powerful in her own right. She is both 'whore' and 'mother' in a family structure which is simultaneously a centre of brutality and yet the loving 'Home'. It's a critical view of family which is very much of its period – *The Homecoming* is contemporary with Orton's *Entertaining Mr Sloane* and Bond's *Saved*. It is arguably more ferocious than either, however. The treatment of Ruth as an object of business negotiation – 'when you were established, you could pay us back, in instalments' – is more brutal than the arrangement around Sloane; nor does it settle into *Saved*'s picture of social alienation. The play's final image is both ironic and inscrutable. Her husband departs, leaving Ruth sitting relaxed in a chair. Sam lies on the ground, possibly dead; Joey kneels at Ruth's chair and puts his head in her lap; Lenny stands. Max walks around, talking about Ruth, warning that she will use them. Then he collapses to his knees whimpering, crawls across the room to Ruth's chair, looks up and asks her to kiss him. She does nothing; Lenny watches (Pinter 1966: 77, 80–2).

The ambivalence here comes from its being apparently real yet simultaneously like a knowing quotation of psychoanalysis's 'primal' family positions. In staging power games around primal family positions – with the competitions of sons and father, the objectification and adoration of the woman – the play is deliberately schematic. It is abstracting from surface reality and teetering on the edge of mythic parables about family. In this respect it recalls another contemporary, Rudkin's *Afore Night Come*, which shows the murder of an outsider by a group of agricultural workers. But Rudkin has the often unspoken, brooding violence expressed scenographically, in a gradually darkening sky. The play gets its power from locking its audience into an inevitable logic. Pinter's scene remains a small family home, the verbal language referring remorselessly to a mundane, familiar and local world: 'I know the kind of man you're talking about' (Pinter 1966: 14). Its power and difficulty come from its refusal to resolve the balance between mundanity and myth.

What is staged is the failure of discourse, the edge of expressivity. The challenge to the audience is to know what to do with what they have heard:

RUTH: I always …
Pause.
          Do you like clothes?
LENNY: Oh, yes. Very fond of clothes.
Pause.
RUTH: I'm fond …
Pause.
          What do you think of my shoes?   (Pinter 1966: 56)

Exchanges become events which disturb assumptions about language's capacity to express. The youngest brother Joey is compelled to talk about a sexual conquest and as he talks Lenny leads him on, supplying detail for Joey to articulate. To speak about the sex is a way of vicariously experiencing it, making it almost actual. But it's driven by a relationship between the two brothers where each is both controlling and dependent. Lenny compels Joey to speak, but needs to hear Joey say it. The focus is not so much on the story that is produced but on the power relations that produce it. An audience watches one man requiring – in all senses – that his brother tell a story of sex. The reality of that story will always remain questionable. More obviously materially present are the power games which underlie the talk, frame it and produce it. While looking at something being expressed, we are looking at the mechanisms which govern the expression. Talk is perhaps less important than the rules of talk.

Only a decade or so later Anthony Howell's Theatre of Mistakes would develop a form of theatre which did away with the representation of fictional spaces and organised itself as a system of rule-bound games and exchanges. In these experiments an audience knows that it is watching the necessary extrapolation from regulated systems. The problem with *The Homecoming*, especially for its first audiences, is that it takes realism to a threshold, leaving it to hover on the edge between domestic drama, mythic fable and knowing quotation of both; where the talk, brought into being by structured behaviours, is a sort of quotation of talk.

Abstracting realism may be said to stage, or give us a sense that we see, the forces and structures that operate under the realist surface. This sense arises from a feeling, dramaturgically produced, that the apparently familiar stage image is somehow strange, beyond normal assumptions. Its oddness leads to its being called various names other than 'real' – plays without incident, symbolic action, abstractionism, theatre of menace. Less a genre in its own right, abstracting realism is a strategy which works on expressive realism and problematises it. So, for example, where expressive realism spawns the chronicle play, an abstraction from this gets altogether more searching and difficult. While Wesker's *Chicken Soup* tracks the lives of an East End family in order to express a sense of post-war Britain, John Arden's *Serjeant Musgrave's Dance* from the following year focuses on a group of soldiers in 1880 in order to stage the relations between exported British violence and domestic power structures.

The situation of the play is that a group of military deserters has brought back the dead body of their friend to the town where he lived. That town is experiencing industrial unrest. The soldiers intend either to warn of the horrors of foreign war or to punish those responsible. The division of motives is part of a set of divisions – between soldiers, pitmen and authorities; between women and men. These then trigger more difficult divisions. In the person of Musgrave in particular the play explores the ideologies that drive actions. Musgrave invokes God and Logic against the muddle that he perceives in human relations; that Logic is either thwarted by accident or purposely ironised in the figure of the cynical Bargee. The ironisation is done by having the Bargee's smirk in tension with Musgrave's passion. More complex is the division of the stage across groups of simultaneous activity: the three soldiers in beds in separate stalls in the stable interacting variously with Annie, Musgrave in the house having a nightmare and visited by Mrs Hitchcock. The juxtapositions establish contrasts and possible interconnections without ever settling on a fixed meaning. The audience has to watch characters as parts of groups, where interrelationship is as important as, and more imponderable than, individual subjectivity.

This complex watching gets polemically challenged in the penultimate scene, first with a direct threat, then with a spuriously 'happy' ending. The direct threat comes from Musgrave and Hurst: their Gatling gun is pointed at the audience, then Hurst – rifle in hand – explains that they have come to deal with those 'higher up'. The 'happy' ending follows the arrival of the Dragoons to arrest the deserters, which leads to all the men in the town dancing in a ring and singing. For the liberal audience at the CND-supporting Royal Court, the unspecified overseas war could have been read as the British suppressing unrest in Cyprus. But the play's challenge – and perhaps unpopularity – came from somewhere deeper, namely its insistence on what we might call a dramaturgy of dialectics, a staging of opposites which always remain tensely connected, of persons both powerfully individual yet always interrelated, of powerful emotion that does not have a single source of expression.

The writing for a group and the strategy for revealing historical effects were developed further in Caryl Churchill's *Fen* (1983), located in a tight community of female agricultural labourers. From the first it is something more than a representation of a specific community in time. As the audience come in they see a boy in a field scaring crows. He gets hoarser, darkness falls. The first scene opens with a Japanese businessman in fog talking about the agricultural value and history of the Fens. He celebrates the farmland, which belongs to a company owned by a trust in which his company has the majority share. This cuts to women and a boy potato picking.

Having suggested a historical frame Churchill then focuses in on the interconnected structures of work and family. Angela uses physical violence to punish her stepdaughter Becky while at the same time invoking the authority of the father, who is off lorry driving. When Becky finally says sorry, Angela '*strokes Becky's hair then yanks it*. No stamina, have you? "Sorry, Angela." What you made of, girl?' (Churchill 1983: 8) There is a priority on being hard in order to survive. In the next scene Becky is one of three girls who taunt Nell, as it were exporting her learnt violence.

These are lives alienated by the hardship of the work and lack of opportunity. In order to render that alienation Churchill develops for the play a stripped-down vocabulary, with attenuated lines, short scenes, silences. Against this there are scenes which feature very long speeches, usually memories or stories of past events. The scene of Ivy's ninetieth birthday has four generations of women present while Ivy reminisces about the brutalities and work of her childhood. The length of the memory speeches give the community's history a presence in their midst. A ghost from the past tells the landowner: 'I live in your house. I watch television with you. I stand beside your chair and watch the killings' (Churchill 1983: 12).

By contrast the attempt to speak of the present moment is strangled:

> I don't want to see you, Val.
> No.
> Stay with me tonight.
> *Silence.*
> No.
> Please go away.   (Churchill 1983: 17)

This is not simply the use of silences on the Pinter model to register incomplete communication. It is also the staging of contradictions, behind which we can, as it were, 'hear' the complexities of desire and entrapment. Angela's hair stroke that becomes a yank is an affectionate gesture thwarting itself. The situation is restated more brutally in her second scene with Becky, where she taunts the girl for writing poems that express her feelings. She also taunts her with loving Frank, who has tried to commit suicide. Late in the scene they improvise a poem together and laugh:

> BECKY: That's quite good.
> *Silence.*
> ANGELA: Becky, why do you like me? I don't want you to like me.
> *Silence.*
> BECKY: Poor Frank. Imagine.   (Churchill 1983: 22)

The silences show the separation, as too the entrapment in self. The single word 'Imagine' hangs ambivalent – it's a colloquialism; it's an activity that has made Becky vulnerable; and, above all, it's a full stop: no imagining happens.

Except in the dramaturgy: when Val is killed she returns as a ghost, speaking about the figures, past and present, she can now see around her. The other characters appear, now in a space that is dreamlike, situated as both present and past: Nell crosses the fen on stilts, as they did in the seventeenth century; Shirley irons the field and speaks about hearing her grandmother talk of her grandmother and the mutilation of cattle when times were bad, remembering 'what it was like to be unhappy'; the scarecrow Boy is there; Val's mother, who never sang, sings. The images are both impossible and yet entirely logical. The community is inhabited by its history. This is a history not just of ownership and economic power, but of learnt human relations, of alienation and desire. The 'real' of the everyday has been abstracted in order to find another real, that of the lives which are lived by their histories. And thus it is also very potently expressive, because what it is expressing is the inability fully to express.

Deferring to the real: theatre as 'document'

From the late 1920s onwards there have been performance events that define themselves on the basis of their engagement with 'reality'. They are not aiming for realism, in either of its main modes. Very often they are not aiming for believable imitation. Instead they claim to present the real itself.

The 'real' is a word that often comes with inverted commas. It is always difficult to know whether you are finally – actually – in contact with it. So in dealing with a theatre that enacts its 'deference' to the 'real' we face a slippery definition, where one term – the real – keeps sliding away. On the other hand, 'theatre' is more precise. In the formulation at hand theatre is, by implication, the thing which is not the real. This logic, such as it is, provides the cue: theatre can enact deference to the real by disavowing elements of its own theatricality. Where a performance can show it has stepped away from, abjured, traditional theatricality it can claim to be getting closer to the real itself. Thus, in cases of theatre enacting deference to the real, the real tends to be suggested by a set of gestures that disavow theatricality. The real amounts, then, to that which is 'not-theatrical'.

The methods of disavowing theatricality can be very simple. Back in the late 1920s the political theatre group that played to an audience at a factory gate or demonstration was performing in a real – that is to say non-theatre – setting. Value was placed on the involvement of or connections with those who were not trained as actors (see pp. 90–1). The performances were driven by an imperative that is not, of itself, necessarily theatrical or even artistic, namely the need to fight for a cause. The place of performance was not simply any convenient found place: it was the site of a purposeful intervention in the political domain. Thus theatre, with its capacity for representation, is a medium that is seen to be put to use in serving the cause. To restate that: it is not just serving the cause, it is seen to be put to use.

The reason for my emphasis is this: if you look at classic political 'agit-prop' (see pp. 94–5) it can look exaggeratedly theatrical, not to say cartoon – the boss in top hat, etc. Devotees of proper theatre art would – and did – reject this mode of performing, and that's the point. Theatre's capacity for representing is being made use of, while the norms of theatre convention are rejected. It was thus possible to create emotive and wild theatre images, while always signalling that the medium was being put to the use of a purpose other than artistic. It is being made to defer to the reality of the cause.

Besides the identities of the performers and the place of performance there is a third way in which deference to the real is enacted – in the function of the script. Theatre that defers to reality is usually seen to take its origin not from a fictional script written by an author but from a series of already existing documents. The show is often 'researched' rather than written. One of the earliest forms that foregrounded the document as source was called Living Newspaper.

Originating in the United States, one of the earliest manifestations of the form in Britain was *Busmen* in 1938. Although Living Newspaper as such did not achieve the same status in Britain as in the US, it put in place some of the key factors that characterise later shows that are based around 'documents'.

Busmen was researched and performed by the members of Unity Theatre in London. It tells of the events of 1937, when the workers on London's buses went on strike in protest against the 'speed-up' which was being imposed, with dangerous effects, on their working conditions. But the play does more than tell of this – it contributes to the busmen's struggle. It conveys information to its audience, and acts out its scenes, in the service of a purpose which was more than artistic, namely the achievement of victory of the workers.

There were, nevertheless, very powerful theatrical effects. In general the staging was influenced by German expressionism. The director, John Allen, said they knew more about Piscator, Kaiser and Toller than Brecht. This is seen in the sharp play between light and shadow, chorus and solo. One scene ends with a silhouetted procession which transmutes, through group movement, sudden light and a roar of sound, into a tube train. In another scene a chorus of women in shadow speak in verse while we watch Nobby's wife receive the news of his accident. Even the Living Newspaper's characteristic method of imparting information, an onstage loudspeaker, is used expressively when it names the passing months underneath a conversation about the negotiations. The different sorts and sources of information produce different modes of text. The formal contrasts between these modes, put into juxtaposition, establish an aesthetic effect which also does ideological work. Based on real events the show's aesthetic prompts questions as to the nature of the document.

None of this constitutes a disavowal of theatricality. Indeed, it is the reverse, in that it is the development of a new theatre language. But this language declares itself as based in the real, rather than realism. Where it draws from other artworks, the reference may be to cinema rather than theatre, as with Merseyside Unity's *Man with a Plan* (1946), which used cinematic 'March of Time' techniques. These are performances made out of the processes of communicating information about, rather than seeking merely to imitate, a real situation.

The new possibility of form was most successfully achieved in Theatre Workshop's *Oh What a Lovely War* (1963). Growing out of research into the First World War, the show was an angry attack on militarism and patriotism which, in conjunction with the class system, led to the largely unnecessary slaughter of the battlefields. Staged as if by a company of pierrots, it incorporated 'documents' from the period. Although there was an equivalent of the loudspeaker in the electronic newspanel and slide projections the show was very different from the Living Newspaper in its relationship to the 'real'. Its fictional company of pierrots provided a highly theatrical framing device, albeit a very ironic one. This tended to lay emphasis on the company and its artistry. By contrast, the attack on militarism was not new. As early as 1918 a London Pavilion revue, *As You Were*, satirised war and profiteers. By 1963 the First World War was back behind another war. Thus, apart from the general cause of peace, linked perhaps to anti-nuclear protest, the show was not serving a particular political struggle or a locality. The centre of imaginative energy in *Lovely War*, indeed the source of its brilliance, is not so much the historical event as the performing company.

As a mediation of Living Newspaper techniques, *Lovely War* came to have a major influence on subsequent shows which were grouped together generically as 'documentary' drama. Sometimes they are also called, or mingled with, a slightly later term, 'community' theatre. Putting the terms together, we can suggest that theatre arising from, driven by, the document promulgates a non-theatrical purpose in service not just of a political dispute but of a 'community'. To exemplify this let's look at one of the most well-known of the type, *The Knotty*, from 1966.

Billed as a 'musical documentary', *The Knotty* was developed and presented by the Victoria Theatre, Stoke-on-Trent, under the direction of Peter Cheeseman. It was one of a series of 'documentary' shows that began in 1964, driven, says Cheeseman, by two motivations. The first was that the theatre company 'were dedicated to the idea of giving expression to the life of our new home community'; the second was that, since they had no resident writer, 'we must assume the function collectively, as a group' (see Collectives). 'The process should be one in which we, the actual practitioners, dominated the presentation of the material' (Cheeseman 1970: x, xi). The idea of becoming an authoring group is attributed to the example of Joan Littlewood, who drew on 'the German and American documentary traditions' (Cheeseman 1970: xi).

Several points should be noted. The 'documentary' presents a topic that is local to the theatre (expressing the 'home community'). It is made by a resident company, who have all researched and written the show, talking to local figures involved in the events. The research thus physically brings together the company and its community. In the case of *The Knotty* one of those interviewed was Len Preston, whose grandfather was a navvy. In the show Len's recorded voice tells how his grandfather was promoted to engineer. Strictly speaking, this scene has little relevance to the overall development of the railway system, the 'Knotty', since it shows merely the career path of one person. Its greater importance, though, comes from its presentation of localness rather than history, in that it is a vehicle for incorporating Len Preston's voice. In this respect it does two jobs of work. Playing back the local voice is part of the process which signifies the company's community connection, placing them as 'local'. Secondly it demonstrates that the company has the power to incorporate local figures, to draw them into the theatrical world and to give them presence there.

This capacity to incorporate, and to perform that incorporation, is embedded in the basic arrangements of the playing space. The company plays out to an audience that surrounds the show on four sides. This layout arranges that the audience is always present to itself. Each member of the audience cannot help but see, opposite them, other people also watching and responding. Over time, this audience comes to be a regular visitor to a space which feels 'theirs'.

Documentary's capacity to incorporate and express locality is a major source of its pleasure. In his account of Ann Jellicoe's 'community plays' in Dorset Baz Kershaw notes that the non-professionals involved in the projects experienced the local references as a source of power – this is 'their' town, 'their' history. Borrowing from a pair of terms first coined by a sociologist, Elizabeth Burns, Kershaw says that the local references are part of an 'authenticating' convention. They are authenticating in Burns's sense because they 'imply a connection to the world of human action of which the theatre is only a part': Len Preston's voice is part of the real world outside the play. Burns's other term specifies a 'rhetorical' convention. This is an agreement between actors and spectators which allows actors 'to conjure up a fictitious world', the means by which 'the audience is persuaded to accept characters and situations whose validity is ephemeral' (Burns 1972: 32, 31).

Burns was a sociologist and her model of theatre, in 1972, was rooted mainly in realist productions. So although it is useful for some shows the model gets more wobbly when applied to something like *The Knotty*. In the scene where Stephenson directs the Engineer and his men to make survey readings, the actor talks always directly to the audience, in language taken verbatim from Stephenson's own reported words. These words and the surveyor activity persuade an audience to accept the fictional world suggested. But there are also two singers, whose song about Stephenson punctuates the scene. They are on a low rostrum not quite in the same space as Stephenson nor quite in audience space. While they sing the story of Stephenson, with verbs in the past tense, direct to the audience, 'Stephenson' speaks Stephenson prose, in the present, also direct to audience. But he will only exist for as long as the scene lasts, since the actor, as is practice, will assume another role in another scene.

There seems to be a layer of 'authenticating' devices superimposed one on another. The overall effect gives primary importance to the company of performers, rather than to the fictional world/s (see Ensemble). These performers are narrators and demonstrators. For the duration of a scene they take on a fictional role, then drop it. The mode of a scene may deal in theatrical stereotypes – a melodramatic villain – or social ones – guests at a posh dinner. This produces pleasure that derives from the fact that these are generalisations, not specifics; quotations that are shared, not fictional worlds that assume belief. The techniques which in other work may operate rhetorically are here contained within the authenticating device of the shared joke. The pleasure is in the handling of theatre conventions not to make fictions but to present what has to be defined as fact.

The capacity to do the rhetorical devices, to set up the fiction, is important. For what *authenticates* these performers as performers is the fact that they can, if necessary, do the *rhetorical*. What authenticates them as members of the locality is that they know where the rhetorical sits within a set of performing conventions. While the most 'real' voices heard on stage are those of the real Len Preston and Fred Adams, these are heard through the loudspeaker. Although thoroughly authentic they are not themselves in a position to show that they can discriminate between rhetoric and authenticity. The ability to discriminate lies, so to speak, with the company, and gives it its power.

In making its discriminations the text of documentary, on the Stoke model, turns scepticism about, or refusal of, 'theatre' into aesthetic effect. After the genre faded from popularity, its work with regard to both the efficacy and aesthetics of that which is 'not theatre' were continued by other, and indeed separate, means. The movement away from the creative role of the dramatist continued. Following *The Knotty*'s interviews, which led to verbatim incorporation of the interviewees, it was a short step to the development of a text consisting entirely of material taken from what had been said in real-life situations. The text of *The Colour of Justice* (1999) was taken from the transcripts of the legal enquiry into the racist murder of Stephen Lawrence. It was the fourth of a series of 'Tribunal Plays' done at the Tricycle Theatre in London. The work of textual production was that of editing. There was no need for individual or company research, or the work of drawing together texts from a range of different sources, or, indeed, the exploration of company response to different materials. The dramaturgic framework and the linguistic register are fixed in advance, in that they are taken from a single original event, with its own mode of performance, the tribunal. In editing down the 11,000 pages of transcript to 100, Richard Norton-Taylor 'set out to include the most telling exchanges for a theatre audience, many of whom [sic] did not hit the headlines at the time' (Norton-Taylor 1999: 8). This produces two effects: it makes more sensuously dramatic the operation of a tribunal; it disseminates more widely information about a particularly shocking case of racism at several levels. These two effects taken together suggest that theatre makes itself an efficiently functional agent of dissemination by theatricalising a previous event. At the same time it has abandoned the need to explore aesthetics.

Norton-Taylor's main aim in editing the tribunal text was to be 'fair, balanced and rounded'. In verbatim text the role of text-manager carries ethical responsibilities. These become even more acutely apparent when the material is based not in the public discourses of a courtroom but in the private experiences of individuals. The act of giving testimony about, or paying witness to, experiences that are deeply traumatic, such as sexual abuse, itself becomes therapeutic work. The speaking is personally difficult and sometimes life-altering. In these circumstances the verbatim editor has responsibility not only to the collected text but also, as respondent, to the speaker. In moving from author to editor, and from aesthetics to ethics, the verbatim mode allows theatre to set at a distance one of the primary engines of fiction, the creative writer.

Creative impetus was instead often supplied by the interest in layered conventions of authentication. This was energised by the use of live camera mediation of stage activity. The audience sees the performing body apparently unmediated; it also sees that body screened in two dimensions. Conventions and assumptions attached to the two media come into juxtaposition. The camera can apparently get 'closer' to the real body, but only ever offers an image of that body. It both services and frames. And its very presence does aesthetic work. The positioning of kit onstage – whether low-tech maps and pictures or higher-tech cameras and mics – involves aesthetic choices. It also produces the technologically equipped – ornamented? – performing body. By these means are produced a documentary scenography.

With its agonising around the authenticity of its material, the onstage camera can be seen as caught up into tensions around mimesis and the work of imitation. Tension around mimesis is at the heart of theatre practice that enacts deference to the real. For such practice specialises in locating and then closing the gap between theatre and reality. It often does so by enacting a refusal of the agencies of theatre – special building, specially trained performers, special writers – and in so doing marks its difference from fiction. It shows its capacity directly to relate to the real, offering greater 'access' to it. The promenade techniques of Jellicoe, as observed by Kershaw, mingled performers and audience and hence 'are designed to make the performances more accessible, by blurring the distinction between "reality" and "play", so that the transition into performance consciousness is modulated by conventions drawn from non-theatrical, social occasions' (Kershaw 1992:192). The question is, though – what is accessed? Accounts of audiences tell of them being delighted by what they recognise and can testify to. The source of pleasure is their connection to that – perforce assumed – reality.

It's a potentially complicated connection. 'Documentary' theatre can have the effect of questioning, and enriching, one's sense of what a document is. Thus, on one hand, there's an enactment of a deference to the real, while on the other hand there's a problematising of the evidence of the real. Documentary theatre may then be said not so much to present the facts of the real world as to present the work of mediating facts.

'Cruelties'

In 1963 the Royal Shakespeare Company funded a laboratory exploration into acting techniques. It was led by Charles Marowitz and Peter Brook. Marowitz was an American reviewer-cum-director; Brook, a graduate of English language and literature at Oxford, had already made a name as a director with the RSC. They were based in premises at the London Academy of Music and Dramatic Art. The outcomes of their exploration were labelled, by journalists and against Marowitz's wishes, as 'Theatre of Cruelty'.

That phrase explicitly invokes the theatrical philosophy of Antonin Artaud, first translated into English in 1958. Like many in Britain in the late 1950s, Artaud had sought, decades earlier, for an antidote to the flatness of European dramatic vocabularies and found it in the Balinese theatre, where the actors, costumes and gestures were 'strange signs matching some dark prodigious reality we have repressed once and for all here in the West'. Its overall effect is 'deep intoxication, restoring the very elements of rapture'. Here was a theatre practice which could reconnect with that which was – in the popular 1950s word – 'vital': a 'theatre that vibrates with instinctive things' (Artaud 1970: 43, 47). This philosophy prompted Brook and Marowitz, and many after them, to re-think assumptions about acting techniques, and, in particular, challenge the dominance of the written text. Their exercises gave importance to movement and improvisation: Artaud's own *Spurt of Blood* was done twice, first as a movement piece.

The 'cruelty' experiment had two major impacts. First, even while writers were busy producing the New English drama (as the Penguin series called it), the emphasis on movement questioned the status of the word. So too the emphasis on improvisation, as with the documentary work at Stoke, showed the performer could also be author. While the English Stage Company sponsored new writing as a form of opposition to the glamour and commercialism of the West End, the really new emergent trend was towards the dissolution of the writer's role – seen in collective writing, devising, company creation – and the dethroning of writing as the primary medium.

The second impact of 'cruelty' came from its formal recognition of Artaud's ideas, and hence the ability to name and recognise a type of stage language. As we shall see, this process itself had two effects. One was an engagement with ideas about representation, the other was the production of 'cruelty' as style.

The Marowitz–Brook interest in Artaud was of its time in that there were explorations of the European dramatic repertoire – seen in the Royal Court's programming – and there were native dramatic experiments with available stage languages: Innes (2002) notes that Jellicoe's *The Sport of My Mad Mother* (1958) and Rudkin's *Afore Night Come* (1960) each explore the irrational and 'primitive'. These various experiments were putting under pressure – or reacting against – the dominant mode of expressive realism as the early 1960s looked for a stage language to speak for its own time. Marowitz spoke of the need for that new language in words which curiously anticipate later generations: 'Our world is fragmented, discontinuous, erratic and uncertain; our theatre is pat, cohesive, arbitrary and consoling' (Marowitz *et al.* 1970: 243).

But there already existed a mode of writing that was 'cruel', produced at an earlier moment of experiment and radical challenge to the dominant. It too came out of an embrace of European theatre. Auden and Isherwood's *Dog Beneath the Skin* (1935) claimed Brecht as influence, but this was early Brecht tilted towards explicit brutality. The Hotel Nineveh Chorus girls, a form of 'culinary' theatre, are offered for literal eating.

As we see in the account of Poetic drama, such satiric scenes produce anger around the exploitation of women, the commercialisation of sex, the drive of capitalism towards objectification and alienation. The parameters of satire are overwhelmed, however, in the episode of Destructive Desmond. He is a hotel entertainer whose act specialises in the destruction of prized works of art. While it's clearly an attack on aggressive subjectivism – I know what I like – the dramaturgy seeks to bind the audience into the savagery. The Desmond role is a good comedy vehicle; the opposition to him is a pathetic art expert; the encouragement of Desmond comes from dinner guests transmuted into destructive crowd, possibly the remembered sound of a Nazi mob. It is a staging of a passionately felt drive towards destruction as fulfilment. 'Grrr!' says Desmond over rolling drums, confronting a Rembrandt painting, 'Take that, you brute! (*slashes canvas with his knife*) and that! and that! (*Finale of trumpets …*)' (Auden and Isherwood 1986: 133).

Dog has two general targets then. One is the objectification and alienation of human relations produced by the economic order which is capitalism. The other is the readiness to accept anything as entertainment without exploring its values. Both these features persist in shows that can be described as various forms of 'cruelty', but they don't always persist together.

A thoroughgoing analysis, in sharply aggressive form, of alienated society was produced in the years immediately following the Marowitz–Brook laboratory. The early plays of Edward Bond scandalised some audiences and reviewers. The scene in *Saved* (1965) in which a baby is stoned to death by a bored gang of youths in a park was banned by the censor. But for Bond this was simply another piece of the casual interpersonal violence that characterised the lives of deprived Londoners. The stoning is conducted with the same flattened language and lack of explicit sensationalism that govern the play. To follow, Bond wrote the wholly banned *Early Morning* (1968): a group of characters associated with traditional 'Victorian' England is put through violent and degrading interactions. Queen Victoria rapes Florence Nightingale and strangles Prince Albert with his own Garter sash, all within the setting of a picnic. A tug-of-war becomes a massacre and the dead reappear in heaven, where they eat each other. Although Bond claimed the play was, like *Saved*, a piece of social realism its focus was less on the culture of alienation and more on the 'fantasy' governing people's lives. This 'fantasy' is better thought of as an ideology of nation and history, dangerous because its values shape attitudes and behaviours in the present. Such ideologies are another aspect of, and fuelled by, social alienation.

For Bond, as for Auden and Isherwood, the attempt to crack open those naturalised fantasies which constitute ideology required a formal tactic for 'making people notice': 'I think it's necessary to disturb an audience emotionally to involve them emotionally in my plays, so I've had to find ways of making that "aggro-effect" more complete' (in Innes 2002: 169). The concept of 'aggro-effect' is a calculated reworking of Brecht's so called 'alienation' – or, more properly, and usefully, 'estrangement' – effect.

In 1968 and subsequent years ideology came to prominence as a target of critique. Marxist thinkers showed how ideology worked as a mechanism for sustaining power differentials. Within the liberationist movements there was a challenge to the assumed, and often repressive, norms which were kept in place by ideology. In his aim to ridicule and make surreal 'fantasies' of nation and history Bond shared an outlook with the early work of Howard Brenton, which was influenced by the Situationist view of 'official life being like a screen' (in Innes 2002: 208). His policemen in *Christie in Love* (1969) speak limericks while they dig for female corpses; the Constable animates a Doll as a whore in dialogue with Christie. Brenton explained the desired effect: 'tearing one style up for another, so the proceedings lurch and all interpretations are blocked, and the spectator looking for an easy meaning wearies', being left only with Christie and his 'act of love' (Brenton 1970: 6). In the multiple-authored *Lay By* (1971), which centres on a roadside pick-up and rape and ends in a morgue, the lurches are even more drastic, with corpses made into jam at the end. The 'tearing up' of styles is similar to the satiric contrasts of *Dog* and belongs with the savagely ironic juxtapositions: picnic and strangling, limericks and corpses. The overall attempt, however, is not to develop understanding but to block interpretation. Repeatedly this is done by presenting sex as a domain of violence. Note, therefore, that this is not seduction of audiences into a dark and deeper reality, as in Artaud's Balinese theatre, but a more aggressive desire, if that's the word, to destroy the surface appearance of 'normality'.

Bond himself had, however, rapidly developed the narrowly conceived 'aggro-effect' by combining it with wider-ranging social analysis in his 1971 play *Lear*. Restaging the events of Shakespeare's *King Lear*, Bond's play has a victorious Cordelia turn out to be as violent, albeit in the name of government, as her brutal sisters. The society is caught up into a mindset obsessed with 'security' and operates to a mechanism described by Bond in his preface. There he argues that societies held together by aggression produce aggression and their main agency for doing so is the production of a 'socialised morality' which governs individual behaviour and encourages people to suppress in themselves liberalism and sexual freedom. The obsession with security is imaged in the huge wall that is built. The ideological assertion of the value of technology is aggressively satirised when Lear is blinded by use of a 'scientific' contraption which draws out his eyeballs. His torturer delights in the device's mechanical efficiency while Lear screams. The scale of the violence, however, takes us beyond the frame of satire and even beyond aggro-effect. At the end of the first act soldiers appear at Cordelia's home, where Lear is. He sits at the back of the stage, opposite the audience, and, like them, watches as Cordelia is raped and her husband is killed and a sheet from the washing line folds around him as, in silence, his head drops back and a bloodstain covers the sheet. There is high-pitched squealing as the pigs are killed. But despite the large visual and aural effects the casual attitude of the soldiers feels even more abrasive. We are not encouraged to be overcome by the effects, so much as to watch violence's process of production. That emphasis on continual process, a continual damage done by recycled violence, is imaged in the figure of Cordelia's dead husband, who becomes a ghost, a ghost who ages and is finally killed, reprising the Act 1 scene, by pigs.

The attack on assumed rationality and 'technology' gained particular new force after the re-election to power of a right-wing government in 1983. That government insisted, ideologically, that its policies were 'realism'. By way of attacking that position, and at the same time attacking what he saw as the bankrupt language of opposition, Howard Barker developed an aesthetic specifically designed to unsettle easy responses. His target was theatre which creates an illusion that human interactions can be readily understood and interpreted by a rational observer, where messages are clear and audiences are 'educated'. This he called 'Humanist Theatre' and against it he set 'Catastrophic Theatre'. In this, his own, theatre, there were to be no messages, no ease of understanding, no totally graspable experience. The audience is to be divided so that it 'goes home disturbed and amazed' (Barker 1989: 91). It is perhaps the theorisation of Destructive Desmond.

As with Bond's aggro-effects, Barker's stage language works emotionally on an audience, making itself incapable of being grasped rationally. Even in his most politically clear early plays, these effects are obvious. For example, *The Castle* (1985) is set in an apparently medieval period. The Knight returns from the wars overseas to find his wife living with a woman, Skinner, and the castle run by women. He reasserts his authority and obsessively fortifies the castle, having higher walls designed by his very rational and mathematical architect Krak. Skinner is punished by tying her body to the man she killed so that he decays on her, but in turn she is worshipped. Krak the architect suddenly kneels to her, describing how a woman 'levered her parts over me … European woman with her passion for old men, wants to drown their history in her bowel … Cunt you lend or rent, but arse you have to will … true ring of marriage … brown button of puckered muscularity … the sacramental stillness born of hanging between pain and ecstasy … **In Shit I Find Peace Is It!**' (Barker 1990: 241). At the end Skinner is given the keys of the castle and she threatens '**Suffering To Be Paid Out, Debts Extracted, Settlement in Yells!**' (Barker 1990: 248). There is a roar of jets flying low and she remembers that once there was 'no government' (Barker 1990: 249).

This draws on the contemporary moment, with the women's peace movement seizing headlines with its siege of the US airforce base at Greenham; with peace actions against nuclear weapons across the country; with challenges to right-wing 'realism'. But the images are also bewildering, 'unnecessary'; the language brutal and shouted; the visual and aural effects claustrophobically insistent. It's a sort of molecular instability which spills across audience territory. Later work would offer even less explicit social parallels, more abstracted positions, interacting across power and desire, both very immediate and yet confusing.

In bracketing off the 'social' Barker was getting closer to Artaud's concept of that which transcended the daily, locking the audience into patterns of sound and movement that were not rationally explicable. For this he was then criticised by some on the left since he seemed to be offering confusion rather than opposition, and hence confirming the triumph of Thatcherism. This criticism, although strange in Barker's case – and probably confirming his views of the 'humanist' left – was replaying a familiar theme in relation to 'Artaudian' or 'cruel' theatre. Its origins come from the time of the Marowitz–Brook exploration, when Peter Brook did his 1963 production in Paris of Arden's *Serjeant Musgrave's Dance*. Arden's play depicts a cross-section of a society as it explores the consequences on the home community of colonial violence (see p. 156), but, to one critic, Albert Hunt, the production moved the focus away from a 'popular' story to a 'generalized nightmare', ending in 'a statement of mid-century despair' (Hunt 1974: 166–7). Brook was to move on to do celebrated productions of plays more suited to his aesthetics of pessimism, such as *Marat/Sade* (to give it its short title) for the RSC in 1964. Thereafter he remained in 'Artaudian' (with inverted commas) mode when he explored supposedly transcultural theatre languages, leading to work such as *Orghast* (1971) at Persepolis.

Without Brook's intellectual project, the transmutation of 'cruelty' into glamorous gloom was more explicit in Peter Shaffer's *Equus*. It dates from 1973, close in time to *Lear* and *Lay By*, and a decade on from the 'Cruelty' season. *Equus* tells of a young man who blinds horses and who is subsequently treated by a psychiatrist. The play takes its audience into Alan's head at the moment when nightmare horses appear – 'archetypal images – judging, punishing, pitiless'. So too it shows the psychiatrist, Dysart, not only establishing connection with Alan's torment but also realising that, in his own way, he is as disturbed as the boy. Famously the play had the horses acted by humans in large horse masks, making them into entities that seemed more than human. Act 1 ends with the horses around the acting square slowly revolving it as the light on Alan narrows down; the horses hum increasingly loudly, and Alan shouts over them. His address to the horses is 'ceremonial', 'ritualistic'. This stage imagery could be said to derive from 'Cruel' theatre, but now positioned as the mindset of a young man in need of psychiatric help. Mutated into an aberrant adolescent problem, this is choreographed nightmare, Cruelty the musical. And this mutation, combined with its aesthetic sanitising, probably paved the way for the play's access to its popularity. It was put on across the land for years after and became parked almost permanently as the love-object of student drama societies.

It seems, then, that the dramaturgy of 'Cruelty' comes with an in-built capacity for aestheticisation and subjectivism, and this, I suspect, is what fuelled the critique of Barker. But that dramaturgy and language also facilitated an appropriate new intensity in the exploration of the person to an extent not available in contemporary realism.

By way of example, Sarah Kane's *Blasted* (1994) appears to return to the stage language of *Lay By* in order to rupture complacence about the distance of the contemporary war in the Balkans. Set in an expensive hotel room in Leeds, which is somehow also caught up into a war zone, the play presents the relationship of the immature Cate, who suffers from fits, with the older, cynical, racist and sexist Ian; then the relationship between Ian and a soldier who brutalises him; then the return of Cate after the soldier's suicide. The soldier's accounts of his killings recall media coverage of Balkans warfare, with its particular focus on domestically local, intercommunity violence. The play brings this violence into a familiar British setting and through its series of encounters tracks the interpersonal transmission of the effects of brutalisation.

The expressive intensity of the play comes from a series of ferocious images – fits and hysterical laughter, a bombed hotel room, male-on-male rape, sucking out of eyes, baby eating. These are combined with a stripping-down of language and persons – all three characters are psychically harmed, replaying their experiences, with their interactions arranged in series. The entry of the soldier comes in the middle of the play, after a sequence of door knocks. This simplification and focus are underlined by a withholding of information about setting. The hotel room is a space apart from wider social interaction. The war that suddenly appears outside is unexplained, a sort of imagined scenography. It all comes close to feeling like metaphor, but it's unclear what it figures. The point about lived and exported violence is made, but it closes off wider social application such as that in Maugham's *Services Rendered*. Indeed it is as remorselessly concerned with the 'personal' as *Equus*. And here perhaps is the reason for its effect. It continues the 'personalising' drift of 'cruelty', but breaks with the arty aesthetics of Brook or Shaffer. That break is, though, a return, to the vocabulary of *Lay By*. And, as Bond had observed, audiences get used to stage languages. The shock around *Blasted* in 1994 replayed, in the same theatre, the shock around Bond about thirty years before. And when that happens, the 'shocking' play slips away from being a challenge to received ideas and turns into the received idea of a shocking play.

When *Blasted* brutally dislocated the personal from the social, echoing dramaturgic rhythm and psychic process, it was turning away from an already existing set of questions around identity, society and politics. The early 1970s had the slogan that the personal was political. Then the 1980s asked a different question, as to how far the political is personal. From this follow others: in what sense is political activity inhabited by desire and fantasy? How far do modes of politics contribute to subjective repression or liberation? Where, in political activity, is the formation of identity and fulfilment? How, vulgarly, does Marx meet Freud?

This is rich, if difficult, material. Its dramatic exploration is exemplified most profoundly by a dramatist who first came to public attention back in the years of the 'theatre of cruelty' experiment, David Rudkin. His 1986 play *The Saxon Shore* is set at a specific historical time and place, with several groups of people co-existing in fraught interrelationship. It is the end of Roman rule in Britain; there are incursions from Saxons on the North Sea coast; the native British feel residual hostility to all others; the Saxon-British, from a previous incursion, have a fragile status. The differences of race and culture are concretised in the languages spoken in the play. In perhaps the most extreme case a scene is played almost entirely in an invented Celtic. Rudkin says that while its sounds must resemble no modern foreign language 'the *emotions* should be clear' (Rudkin 1986: 52).

The scene produces a barrier to understanding. The audience can in general terms follow what is going on, but more from relying on the visual imagery and music of the scene than the literal meanings of every word. The capacity to interpret, to arrive at intellectual understanding, is withheld in favour of exposure to sight and sound. The audience is invited not to work with its brains so much as its senses, to give itself over to that which is both prodigious and dark.

Rudkin asks that the actors don't use regular accents in dealing with the various languages. Similarly he is cautious about the play's werewolves, who are enemies of the British. They are not to be in wolf costume. They are human characters who '*experience* themselves as wolves' (Rudkin 1986: 52). Not masked rebels, then, these are people in a specific situation who transform.

The psychic difficulty of the transformation is played out in the scene where the central figure Athdark is compelled to return to werewolf status. Athdark has moved between cultures, learning words of Latin, being healed of a wound by Ceiriad the British queen, becoming alienated from his own skin. In his reversion to werewolf status he is told 'a deeper Athdark has to waken' (Rudkin 1986: 37).

The play refuses to 'translate' this werewolf condition into a sign for something else or to pin it down within a rational reading. In this respect it is rather more than an account of the effects of colonialism and enforced movement of peoples. In part it certainly is this: Rudkin's approach here and in other work is informed by a (proto)Marxist understanding of how identities are produced within specific social circumstances. But that approach is accompanied by an effort to stage, to push out into public space, the more inchoate drives and passions that work within human beings. That staging is felt most strongly in the play's visual and musical organisation. The dark peoples with 'illseen forms … From gathering forms, a like mimicry, as they tune into the sounds of the night' (Rudkin 1986: 36–7). At the centre of the picture are figures who feel alienated both from their society and from their own bodies. The audience too experiences a form of alienation, in that it is denied the wherewithal to explain within known points of reference. It is subjected to obscurity, in a fairly literal sense. But the invitation to respond sensually is never just that, for there is, simultaneously, the overview of specific groups interacting at a specific point in history. The strain between two modes of response is calculated. Both are at play in the closing moments, as Athdark sorts his way through his Romanness and his wolf identity: 'So cold … Spathum, sword: shall be a spade.

To this stage language one other element was added. In Forced Entertainment's *Emanuelle Enchanted* (1992) they used rails with jumble on, a translucent curtain, wheeled theatrical flats and wheeled televisions rigged to a video. Although here it's part of a 'makeshift' feel, the onstage presence of imaging apparatus has become one of the regular tropes of contemporary work. Clearly the increase in flexibility and precision of this equipment has been one of the major developments of the modern period. But that is not itself a reason for its being staged. For much of the early part of the modern period the objective was to combine – often seamlessly – the effects of different media. Such combination is primarily associated with the effort to produce a stage picture that would be an accurate copy of recognisable reality. With the development of technologies around digital imaging the performance acquired the mechanism of reproducing 'reality' – through recorded images – without itself needing to imitate. This development came within a reaction against the realisms of the earlier part of the period, and embraced a conscious separation of the elements of the show – placing the lighting effect, for example, in tension against the onstage activity. The aesthetic excitement around the forced interrelation of separated elements is articulated in a favoured word of the 1990s – 'hybrid'. The development also has a political nuance in that it comes the other side of extended debates, through the 1960s and 1970s, as to the relationship between theatre and film and television. With imaging technologies on stage the theatre performance can itself enact – can retake possession of – the relationship between live performing and recordings/broadcasts of it. This work has been called 'mixed' media but, to reflect that element of separation in the rhetoric, it may be more appropriate to call it 'cross-media' theatre.

It's worth asking now why this mode might have emerged and how it works. In a general sense the collaging and mingling of images from diverse sources, together with the display of the equipment that generates them, operate as a form of mimesis. What is being imitated, or expressed, on stage is the feeling of modern society. This is a version of the 'modernity hypothesis' (Singer 2001), which notes how, late in the nineteenth century, there was a feeling that life was becoming faster, more technologised. The polemics of Futurism or biomechanics are one statement of this feeling, the scenic transformations and suspenses of melodrama another. The conspicuous use of 'technology' on stage, as a rhetoric of cross-media, can be seen as a continuation of this process, a way of expressing the general experience of contemporary living and, more particularly, media process.

There is, however, a political choice about what you express. James Yarker, founder of Stan's Cafe, explains that in *Be Proud of Me*, despite the possibilities of digital equipment, they decided to use older technology, a slide projector.

The decision was in part aesthetic: 'There is a quality to a slide's enforced still-ness, a seductiveness to the gaps that lie between them, a "thing-ness" to their substance.' But the issue goes wider: 'I feel we must be careful about placing the means of production centre stage as the main attraction' (Yarker 2004). Where the projector is as much the spectacle as the film, then limits are imposed on the cinema as art. The theatre can exhibit its technology as a natural feature of contemporary life or it can make a problem of its relationship with this tech-nology. A stage that gleams with the shiny texture of kit is expressing not only an attitude to the contemporary but an assumption, also, of competence.

By contrast, the fragments that comprise *Marina & Lee* are such things as 'adverts for Toyota, fragments of sex shows, TV thrillers' (Etchells 1996: 112), the cultural world of modern society, where images flow together in an undif-ferentiated way, and have to be 'exorcised'. That's an interesting verb. It implies a subject who is inhabited or haunted by these media effects, for whom the pro-cess of the show is a way of dealing with this experience of modern life: 'This notion of an onstage community pitching itself against a system of texts or images ... and the progress of the community ... is', says Etchells, 'almost a con-temporary version of plot' (1996: 115). In this formulation the work of mimesis shows the tense situation of individuals in mediatised culture. Those individu-als are played not as 'characters' in the old sense but as versions, more or less fictional, of the performers' own selves. And the spoken word, although appar-ently less important, keeps returning in fragments and quotations with enough obsessiveness to indicate that spoken text still has major potency. In various respects, then, I think what we are looking at here is a sort of realist mimesis, and as realism its job of work is to be expressive. When the theatre language of Forced Entertainment became a dominant mode it was perhaps not surprising in that this was a continuation, by other means, of expressive realism.

Being physical

Alongside the development of this new theatre language, another strand of work had emerged from the 1970s. When he founded the dance company DV8 in 1986 Lloyd Newson defined it as 'physical theatre'. This set it apart from dance, often understood at that time as 'ballet', and also from theatre, which was still primarily word-based. Replacing terms such as 'new mime', Newson's phrase felt novel, and it took off, coming to describe a range of activi-ties and provoking convolutions of academic prose. In its origins, however, as Heddon and Milling (2006: 177) suggest, there were two basic models: an extension of dance; an exploration of clowning (usually anchored in Lecoq's method). In general 'physical theatre' is a theatrical rhetoric that foregrounds corporeal physicality. When he was asked about the abilities of the performers in Complicite, Simon McBurney said that their physical fitness was in fact an illusion produced by the shows (Giannachi and Luckhurst 1999: 76). In other words the shows have us attend to – they set a framework of expectations around – the importance and productivity of the performing body. By contrast the rhetoric of naturalism foregrounds the relations between people and their environment through a staging in which rooms and bodies seemed to interpenetrate.

The physical rhetoric can be seen at work in Complicite's *Street of Crocodiles* (1992), based on Bruno Schulz's short stories about his family and upbringing. Schulz's experimental prose, combined with the 'atmosphere of his time and the mechanism of his dreams', provoked a creative response in which the whole company, bar the one playing Josef, operated as a scenographic entity as much as individuated characters. They became birds and books; a classroom that mutated into a forest of chair-legs. Their trained ability to interact physically produced surprising and wonderful transitions which depict fantasised or nightmare sequences. But although sound and visuals were crucial, the principal expressive work was done by a group of bodies, as a group. In them we watched more than dexterity, for in the sequence where the ledger apparently moved on its own around the group the normal relationship between humans and objects is inverted. The bodies appeared to be controlled by objects. These inversions were both a representation of nightmare – as it were a mimesis – and a display of physical dexterity, materially here and now. That emphasis on the corporeal gains force to the extent that it deviates from social norms. The bodies are apparently not governed by the rules which normally obtain with regard to consistency of physical identity, relationship with objects, norms of interpersonal relations, even (as Father walks up a wall) gravity.

The core of the show, in narrative terms, had to do with Josef's experience of the loss of childhood and his father. For the director the show was about memory, and its atmospheres were imbued by loss, that which is irrecoverable, that which is absent. At the same time the core of the show was – both materially and imaginatively – the work done by the performing group. The subject of 'memory' allowed them to make representations that were both non-realist and non-static: one image dissolved into another. Strange and seemingly subjective as the images were, what was clear and graspable was the movement between images, the activity of transformation. In this activity the group process of devising had itself transformed into the structuring aesthetic of the show. Indeed the protagonist was not so much the fictional character as the trained group. The centre of the Complicite show was, both materially and affectively, Complicite.

And thus they had their influence. Once again a theatre language has been adopted by enough people to give it a dominant position, indeed to be on the school syllabus. Complicite's work is powerful in part because it demonstrates a group closely working together in conditions of physical trust. In a society of alienated labour, that image is pleasurable because it is a vision of how things might be different … being handled differently in the world. The other source of power is the work's enunciation of a clear company identity. Complicite have a readily recognisable signature. In the flow of mediatised society their authorship is distinctive. Those working with written text have produced similar pleasure from both the impossible eloquence of the spoken and the sense of clear singular authorship. This we have observed in work from the readable tradition. Complicite might be said, albeit paradoxically, to have created a physical tradition which has the pleasures – and status – of readable theatre.

Provisional Fictions

One other strand emerged from the late 1960s/early 1970s. This was theatre made by visual artists. We have seen elsewhere (see p. 43) that sculptors put their own bodies into the frame, but visual theatre as such is something more extended. There are two general features: one is the emphasis on visual media in the performance – thus John Fox made puppets for Albert Hunt's *Russian Revolution* in 1967; when he founded Welfare State, the company worked with communities to build structures and objects; the resulting performance in 1971 might be a procession with objects or an exhibition in a maze. The second feature is an approach to composition which derives not from plot and action but from the deployment of a system of rules, much as a painting might be structured by colour values or geometric balance. The prime example of such rule-based performance in its early phase is Anthony Howell's Theatre of Mistakes (see pp. 96–7).

After working with Theatre of Mistakes Julian Maynard Smith, himself trained as a visual artist, founded Station House Opera in 1980. The company's work has experimented with a range of media and materials, where the internal dynamic of the material in question shapes the logic of the event, whether as mechanical pulley systems, breeze blocks or projected media. Describing a show in which the performers were suspended from Brooklyn Bridge, Maynard Smith notes: 'It is the unpredictable behaviour of the construction that will necessitate its own, functional music' (Maynard Smith 1983: 24).

In taking the model of rule-derived performance Maynard Smith moved it from abstract rules to rules derived from given physical materials and circumstances. While The People Show were interested in the relationship between the visual artist and 'his materials' (Time Out 1971), Maynard Smith intensifies the presence and intractability of those materials. This takes us somewhere new. One strand of contemporary work has ended up pretty close to expressive realism; another has settled on the performer as auteur. Rule-derived work has managed to take a different position on the real and at the same time has unsettled the concept of performer.

Let's track this through two works from two different companies, spanning a twenty-year period. In Station House Opera's *Bastille Dances* (1989) a group of performers worked with forty tonnes of loose breeze blocks: 'resident at this site, unable to leave, obliged to construct their stories with the material available'. The breeze blocks are 'part of the conditions the performers encounter' and the effort to move them is 'natural work in the course of gestural expression'. The performers' bodies are entrained by that effort; particular groups of muscles have to be used and become exhausted, hands bleed. The concept of performer falters: 'Given the nature of their situation, it is obvious they cannot pretend they are characters in a play.' Nevertheless they act out roles as they build their structures and interact. It is an image of both agency and constraint: 'Each performer changes role as the situation demands, and as the configuration of the blocks allows.' Similarly in the shows on pulley systems there was a tension between the weight of the body and the desire to be free. The structures are both beautiful and unstable. Driven by dialectic tension, there is no 'grand design' (Maynard Smith 1994/5: 60).

Which doesn't mean to say there is no meaning: 'the performance became a metaphor for a complete system, a world'. Because the interactions between the performers were expressed through the handling of the blocks, 'the structures built are narrative ones'. Blocks are piled on a singer until singing becomes impossible. As blocks are assembled, small narratives, vignettes, seem to appear – and then disappear as another phase, another construction, develops: 'Ideally, every action is both constructive and destructive, taking away one thing while building another' (Maynard Smith 1994/5: 62; also Quick 1998). The interest in working with 'found' materials is that these materials – the breeze blocks – are both familiar, recognisably real objects in their own right and, at the same time, capable of apparent transmutation into something else. Pleasure comes from watching transformation. The raw materials are difficult, heavy, rough, but they become taken up into games, small narratives which keep changing. Full of transitions, the work is both heavily awkward and ephemeral. It stages narrative and its destruction, the physical investment in labour and its fragmentary nature. As relationships develop, and stories unfold, we know that they are highly provisional. It might therefore be appropriate to say that what is produced here is a provisional fictionality.

A similar sort of provisional fictionality was staged in Blast Theory's 2007 event at the Barbican, London, *Rider Spoke*. Participants rented headphones and a bicycle equipped with a computer, which tracked its position using WiFi networks. The reason for this method of tracking, rather than GPS, is that, as Matt Adams says (private communication, 13 March 2009), 'WiFi positioning is ubiquitous and inherently mutable', characteristics which set the tone for the event. Thus equipped, participants were invited to ride off on their own into the surrounding streets, to select a suitable place to stop, and then to record their answer to a personal question. If they tried to stop somewhere where others had stopped previously, they were told to continue cycling. Once they had recorded their first answer they could opt then either to answer more questions or to find where others had stopped and listen to their answers.

For participants the activity was on the edge of everyday behaviour. The cycling and headphones are ordinary; stopping on the street to answer a personal question is perhaps less so. Some investment is required from the participants – the work of cycling and negotiating traffic, selecting stopping places, choosing how – and indeed in what persona – to answer the questions. That investment is already teetering near to activity that can create a fiction. The space where one records one's own answer can become special. More so, perhaps, is the space where an individual listens to the voices of others, telling 'personal' thoughts about themselves. The city, in all its intractable rhythms and processes, carries on around. Momentarily, in an ordinary street, a cyclist hears another voice speaking 'personally', which, for a few moments, might make the ordinary city space a bit less ordinary. The fiction is that one is in touch with other real individuals' thoughts and feelings in the alien urban environment, connected through participation in something which is – what? – game? performance? theatre? The participant is audience for those other voices and scriptwriter for people yet unknown. The elements are all seemingly transparent – the apparatus, the city, the cycling. There is never any guarantee that it is not going to be just rather dull or twee. The random, and not always interesting, conjunctions of recorded voice and setting; the risk of recording a private statement in a space never wholly reliably disinterested – all of this suggests possible access to a different world, with its own limits, its own provisional narratives.

There are, then, loose similarities between *Rider Spoke* and *Bastille Dances* in terms of their play with provisional fictionality. That said, the shows come nearly twenty years apart and there are major differences. Blast Theory can count on both the technology of, and the cultural familiarity with, 'gaming', in the sense of computer games. These allow games-players to immerse themselves – the mechanism is no longer driven by empathy with a witnessed event but by submission to a structure of rules and risks. Either way, the accurate word would still be 'involvement'. The most crucial point of difference, however, is that the concept of the audience as such has disappeared from Blast Theory's work. The audience at *Bastille Dances* watched small narratives come and go. In *Rider Spoke* it is participants (see Audience) that become engaged with found moments of seeming interconnection in the alien city. What is being represented here, we might say, is the apparatus of interconnection. And the invitation to inhabit it – indeed to empathise – is in part developed by old-fashioned theatrical means. The tone of the voice in your ear as you cycle round has all the acted signifiers of intimacy, privacy, closeness.

Underlying both examples of provisional fictionality we can note, here and elsewhere, the persistent presence of 'fragments'. For Forced Entertainment the 'fragment' was a bit of media culture, a dislocated image. From these the performers were trying to exorcise themselves. But for Station House Opera and Blast Theory there's a different take on fragments. The small narratives that come and go, the anonymous voices heard in a found space: each invites engagement with – cathexis of – not just the momentary but its transitoriness. Back in 1979 three feminists described their sense of a changed politics – the decline in potency of the monolithic Party, the defeats of organised labour, a need for networks of connection between 'single-issue' campaigns: they called their book *Beyond the Fragments*. The structures and thinking that disappeared then have not returned. Instead, through the 1990s, resistance not so much to a ruling Party but to a dominant corporate culture was expressed in networks of seemingly spontaneous gatherings to dance. Clusterings of intense energy, dissipation, reconfigurings – the strength was in transitoriness, networks not structures, not the Party but parties. This was as much about potency in, as subjugation to, mediatised culture. It was about finding new spaces within the already existing.

Duress and duration

Something new enters theatre languages of the 1980s and 1990s as they grapple with staged process and fragment. We have already encountered a couple of repeated tropes.

The spectacle in *Bastille Dances* is of performers engaged in working with intractable materials. The performers of Brith Gof's *Gododdin* battled tons of sand and water, becoming implicated in the material. A panicking 'performer' raced through streets against time to find Uncle Roy's office (Dixon 2007: 663–9). In these cases the performers are engaging not so much with the given circumstances, on a Stanislavskian model, but with the specific weights, textures, dynamics of what we can call given materials. We have also seen that these engagements produce, in passing, a sense of provisional fictionality.

Underlying these tropes are more general areas of repeated interest in the work of this period. The grappling with given materials, especially where those materials are intractable, involves actual hard work. Lifting weight or maintaining balance, repeating movement until exhaustion, staying at it over long periods, panting, bleeding: the body is under duress.

Where provisional fictionality happens, the fictional is an effect of a larger process. The work is not governed by story, linear or not. Instead it takes the time it takes to do what needs doing, or to fill the time given. A cycle ride in *Rider Spoke* was cut off after half an hour; Forced Entertainment's *Speak Bitterness* (1994) can last up to six hours; a Welfare State procession may have taken a month. The suspense narrative introduced by melodrama was a response to new feelings about time, speeding up and slowing down the sense of time passing. Another response might be the performance organised to foreground time, where the ability to interfere with a sense of time passing is prevented. In this sort of performance a key element is duration.

Duress and duration in their separate – and often connected – ways indicate new modes of thinking and imagining about performance. Each has us attend to the limits of performance. The performing body may become exhausted and less able to continue, the show may have an inability to organise time on behalf of its audience or participants. Rather than taking a delight in the capacity of theatre to manage and seemingly transcend the limits of the physical and temporal, theatre becomes fixated on those limits. For those who may wish to evaluate this politically there are several considerations. Are duress and duration resistances to a 'fast' society with its notions of how individuals can 'make over' their bodies? Are they an abandonment of theatre's capacity to exercise and celebrate human agency? Are they a denial that theatre works by illusion and signifying? Are they a failure to do anything significant?

Perhaps all of these, in different work and different places … bits of it merely evidence of the political bankruptcy that some see in the culture of the 1990s; other bits of it evidence of an attempt to speak of a changed world and, in speaking of it, perhaps, starting to make it.

Theatre and Technology: staging a relationship between bodies and technologies; living a relationship between bodies and technologies. What are the points of penetration? Is the penetration mutual? Definitions of technology are apparent, but so too definitions of performance and indeed work.

12. Welfare State International, *Parliament in Flames*, Burnley, Lancashire, 5 November 1976: preparations for the fire spectacle.

13. Complicite, *The Elephant Vanishes*: original production (2003), a Complicite co-production with Setagaya Public Theatre, Tokyo and BITE:03 Barbican, London.

14. Victoria Theatre, Stoke-on-Trent: rehearsal for *Fight for Shelton Bar!* (1973). The process of steelmaking, which formed an intrinsic part of the documentary performance, was studied by the actors both at the works and in rehearsal. Actors (*l to r*) Graham Padden, Alan Gill and Bill Thomas watch as steelworker Phil Rogers demonstrates how they take a sample of molten steel from the furnace.

15. Blast Theory: Dicky Eton performing in *Can You See Me Now?* in Cologne, being chased by local children.

Chapter 4

Why they do it

This section is concerned with people's ideas about why theatre should be made and what impact it has. The largest part deals with groups of people who have used theatre to try and do something in society. A much smaller part describes the processes of allocating value to – or removing it from – various theatre practices.

Movements and manifestos

The modern period has seen a wide diversity of performance practices. But that is not what makes it necessarily more significant than earlier periods. Its particular character comes from the self-consciousness of this diversity, the diligently sharpened contrasts between one practice and another. More than other periods perhaps, it is a time of conscious 'movements' in art and politics.

Most theatrical movements come into focus because they define themselves against a norm, a mode of drama or practice of theatre. Some result from philosophical or formal arguments among artists and makers. Celebrated European movements such as symbolism, expressionism and surrealism had little effective operation, as movements, in Britain however. By contrast most of the movements examined here tend to be motivated by, and seek to express, wider social and political campaigns. In some ways this is a very British phenomenon.

Responsible theatres: the Whig tradition

Deeply embedded in writings about British theatre history there is a recurrent narrative. It comes to the surface most clearly in the early Victorian period. When scholars of the time wrote accounts of the Restoration theatre of the 1660s onwards they viewed it as licentious and elitist. They regarded it as the product of a royalist court and, as such, a temporary and deplorable aberration in the history of the Parliamentary democracy that had been initiated in the puritan revolution of the 1640s. In this, the 'Whig' view of theatre history, Restoration drama was characterised as theatre that was socially and sexually irresponsible, created by a minority for a minority, undemocratic and indulgent. It was positioned as an archetype of theatre that disavows social commitment and ethical responsibility. From here its shadow falls over subsequent theatre practices. You can see that shadow lurking behind the belief that a form of theatre that does not demonstrate its engagement with wider society must be a theatre that is elitist, decadent and irresponsible.

The theatre and performance activities reviewed in this section of the book are all stridently conscious of their social responsibility. An agitational sketch from 1932 called *Their Theatre and Ours* (Thomas 1985) quotes and mocks the characteristic features of dominant theatre of the day – the patriotic music hall song, the gangster play and celebrity performers ('Miss Greater Garbage'). This theatre is unhealthy, it argues, because it encourages illusions about the world. 'Their' highly entertaining songs and dramas do treacherous ideological work. They conceal the struggles of workers against the system that oppresses them. 'Our' theatre sees the world clearly, refuses the treacherous attractions and thereby works towards a more just society.

The Workers' Theatre Movement

The 'us' here, attacking 'them', would be a small troupe affiliated to the larger network which is collectively referred to as the Workers' Theatre Movement (WTM). These groups, who were often members of the Communist Party, were most intensely active around 1931–2, using the methods of drama to promote arguments for social revolution. Their arguments had to be readily transportable to a range of venues where they would get a working-class audience, preferably one actually engaged in industrial and political struggle. The Red Megaphones in Salford, following the cotton strikers, played outside factories and in market-places, so they needed a form that could be written and rehearsed quickly, in response to developing situations – the form generally known as agit-prop (see pp. 94–5).

---

from: Workers' Theatre Movement first National Conference, London, June 1932

the Workers' Theatre does not pretend to be above the struggle. It is an expression of the workers' struggle in dramatic form. It is consciously a weapon of the workers' revolution, which is the only solution of the present crisis.

> It not only unmasks the capitalist system but organizes the workers to fight their way out.
>   Because it deals with realities it escapes from the emptiness of bourgeois drama and becomes the first step in the development of proletarian drama. (In Samuel *et al.* 1985: 100)

Although it is reputed to be incapable of subtle analysis, the form was crafted so that its stripped-down qualities were aesthetic as well as functional. This 'Propertyless Theatre for a Propertyless Class', as Tom Thomas called it, embodied less a political position than an attitude. Sketches prided themselves on being fast, rhythmic, disciplined. In a note at the top of *Their Theatre and Ours* Thomas says, 'It is vital that the strongest contrast in style be made between the burlesque inset scenes of the capitalist theatre and films, and the serious passages' (Thomas 1985: 138). This required accurate and disciplined performing of different sorts. As the text defines it, however, the key quality of workers' theatre is not that it is highly 'theatrical', but that it has something 'the boss-class theatre' hasn't got and can't buy – 'The spirit of the working class that is changing the world' (Thomas 1985: 144). In other words, quite a lot of aesthetic effort is put into getting an effect that is clear-cut and simple. This acquires value to the extent that it doesn't look like aesthetic effect for its own sake but is instead experienced as efficiency and commitment.

As such it was potentially very powerful. The ideologues of the WTM knew that 'The direct approach to the audience, together with the fact that the performance is surrounded by and part of the crowd, is of great value in making the worker audience feel that the players are part of them' (in Samuel *et al.* 1985: 102). The troupe that does *Their Theatre* begins by marching on, singing 'in well-marked rhythm'. Then they stand in a line and shout in unison: 'Workers' Theatre! Workers' Theatre! Workers' Theatre!' (Thomas 1985: 138–9). In that entry there is attractive discipline of body and voice, a rhythm which is sung. The unison shout alternates with individual lines, as it were anchoring individual utterances in the group, and giving that group a solid presence not just in its unity but through its production of vocal energy. When it feels this performance is 'part of them', the audience is not only shown but drawn into an ideal version of its own unity and potency. For the professional director André van Gyseghem the experience in Moscow of workers' performance from other countries was an introduction not to politics but to an aesthetic: 'mass movements, individual movements contrasted, a montage of effects which create a third thing … using the … shape of the body in space, and … levels, flags, poles, whatever props you had, using patterns' (in Stourac and McCreery 1986: 241).

For others, however, the experience of performing alongside other groups in Moscow in 1933 came as a shock. The British were criticised as amateurs, 'our plays were too raw, we kept shouting slogans' (in Stourac and McCreery 1986: 241). While for the WTM in general this conscientious – and political – preoccupation with the artistic forms and standards of its work was a distinguishing feature, there was resistance. One criticised group (Castleford WTM) argued that it was less the aesthetics than worker involvement which was important. This response takes everything into new territory.

Hitherto the dramatic form could be criticised for not being sufficiently effective, for alienating those who should be engaged. Such judgements are predicated on the assumption that the form has a usefulness in its own right. But to argue that formal standards are less important than the involvement of the members is to move to a different sort of usefulness. As community theatre practitioners of the 1990s would later put it, what matters is 'participation'.

As an initiative the WTM can be seen to anticipate the shapes of practices which were to follow. It was classically modernist in its belief in a political and artistic vanguard whose job was to convert others. Irrespective of existing political hierarchies, it aimed to provide a form of leadership that was an embodiment of advanced thinking and active energy for change. Its tense relations with both its own political masters and its projected mass audience served to confirm its status as artistic and political vanguard. As such, its discussions about the art of performance were perhaps more extensive and deep than in almost any subsequent set of groups. In turn, the WTM's awareness about, and analysis of, the ideologies of dramatic form set a pattern for later practices. But it also anticipated later practices in those moments when it was less confident as modernist vanguard, namely when there were suggestions that standards of art were less important than the fact of creative participation. Here the WTM's power might be said to lie not in its role as leader but as facilitator. Whichever of the two, by the end of the 1930s the revolution had been neither led nor facilitated, and the WTM had vanished.

Until, that is, it was rediscovered in the late 1970s. As he was dying, in 1976, Tom Thomas asked the socialist historian Raphael Samuel to visit him, so that he could pass on the archives of the WTM. This bequest led to the publication in 1985 of *Theatres of the Left*, co-edited by Samuel, Stuart Cosgrove and Ewan MacColl, founder of the Salford Red Megaphones. In the following year another account of the WTM appeared in *Theatre as a Weapon*, edited by Richard Stourac and Kathleen McCreery. McCreery had helped to found two theatre groups, Red Ladder in 1968 and then the break-away Broadside Mobile Workers Theatre; Stourac had worked with both groups. The publication of *Theatre as a Weapon* suggested a precursor for 1970s political troupes and thereby established a lineage, albeit one half-hidden or indeed actively suppressed, for workers' theatre.

By this time, however, workers' theatre was also having to find its place alongside feminist, gay, black and, latterly, disability theatres. All were engaged in altering a worldview which privileged a specific and narrow set of norms.

Feminist theatres

Feminist performance, like twentieth-century feminism itself, comes in two phases. The first coincides with the campaign for voting rights for women in the Edwardian period. The second, and longer lasting, comes at the very end of the 1960s, emerging within a general climate of political militancy.

Suffrage

The long simmering campaign for equal rights for women boiled over into spectacular activity in the early years of the twentieth century. In 1897 the formation of the National Union of Women's Suffrage Societies sought to draw together into one organisation various different campaigning groups. But the crucial move came in 1903 when a break-away group was formed, the Women's Social and Political Union (WSPU).

Arguing that the old-style techniques of legal wrangling and persuasion were getting nowhere, the WSPU committed to direct action, fighting the campaign by any means necessary, legal or not. The battle for women's suffrage was suddenly in the headlines. It led in 1908 to the formation of the Actresses' Franchise League (see Actors as activists) and the Women Writers' Suffrage League, the objective of which was, as the *Suffrage Annual* declared in 1913, to obtain the vote for women by 'the use of the pen' (in Stowell 1992: 40). In the same way the Pioneer Players, founded by the suffragist Edith Craig in 1911, had two general objectives: '1. To produce plays dealing with all kinds of movements of contemporary interest. 2. To assist societies which have been formed all over the country in support of such movements, by helping them to organise dramatic performances, it having been asserted that "one play is worth a hundred speeches" where propaganda is concerned' (in Stowell 1992: 69).

The simple proposition that writing should advance the suffrage cause had more radical implications than first appear. The dramatic writing for women's emancipation took various different forms: short realist sketches, full-length plays, satiric sketches, masques, pageants. These different works were performed in an equally diverse range of venues. Elizabeth Robins's *Votes for Women* was done in 1907 at the Court Theatre. Gertrude Jennings's *A Woman's Influence* was done as part of the WSPU's Women's Exhibition at Prince's

Skating Rink in 1909. Cicely Hamilton's *Pageant of Great Women* was the Actresses' Franchise League's first matinee at the Scala Theatre the same year. Gertrude Vaughan's *The Woman with the Pack* was done in 1911 at a WSPU Christmas fête. Elizabeth Baker's *Edith* was part of a Women Writers' Suffrage League matinee at the Prince's Theatre in 1912.

Elizabeth Robins, addressing the Women Writers' Suffrage League in 1911, repudiated the criticisms of women's writing: 'Ladies, what shall we say of many of the girls drawn by men? I think we shall be safer *not* to say. But there she stands – the Real Girl! – waiting for you to do her justice. No mere chocolate-box "type", but a creature of infinite variety, of curiosities and ambitions, of joy in physical action, of high dreams of love and service' (in Stowell 1992: 13). In 1911 the word 'girl' had pretty precise cultural overtones. The world of musical comedy specialised in shows about 'girls' (see Bailey 1996). Like many of her fellow campaigners, Robins was concerned with women's representation in every sense.

This did not always result in sympathetic characterisation. Jennings's sketch *A Woman's Influence* is a realist parade of a set of contrasting positions. There is the wife, her secretary and friend, the female factory worker, the woman who believes her feminine charms can get things done. When the latter attempts her persuasion she discovers that her own wealth is implicated in the factory with appalling conditions, and rapidly backs off compromising her income. The ending both rejects this woman and brings middle-class husband and wife into alliance to change conditions for the factory workers.

The issue of representation on stage went rather further than representation at the ballot box. As Cicely Hamilton put it:

> If I worked for women's enfranchisement … it wasn't because I hoped great things from counting female noses at general elections, but because the agitation for women's enfranchisement must inevitably shake and weaken the tradition of the 'normal woman'… with her 'destiny' of marriage and motherhood and housekeeping.
>
> (in Fitzsimmons and Gardner 1991: 30)

In her 1908 play, *Diana of Dobson's*, which she described as a 'romantic comedy', she uses the contemporary archetype of the working woman, here in a drapery establishment, to tell a fantastic tale of sudden wealth and its loss. Diana, employed in oppressive surroundings, finds she's been left £300 and decides to spend it all to give herself one good time in her life. She buys fashionable clothes, stays in a swish hotel in Switzerland, and attracts rich suitors. When the money runs out, she meets one of these suitors again and agrees to marry him.

The play's two central acts, set in the Swiss hotel, are sandwiched between the shop girls' dormitory and the Embankment in London. The first act ends with an explosion of rage and defiance from the newly moneyed Diana against her dislikeable superior. The hotel sequence gives plenty of space to the well-dressed, witty Diana, who, although faking it, seems entirely at home in this setting. Up to this point the play is a staging of the pleasures of blowing everything. To this then is added a fourth act with its destitute characters sleeping on benches or wandering the Embankment. After the party this is abjection, though it is nevertheless abjection safely embraced by the harmony of comic narrative. Together the whole thing works as an imaging of appetite, of the need to do what is not necessarily sensible ... the insistence on being the thing one always might be, both impossibly charismatic and impossibly abject. As such the play, while never really being political, gives an expansive account of what is deep at the heart of emancipationist thinking.

Second-phase feminism
In second-phase feminism political demonstrations and street manifestations preceded the making of shows in theatre spaces. The first formal conference of the British Women's Liberation Movement took place in Oxford in 1969. In 1970 and 1971 there were protests against and disruptions of the Miss World contest, led, in 1971, by the Women's Street Theatre Group (WSTG) and the Gay Street Theatre Group. In the same year women and gay men disrupted the Christian Festival of Light. Founded in 1970 WSTG had accompanied political marches and done a show satirising representations of women (Wandor 1986: 38). They later regrouped as the Punch and Judies and did *The Amazing Equal Pay Play* (1972), based on a strike at Ford's car plant. This again was a street show, and it was on this model that sexual liberation performance spread in its earliest days. In 1973 the Oxford Women's Action Group and the Oxford Gay Action Group made a show about gender for a shopping mall.

Note some features of these beginnings: two targets in parallel – the representations of women and the conditions of work that structurally underpinned sexual inequality; anger about representations of women viewed as a gay issue as much as a feminist one; very little concern with 'art'. The first step towards the production of an identifiable feminist theatre in its own right came in 1973, when the Almost Free theatre mounted a Women's Season of plays. Although it was in the West End of London, home of commercial theatre, the Almost Free – where you paid what you could afford – was part of Inter-Action, based in the less grand Kentish Town. Founded by Ed Berman, Inter-Action was very much a product of its moment, 1968. It was a cooperative organisation formed 'to stimulate community involvement in the arts', giving opportunities to young theatre workers and providing a platform for 'oppressed' groups. On the basis of the success of two fairly angry plays written for him by Pam Gems, Berman conceived the idea for a season of plays devoted entirely to the issues of the newly emerged feminist movement. The success of this season showed the keenness of the hunger for women's work, and other festivals followed: at the Haymarket, Leicester, in 1975 and the Drill Hall, London, in 1977.

As a result of the Almost Free season two companies formed in 1974 – the Women's Theatre Group (WTG) and the Women's Company. WTG largely consisted of political activists from the feminist movement; the Women's Company consisted mainly of feminists from the professional theatre. That contrast mobilises two others – between amateur and professional, and between the claims of politics and art. As such it reverberates through political and community theatre in general, as well as shaping feminist work in particular. When, for example, Monstrous Regiment was founded in 1975, it largely worked the art circuit as opposed to WTG on the political circuit, and while WTG explored theatre as education Regiment interested itself in cabaret.

Two words which have been silently sitting alongside one another now need pulling out. The relationship between 'women's' theatre and 'feminist' theatre has been much debated. In 1984 Susan Bassnett attempted to clarify usage. Feminist theatre, she argued, was based in the 'seven demands' of the organised women's movement: 'equal pay; equal education and job opportunities; free 24-hour nurseries; free contraception and abortion on demand; financial and legal independence; an end to discrimination against lesbians and a woman's right to define her own sexuality; freedom from violence and sexual coercion.' She then notes that the first four demands were articulated in 1970, and had to do with re-evaluating women's role in society. The other demands, articulated in 1975 and 1978, show a shift, she suggests, towards 'a more radical concept of feminism', where recognition of lesbianism and the assumption that all violence originates from men point towards the need for a new definition of male and female roles (in Goodman 1993: 30–1). In other words, it seems, even on the point of clarifying what feminist theatre might be, another potential debate arises.

Here, though, we have to acknowledge the interval of at least ten years between the founding moment and Bassnett's commentary. By 1984 the debates between socialist feminism and radical feminism had become hotter. Deep inside these debates was an apparently irresolvable division: while socialist feminism concentrated on changing the world through a redistribution of the power between the sexes, radical feminism contended that men were not changeable – that they were impelled by nature towards oppressive behaviour and violence. 'Theoretical' short-hand summarised this debate as 'constructionism' versus 'essentialism': the first term indicated a belief that identity, including sexual and gender identity, is a social and cultural construct, and can therefore be changed where social conditions change; the second term indicated a belief that sexual identity was shaped by biology, by nature, that it had an unchangeable essence, so that, by this argument, women are naturally predisposed towards caring, nurture and peace.

Like many fundamentalist positions the essentialist orthodoxy had roots in painful experiences of oppression. For women involved in supposedly collective theatre companies, the men appeared to be louder and more insistent in discussion. Even where a company began deliberately as mixed, such as Monstrous Regiment, when, through natural process, the men left, the women seemed to experience a change to their working relations. This change contributed to the creation of an autonomous voice for women, a fundamentally necessary step. It underpins WTG's first play, aimed at non-theatre-going teenagers, *My Mother Says I Never Should* (1975). Dealing with contradictions around attitudes to young women's sexual choices, contraception and desire, it produces effect by having women on stage say things that were conventionally unexpected from women: the oldest woman, Gran, speaks in defence of promiscuity: 'you should see about them tablets they have – no point in taking risks'. Mother and daughter show shock as Gran continues: 'for stopping babies, so you can enjoy yourself' (Women's Theatre Group 1980: 127). Revealed, or brought into being, at these moments is a shared basis of experience between stage and audience. But there is also a staging of difficulty in speaking, in a scene between daughter and mother: 'They don't tell you what really happens.' 'Look, Terri, it's just part of being married' (Women's Theatre Group 1980: 133). This makes for a play about more than gendering. In worrying around reputation and understanding, it images the effects of ideology. Attempted explanations about sex become metaphors for conversations that don't know how to happen, the gap between words and desire.

In material terms theatre feminists ensured they were heard by forming their own companies. The story of the origins of early feminist companies is that of conscious secession – leaving Belt and Braces to form Monstrous Regiment, leaving an undifferentiated Gay Sweatshop to form a women's Gay Sweatshop group. This reflected a general pattern in the leftist groups, where differences of analysis, emphasis or perhaps personality could lead to secessions and re-formations: the Cartoon Archetypal Slogan Theatre gave birth to the Agitprop Street Players in 1968; these transmuted into Red Ladder in 1973; Red Ladder gave birth to Belt and Braces; and from there … as above. Where individuals are in charge of their own structures they can discover how to change those structures to produce different conditions of work and relationship.

Within the early feminist groups, as with the others, the political – and indeed emotional – focus on appropriate organisation and working conditions seemed to be as important as the statement of feminist demands. This was logical, in that, for feminists, the 'personal is political': the problem had precisely been an oppression predicated upon uninspected assumptions about women's 'place'. There was, consequently, a deep interest in how a group could work together. Where that group was all-female the excitement came from the discovery of new circumstances that had hitherto not existed in their own lives, namely the chance to invent structure and processes for themselves. WTG announced that as a 'by-product of the Women's Movement' they functioned in a 'totally collective manner, trying to avoid leadership and hierarchies' (in Wandor 1986: 51). In some ways this job of organisation was the most creative aspect to feminist, and perhaps also wider leftist, theatre at this period. It invented the processes that could make the conditions that would shape the theatre. Feminist groups laid stress on consciousness raising – sharing and reflecting on their own histories and experiences. They resolutely insisted on forms of power sharing which were equal. And from here they committed to creative processes which were equal – group devising, collaboration, collective writing. And finally, in order always to attend to new voices that were trying to be heard even where money was short, they pioneered that development of the modern period, the rehearsed reading.

I suggest that this focus on structure and process was possibly the most 'creative' aspect of the work for a couple of reasons. First, and more locally, it is suggested by a number of commentators that the political work of the early 1970s did not see a great deal of formal innovation. The earliest work was heavily influenced by traditional agit-prop, and for good reason, in that it had an urgent political job to do. This mutated into a sort of realism, partly to deliver more complex argument and partly to reach audiences brought up on television. So in writing *My Mother Says* 'there was a wariness of experimental "artistic" theatre as well as of stark agitprop forms' (Mica Nava in Women's Theatre Group 1980). The function of reaching out to people establishes constraints on artistic form. This is a very different mind-set from that of the cultural 'underground' which only about six years before was experimenting wildly in places such as the Arts Lab.

The rather larger reason why the emphasis on structure and process was importantly 'creative' is this: it explored, and then demonstrated, new ways in which people could make work together. This politically driven initiative had an impact on many later theatre groups and their methods of work. But it is larger than that. In the domain of independent small 'alternative' theatre companies people can, largely, invent their own structures and process (although the manipulation of funding mechanisms often works, significantly, to disallow certain sorts of structure – collectives become 'management collectives'). This small-company domain can be seen as a space for trying out new ways of organising people, an opportunity for rehearsal of possible utopias. It was not any one show that was important, perhaps, but the work of shaping roles and rehearsing relationships on a larger scale. And through this rehearsal different ways of thinking were coming into being – structures were demonstrably not naturally given, they enshrined values and positions, they were changeable. Things could be as they were constructed. A new sense of relativism was coming into being. And the fundamentalists were the voices trying to resist it. They were clinging to a belief in the naturally given: while their enemies said women were by nature weak, dependent, etc., they said men were by nature aggressive, domineering, etc. The fundamentalist argument is a mirror-inversion of the oppressor, a conservative clinging to old structures of thought.

The full-on critique of representations of women potentially carried within it an orthodoxy about what the norms should be. These norms were kept in place at a deep level by an earnestly functional realism which, while it might have argued about women's control of their own bodies, had a fairly narrow notion of what the body is and does. The challenge to this orthodoxy came from the emergence of women's clowning and comedy. When Iris Walton and Jan Dungey formed Cunning Stunts, around 1977, there were very few women's theatre groups and these were not explicitly humorous. Stand-up comedy was only just beginning, and it was all male. Stunts developed performances which dealt in large physical gags, silly puns, acrobatics, music, singing, wild costumes and grotesque and uglified personas. This vocabulary was cross-fertilised from Circus Oz but aware also of the late-1960s experiments (they shared their initial base at Oval House with The People Show). This new women's physical comedy was thus a sort of continuity. But it was also a new theatre politics.

Stunts deliberately took on gigs at working men's clubs – being booked, of course, because of their name – in order to push the theatrical and gender boundaries where they were at their most conservative. What was more distinctive, however, was, first, that they aimed to involve audiences not as individuals but *en masse*, doing silly things. I remember cabbage leaves on a very long piece of string weaving across the audience: the Cabbage Forest. At one level this was a reprise of a late-1960s technique, but it was very different in its playfulness and generosity. By enacting women's capacity to lead crowds of people to be hilariously daft, they proposed theatrical and political relationships that broke from the earnestly functional realism. Rapidly other groups began to develop in a similar mould.

Second, and more testingly, they were somewhat problematically 'feminist'. They were not doing functional education shows nor reappropriation of glamorous forms such as cabaret. A reviewer in the feminist *Spare Rib* magazine noted that as an all-women group they were under 'an obligation to the women in the audience'. That 'obligation' should involve discussing women's issues, rather than being silly in big hats. But that silliness was, arguably, opening a space for onstage women to be physically inappropriate, messy, non-functional even: making space for a new feminist body. There were, however, tensions in the culture around definitions of that body. Most notoriously, in the mid-1980s there was major, and violent, uproar at the London Lesbian and Gay Centre over an attempt to ban lesbian sado-masochists. More trivially – perhaps – a woman arts officer sniffed scathingly at Stunts' 'finger-up-the-nose' humour. Putting these things together it becomes apparent that ancient conservatism around the body together with prejudices about proper art were begetting between them a new monstrous progeny – acceptable feminism.

Gay theatres

From about 1970 there was organised and public action by homosexuals against institutional and cultural oppression of homosexuality. The Gay Liberation Front (GLF) was founded in London in 1970 and went on to spawn, as it were, groups across the country. Gay theatre formally announced itself in a season of plays put on at the Almost Free Theatre. Following the model of the successful Women's Theatre season in 1973, Inter-Action encouraged the forming of a gay theatre group to mount a gay season. The emphasis, note, was not simply on doing plays, but – for this was the early 1970s – on building a company.

That company was Gay Sweatshop. Drawing committed performers together, often from professional theatre, the Almost Free plays were used to encourage others to come out. After the season finished Gay Sweatshop's first independent production, *Mr X*, was commissioned for the conference of the Campaign for Homosexual Equality in Sheffield in 1975, and thereafter toured nationally (see Actors as activists). The next production, *As Time Goes By*, although intended for the Edinburgh Festival, also premiered at a CHE conference, in Nottingham in 1977. Simultaneously gay theatre was also developing a life in 'art' venues. A second series of Gay Plays took place, at the Institute of Contemporary Arts (London), in 1976, and in 1977, in association with the Royal Court, a mixed-sex group did *Age of Consent* for the Royal Court Young People's Theatre Scheme. Nevertheless, in the eyes of the funders, gay theatre was clearly a lesser form of art: while Women's Theatre Group and Monstrous

Regiment got annual grants from the Arts Council, Gay Sweatshop only got project funding.

Another sort of problem emerged with the move into art venues. Unlike other oppressed groups, gay people are not necessarily visible on stage as gay. This invisibility allows the fact of difference to be ignored. As a reviewer in the socialist gay paper *Gay Left* noted: 'It is not the form of [Stephen Holt's] "Men" which challenges traditional theatre, but its content and the way it is produced. Unlike [Martin Sherman's] "Bent" which is written by an openly gay man, but performed by men who did not state their sexuality, "Men" was a specifically gay production and one to which we could respond without ambiguity' (Cooper 1980: 39).

This takes us back to a recurring issue in much of this movement-driven theatre. The 'form' or art is sometimes less important than its production process. Cooper celebrates the production where the actors are known to be gay. In the disabled company Graeae, formed in the same year as Cooper was writing, the importance was to have disabled performers on stage, even though the theatre piece may not have been 'satisfactory' (as Tomlinson 1982 put it) in conventional terms. The audience may often be there in order to watch something being made by people who are of their own community. And the show may make it clear that it is interested in speaking only to that community, as with some feminist shows for women-only audiences. The event of the show is less about engaging with an art work than with being there as witness to the achievements and agency of the political movement itself. And in this respect, where a movement was insisting on its presence against a dominant culture, then, whatever the art was like, each event of witnessing mattered, again and again.

But what the art was like was, for gay theatre perhaps more than for others, a key political question. Michelene Wandor comments that, by contrast with the women's season, the plays in the gay season were more 'literary' (Wandor 1986: 53). It's a remark that activates some old assumptions: the gay season was basically male, gay men have male privileges, they have ready employment in artistic professions, the economic security of their employment allows them space to be interested in art. This division between women and men, gay or not, appears to be manifested in the two productions which followed Gay Sweatshop's temporary split into male and female groups. The first women's show was about custody of children, called *Care and Control*. Based in the experiences of the women who made the show, the first act realistically tracked parallel stories and the second showed, in more agitational form, a set of images of women abused by the legal process. The men's show was *As Time Goes By* (1977), by Drew Griffiths and Noël Greig, a history of the modes of gay oppression ranging from late nineteenth-century London, through Germany in the 1930s to the American west coast in the early 1970s. It tries consciously for an epic sweep rather than a localised focus on issues. As Greig later said, 'To our knowledge there had been no other play which had attempted to place Gay men at the centre of a broad, historical narrative' (Greig 1997: 39).

The political drive in *Time* is the need to reveal, and hence understand, all those invisible historical links which together constitute the naturalisation of oppression. In this respect it coincides with other contemporary attempts to recover what was, in the feminist historian's words, *Hidden from History*. From this starting point Noël Greig later went on to write a series of shows, for general audiences, that worked rhetorically as an uncovering of ever more intensifying links between characters and events. But while Greig continued to work for political and community-based companies, as a matter of principle, the way had opened up for gay theatre to enter mainstream art houses. It was clear, now, that 'gay theatre' could mean two rather different things: theatre about gay issues or theatre done by gays. Each could be politically justified. Within the general leftist drive towards 'strategic penetration' of dominant culture, there was a value in having gay issues staged in a range of venues. But so too there was a need to ensure that the newly emerged gay voices would still be heard – as gay.

Built into gay activism from its founding moment was a commitment to making visible that hidable sexuality. Activists such as the Bethnal Rouge Bookshop Collective would often put on 'radical drag' as part of a political action. Even when invited as guests to a 'disco' at London's Goldsmiths College, they turned up dressed for the occasion – and were attacked by college security guards. This aim to make visible produced a form of direct political action which differed from other forms precisely in what we have to call its theatricality. GLF activists refused what they saw as the repressed mechanisms of 'normal' political contest and in the invention of the 'zap' they made front-on challenges to oppressive forces. The zap was an unannounced intervention, usually involving costumes and effects; nuns were highly favoured. One of the Gay Lib street theatre group's most famous, near-legendary, zaps was against the so-called Festival of Light, a gathering of Christian morality campaigners.

The Festival of Light zap (1971)

Mice were released. Stink bombs were thrown. Bubbles were blown by a pretty girl in a girl-guide uniform … A banner went up proclaiming 'Cliff for Queen' … At about this time a phalanx of flying nuns – the same ones we weren't sure about in the queue, and who'd been warned by the organisers about disturbances and asked to pray for the people involved – charged the platform, a fantastic vision of hurtling white and blue figures. They tried to dance in the narrow space available, one of them – only one? – a man, all surprising the bouncers with their non-nun-like energy … The brother who'd been getting into drag at the back of the balcony now prepared to come out, and as soon as the singing stopped … he got up shrieking: 'I've been saved, hallelujah!'

(in Walter 1980: 125)

Radical drag and zaps were a long way distant from literary realism. In that distance lies a political argument that sat at the heart of the gay movement. Some gay men viewed the matter of oppression as largely 'personal', and aimed to solve it by achieving equal rights for the individual. Others, such as GLF, viewed gay liberation within a wider context of revolutionary struggle, aiming not so much for equality within the system as a dismantling of the 'system' itself. The former were regarded by the latter as 'straight gays'. Wearing radical drag in the street was both more risky and more polemical than putting on plays for a self-selecting audience. Six years after the uniformly realist gay plays at the Almost Free, in 1980 a gay season at the Oval House theatre showed how far gay political arguments were also being conducted by means of diverse artistic forms. There was Stephen Holt's *Men*, in a realist mode; BLOOLIPS' cross-dressed clowning; the Sexual Outlaw Workshop, which polemically contrasted images of harassment and liberation. The political 'community' group Brixton Faeries did a show about sex in men's lavatories which juxtaposed high camp and realism. It looked at how gay men 'are lured, mesmerized and even terrified by cottages [public lavatories]', and ended in a toilet 'transformed by chandeliers and decorations' (Cooper 1980: 39). But despite their brief coming-together at Oval House these different forms were to become progressively institutionalised in different places. One of the most successful plays about gay issues was the American play *Bent*, by Martin Sherman, a realist text about persecution of homosexuals under the Nazis. The story is engagingly grim, and its mode encourages distress, if not anger, about the brutal homophobia. Its focus is relentlessly on individuals rather than systems, however, and making audiences angry about Nazis tends not to be a contentious activity, yet. Coinciding with the *Bent* triumph was something that looked altogether more trivial: a male performer walks onto a stage in a dress closely copied from an oil painting of Elizabeth I. Its layers of encrusted ornamentation are made out of egg boxes. He looks at us.

This is Diva Dan. The company is BLOOLIPS. And the dress and the look are the sorts of thing the company was famous for. With costumes that they described as coming out of skips – lampshades as hats, a dress decorated with row upon row of tea strainers – and always in clown white-face, the gay male company developed a hallmark style that played with the edges of excess.

With dreadful puns, propensity for musical numbers and those monuments of dresses, BLOOLIPS were billed as a drag clown group. This, put alongside the tragic seriousness of *Bent*, looks like gay men up to their old 'camp' tricks. But BLOOLIPS had their origins in the GLF.

In 1969–70 Bette Bourne, founder of BLOOLIPS, was living in a drag commune and working with the GLF steering committee. Already shaped by GLF's theatrically political activism, in 1976 Bourne saw the American gay group Hot Peaches at Oval House in London, briefly joined the company and then in June 1977 mounted the first BLOOLIPS show, *The Ugly Duckling*, done at a church hall in west London. The style of the show, including the white faces, was derived from Hot Peaches. But it remained throughout all those which followed, such as *Cheek, Teenage Trash, Get Hur, Lust in Space* and *Gland Motel*. The titles give a flavour of the puns unendingly supplied by the BLOOLIPS writers Jon Jon Taylor and Ray Dobbins. They don't, however, suggest the quite careful articulation of issues that directly connected with gay liberation – the first show was about coming out, *Just Myself* was about refusing gender ascription, *Cheek* was about the Christian 'family values' campaigner Mary Whitehouse. Soon after Margaret Thatcher came to power BLOOLIPS were telling a narrative about how their dragged-up bodies were becoming possessed by an entity that compelled them to wear suits.

And their audience, of course, wanted them to escape the suits and to come out in even more monumental skirts. When Diva Dan walked on to sing 'Scream Yer Tits Off' the effect was designed to wind up the audience, make them noisy, seduce them into behaving in – how should we say? – very unsuitable ways. This wasn't, though, an easy communal romp. Bourne trained the performers and insisted on rigorous company discipline. These were neither politically committed amateurs nor closeted theatre professionals. It was an exercise in playing with the theatrical pleasure – punctiliously exploited by managements, revered by commercial musicals and frozen with seal-in freshness by drag artists – of a glamour that is beyond the everyday. But they were not quite governed by the appropriate glamour rules – the costumes were too large, were insufficiently tasteful, revealed too clearly their origins. They were bound up into narratives that were full of constant innuendo and pun. These positioned the performers as always one step ahead of the audience. Using a meticulous rhetoric of looks, they would sometimes offer a double meaning to be shared, sometimes not acknowledge it, sometimes leave it undecideable. That rhetoric of looks was always looking back, watching us watching them. The eyes that looked out from the white-faced costumed entity were aware very precisely of the size of that entity and its effect. Watching us watching them, waiting for the pun to work: it was a sort of vigilant attention to the audience's own alertness. For when it responded the audience displayed its own readiness to understand double meaning and enjoy disruption of rules. Letting go of your inhibitions, and being watched by gay clowns as you do it … this was a continuation of the zap by other means.

BLOOLIPS' effect on their audience, like that of Cunning Stunts, was like an infection of liberation. Or, as some might say, a gay plague. Coming only a few years after BLOOLIPS' theatrical heyday, elsewhere in London, at the rather more literary Royal Court, a rather more realist young gay man is fucked viciously by a man he wants to think of as his father. The play was Mark Ravenhill's *Shopping and Fucking* (1996). Propelled by its apparently scabrous images, like many accounts of alienation, it became a huge success. Gay issues had shown definitively that they could be dislocated from gay activism and turned into money spinners, producing a neat combination of what we might call shocking and funding.

'Black' theatres

In the spring of 1981 the journal *Plaform* devoted an issue to 'black' theatre in Britain. Here Mike Phillips argued that there was not yet anything in Britain that could be called a black theatre. His provocation was then opened to debate, with one dramatist, Mustapha Matura, refusing to accept the label 'black'. This deviated from conventional usage by which, as Jatinder Verma points out elsewhere, although theatre groups may have a range of racial identities, they are all 'black' insofar as they are structurally positioned in the same place: outside white control, opposing a white racist mainstream, dealing with contemporary or historical 'black' issues, demanding an equal share of funding (Verma 1996: 56). Matura's refusal activates a debate around cultural specificity versus structural politics.

This debate also surfaces in the matter on which the *Platform* contributors were agreed, namely the problem of reaching, or developing, an audience that connected with the subject matter of black theatre. It was picked up the following year, when Phillips chaired a Greater London Council conference on racism in culture. There Verma, of Tara Arts, identified two sorts of Asian theatre, an Asian-language one, closely connected to specific communities and their cultural and religious events, and an English-language one which was more metropolitan and cut across cultures. The issue of specific community versus national audience was similarly opened up when Farrukh Dhondy, of Black Theatre Co-op, proposed that a way to ensure institutional permanence for 'black' theatre was to concentrate funding into two companies, one Asian, one Afro-Caribbean. The proposal was opposed on the grounds that a 'national' black theatre would destroy the specific culture of communities.

Both discussions, in *Platform* and the GLC conference, came hot on the heels of the Brixton riots of April 1981. For the *Platform* editors this was a watershed moment. But a later black commentator viewed it as part of a process: 'black arts practice emerged as part of a wider response to debates and campaigns against ongoing racist immigration laws, police and state brutality and marginalisation in the housing, education and labour market. These struggles culminated in a number of revolts, from uprisings at the Notting Hill Carnival in 1976 and in the inner cities in 1981 and 1985, to a strike at Grunwick in 19[8]7' (McMillan 1995: 192). This process of resistance led to what McMillan sees as a 'black arts cultural renaissance' through the 1980s.

At the start of that period Mike Phillips had suggested there was not yet a coherent entity that could be called 'Black Theatre'. Using as his model the United States, he outlined the criteria necessary to establish black theatre as such: the '*emotional relevance*' of the material to its audience; the accurate description and analysis of what a black person *is* – 'what it means to be a black person'; allowing for flexibility in the term 'black', a black theatre is 'rooted in and springs from the *fundamental concerns of a black culture*'; the black audience needs to be 'an entire cultural envelope', where, even for those who do not go to the theatre, in their consciousness 'theatre's expression of their concerns will be re-articulated' (pp. 3–4). While these criteria did not exist, according to Phillips, in Britain in 1981, black playwrights seemed to be proceeding towards establishing them. This, he says, distinguished them, with the exception of Matura, from their Caribbean precursors.

Those precursors fall into three main phases: individual voices in the 1940s, embryonic networks and groups in the 1960s, then the ideological break-point of Black Power in the late 1960s/early 1970s. Among those voices in the 1940s Robert Adams challenged Equity to take a stance against the importation of 'American Negro material' because it had the effect of relegating British black actors to a lesser role, producing an 'inferiority complex' (Adams 1947: 11). Alongside this view of a discriminatory industry, Frank Silvera suggested that the 'Negro artist' should be more thoroughly integrated – a first step might be a black *Hamlet*, leading to black actors playing major roles in such plays as *King Lear* and *Ghosts* (Silvera 1948: 19). In later years each of these models was both tried and criticised: Yvonne Brewster's Talawa specialised in doing the classics with black casts, producing for some new insights into Cleopatra's real racial origins (1991); while, on the other hand, Mike Phillips criticised an all-black *Measure for Measure* 'as a sort of apprentice in the business of learning about [white] theatre' (Phillips [1981]: 6) and ignoring Black concerns. This sort of 'blaxploitation' has a long tradition: at the Edinburgh Festival Fringe of 2008 there was a black rap *Much Ado about Nothing*. Even more problematically, while the manager of the Theatre Royal, Stratford East, Philip Hedley, celebrated the importance of casting despite race, the counter-argument proposed that 'colour-blind casting' effaces racial specificity, and indeed apes the habits of white theatre where an Afro-Caribbean may be cast to play an Indian.

In this white theatre, in the late 1950s/early 1960s, black playwrights watched their work being whitened. Errol John thought his *Moon on a Rainbow Shawl* was sentimentalised by a white director in 1958. Barry Reckord's *Skyvers* (1963), about kids in their final weeks in a comprehensive school, was staged by the English Stage Company with an all-white cast. This began to change with the founding of the first 'black' arts centre, Keskidee, and the formation of 'black' companies such as Black Theatre Co-op, Talawa, Tara Arts, Temba. But by 1980 Keskidee had closed and in 1981 the Brixton riots happened, leading the companies to wonder if their theatre was appropriate to their communities. The issue was not simply about employment and money, but also aesthetics. The need, as Kwesi Owusu put it, was to resist the 'cultural domination of Western theatrical traditions' and engage with traditional 'black' forms (Owusu 1986: 93). The consequence of not doing so was the alienation of black audiences from the theatre.

The work of ensuring a bond with the community led to two main aesthetic initiatives. One was the explicit use of traditional, and typical, black forms; the other was the persistence of a form of realism, even as white theatre was turning against it. This realism worked because it enabled recognition while at the same time, in its most potent mode, expressing problems around identity. In Mustapha Matura's *Welcome Home Jacko* (1979), centred on a group of boys in a youth club, the Caribbean, and indeed African, traditions are made tense. A new club worker, Gail, a young black woman, talks to Zippy, who is wearing an Ethiopian robe. He rejects her offer to go and see African exhibits: 'dat not Africa, dat a white man ting, dem a hypocrite, dem not genuine Africa, is Africa we want ter see'. And in part he is right – but in part he is gripped by religious posturing. When Gail asks him if he was born in Jamaica, because he talks Jamaican, he owns to being born in London: 'me could talk London if me wanted to but me is a Rastafarian so me talk Ja' (Matura 1992: 261–2). The unsettling of the distinction between Caribbean and black British is followed later by a dissolution of 'black' as a natural or coherent category. Referring to Gail, whom he has attacked and wounded, Marcus says 'She a black just like me': she is, though, a woman and she has different values. Shortly after, dismissing Jacko's attack on Rastafarianism and the depoliticisation of Black people, Marcus says 'He en no genuine black man' (Matura 1992: 289, 292). This brings the play to a point where it seems that it can't resolve itself: after a scuffle between Marcus and Jacko, the white liberal woman is left alone on stage while the black characters depart, taking their contradictions with them.

This ending does, however, remind us that, whatever the contradictions, the main framing contrast is between black and white. Tunde Ikoli neatly plays with this in an exchange between Trevor and his white mother in *Scrape off the Black* (1980). She has left his black father and remarks cynically on the behaviour of 'Africans' as sexist, brutal and lazy fathers, despite their initial charm. To which Trevor responds: 'If my dad was so cruel why didn't you leave him and find yourself a nice Englishman ….' 'Me' says his mother 'go with an Englishman …? Don't be silly' (Ikoli 1998: 58–9). The play then introduces a new division as profound as that between black and white: Trevor's brother Andy, just out of prison, recalls the last things he heard his parents say to each other: 'Get back to Africa you black bastard' and 'May you burn in hell, you pink-face cow' (Ikoli 1998: 82). Through much of the play the dominant contrast is between the sexes, with the diligent Trevor juxtaposed with his selfish, self-pitying mother, who is addicted to bingo while her friend Mary is addicted to alcohol. When the two brothers recall an upbringing spent in foster homes, Trevor speaks of a deep childhood desire to be white. It is as if the mother's neglect, the woman's selfishness, alienates the child from his own racial identity. As a grown man Trevor is proud to be black and it's this pride that allows him finally to confront his mother: 'you're half white,' she says; 'I'm black,' he replies (Ikoli 1998: 102). And he goes on to say that he has a black wife and son and doesn't want them to hear 'that racist bullshit' from his mother. He leaves, with his mother in a fit of temper throwing her bag at the door and her bingo winnings spilling over the stage. Again a white woman is left alone, but now marked as greedy and alienated as against the proud black identity. In 1980, after feminism, that contrast was very insecure, if not deeply problematic.

These plays were in their separate ways addressing the question of what it 'means' to be a black person, and their realist dramaturgy makes for 'emotional relevance'. Looking back at this period, McMillan, with others, argues that realism was a necessary phase: 'Quasi-naturalist/realist aesthetics in black theatre/performance was an overt protest against their marginalisation, and an emphatic insistence on the real to "correct" the reproduction of colonial fantasies in mis(sed) representations of the black subject and their communities.' The later 1980s then saw a reaction against this phase, with realism being seen as incapable of providing 'the tools necessary to investigate the black experience' (McMillan 1995: 195, 196). The critical narrative that begins to appear tends to bracket off drama like that we have just looked at. For those plays don't deal in positive corrections to colonial fantasies, nor do they deal in a simply defined coherent blackness. They seem to be doing something, albeit as realism, which is not recognised.

That response to stage realism seems to be connected to the status of theatre in relation to the rest of black culture. In feminism theatre seemed to be an unproblematic tool for developing political education; in gay politics the mode of theatre became politically problematised. While realist black theatre has persisted, it has done so alongside a perhaps more dynamic presence. In the mid-1990s what dominated the subculture were the idiom and production modes of black music. New work consciously integrated black theatre with wider black culture – as opposed to a wider theatre culture. McMillan describes Double Edge's *Ragamuffin* about 'an archetypal young Black urban warrior on trial in a court of African justice, with the defence and prosecution making lyrical social and political commentary over records, in the style of competing MCs … The theatre spaces were transformed into the social space of a dancehall … The audience were transformed into a congregation' (McMillan 1995: 198). In turn this also worked as a throwback to a much earlier pre-realist – and indeed Caribbean tradition – ritualised performance.

The repudiation of the realist tradition was intensified in the late 1980s by the effects of cuts to arts funding. As in other contexts the gap was filled by the generally cheaper forms of live art, announced – typically – as a breakpoint, 'a critique of the timidity and the unadventurousness of a large amount of the output of black performance and theatre in Britain in recent years' (Ugwu 1995: 82). This cultural shift also facilitated the emergence – or, more accurately, return – of oral practices which came from a deep tradition, that of orature. Within the tradition, and unlike the separation produced in Western white society, Owusu argues (Owusu 1986: 138), poetry, song and dance can be explicitly politically expressive. Furthermore, orature brings together art forms, and has a structured relationship with audiences through call-and-response devices.

The challenge for black performers, in parallel to the growth of a somewhat apolitical white performance art, was to produce a politically invested union of the visual and performed, with an emphasis, unfashionably, on the word. SuAndi, Cultural Director of the Black Arts Alliance, notes how, before 'Live Art' emerged as a funding category, her own medium of performance poetry was an unrecognisable entity. Yet this work needed to inhabit mixedness of category in order, precisely, to throw into dialogue the various elements which have framed discussions of black performance. In *The Story of M*, SuAndi draws from the traditional orature form of the poem while incorporating specific visual documents, photographs of her dying mother. While she speaks the poem as M, towards the end M becomes both her mother and herself. This mother, it turns out, is a white woman. Even while the poem works as testimonial, powerfully expressing the feelings of a woman dying of cancer, it also conceptually unsettles any fixed notion of what blackness might be. It is both very immediately present, a specific testimony, and, yet, a complex woven history.

In its restless reinvention of itself, driven very often by the question of what 'black' might 'mean', black theatre has embraced and recycled forms that are definingly associated with black arts practice and, hence, not available to white theatre. In its staging of them, therefore, black theatre may be said to have developed forms that extend the language and practice of all theatre.

Theatre of disability

The best known disability theatre company, Graeae, grew out of work done in the early to mid-1970s in Hereward College, Coventry. These origins are characteristic of the time, when there was much experiment with and within education. The development of disability performance was led by Richard Tomlinson, a lecturer without disability, often in partnership with Nabil Shaban, a wheelchair-using actor. Their work took as one of its reference points the black theatre which was emerging out of South Africa, but disability, as Tomlinson says, comes with its own particular issues and modes of work.

For each movement, theatre as a medium brings specific opportunities. Thus feminist theatre made representations of women that challenged dominant assumptions. For the disabled, Tomlinson argues (1982), power comes from the work of performing – because all performance bestows a sort of power. This power in turn gives status, because it changes expectations as to the capability of disabled people. A performer takes on responsibility – to the company and to the audience – and also the risk which comes from appearing in a public show. Participation in the show precedes, in importance, the making of representations. As Tomlinson says, if access to drama training and to parts was totally open, there would be little need for disability theatre.

Here, though, we note a difference from other 'movement' theatre. This comes from the status of the disabled. Contrasting them with women's groups or gay groups 'whose very existence is a political statement', Tomlinson suggests that 'disability is not so easily and readily identifiable. It has no ethnic, class or cultural roots. It is part of all sections of society and yet it is seen as apart … Political consciousness about disability amongst disabled people is notoriously low; disability gives no sense of pride or of belonging, and many prefer not to be labelled in that way' (Tomlinson 1982: 39). When Graeae was founded in February 1980 it articulated three general principles, which are a response to this sense of the relationship between politics and disability: 'to encourage the active participation of disabled people in exploring their aspirations', 'to develop, for the time being, our own material', to tour the work (Tomlinson 1982: 52). While there was a considerable amount of engagement with the 'issue' of disability in theatre-in-education (see pp. 214–15) companies at this period, next to none were working with the disabled. Graeae deliberately chose to make a theatre of the disabled.

Further, it accepted that there is no common 'disabled' condition – deafness is very different from cerebral palsy. These elements all give sharp importance to questions of aesthetics. Just as with some elements of gay culture, amongst the disabled there was caution about being 'political' – only one member of the original Graeae thought the group should do political work. This status of disabled politics led, in Tomlinson's view, to a preference for the 'proper' scripted theatre repertoire. This wasn't entirely a matter of conservatism, of embarrassment about the 'label' of disability, however. It could also be seen as an effort to make disability irrelevant, to make it less important than the art.

Where companies confined themselves to one group – such as the Venturers Club, for blind people, or Theatre of the Deaf – the particular shared condition can be transmuted into a 'house-style', for example the aesthetic presence of signing and miming in deaf shows. But where you play across, and with, different disabilities, the problem increases. A wheelchair user learns to work with a blind person. For Graeae, as for any disability company, to work with various different bodily conditions in its five original performers, and particularly to tour with them, meant real material difficulties. But it also led to a whole different way of being on stage. The encounter between differences of, for example, speech and mobility raised awareness of different sorts of physical possibility and in doing so generated the material and aesthetic stuff of theatre. In his description of the improvisation work which created the show *M3 Junction 4*, Tomlinson describes how, when the cast were allowed to develop their own characters, most of them specifically challenged their own particular bodily ability. Jag Plah, with cerebral palsy and a thick Indian accent, became 'Roger' Singh, a dodgy barrow-boy made good who will only go out with white girls; Elane Roberts, blind, played a blind daughter of a high-court judge who gets expelled from school and opts instead to model and prostitute.

The aesthetics of disability theatre raise issues around representation that can, in all senses, be very uneasy. Graeae found that they often 'confused and contradicted' people's perceptions of disability, leading to theatre that was more difficult than satisfying. At a simpler level Tomlinson asked himself the question of the extent to which he was being exploitative, as a director without disability. This reflection was then put to use in exercises where disabled performers teach something to able-bodied carers, or where each group is led to articulate the tensions between being patronised and used. Slightly more complex is the telling of disability jokes by those who are disabled. Still more ethically vexed is the use of material generated from the real-life stories of the company, where a disabled actor speaking of a disabled person may – or may not – be telling her own story, may – or may not – be 'really' weeping.

For, to rework Tomlinson's phrase about women's and gay groups, the very existence of the disabled person is a theatrical statement. In the western tradition audiences are used to the idea that almost all apparent bodily aspects of a performer may be fictional – even biological sex can begin to be rendered uncertain by make-up and learnt muscular regimes. The disabled performers cannot divest their disability. They are thus more thoroughly anchored in the physical real, which then has effects on the way that they are perceived. At one end, audiences can note – usually obsessively – that a fictional text is being delivered 'despite' the disability. At the other end, the disability can make the performance theatrically present – insistent, sensuous, wild – in a way nothing else can. I recall Diva Dan, a deaf performer with BLOOLIPS, in a big dress and hat standing centre stage, singing. The fact that many of the notes were musically distorted because of his difficulties in enunciation simply made the thing more huge, more storming. The audience screamed with pleasure.

The aesthetic complexity that comes from working with different abilities can in turn enrich the effects of pre-scripted drama. In Tomlinson's production of Pinter's *The Dumb Waiter*, the killer Gus was played by a wheelchair-user. At the end he stumbles back into the room, stripped of 'jacket, waistcoat, tie, holster and revolver'. This time he was also without his wheelchair, crawling in. This creates layers of meaning not immediately available in the Pinter script – sudden vulnerability, an 'authenticity' to that vulnerability – of actor as well as character, risk and heroism.

Although at the time he published his book, 1982, Tomlinson thought working with scripts was some way off, the theatrical dialogue between scripted drama and its physical manifestation is now thoroughly present in the most modern work of Graeae. Thus, in their 2007 production of Kane's *Blasted*, after a workshop with two blind directors the company experimented with delivering the stage directions alongside the text spoken by characters. From here they interested themselves in how the production might become accessible for both deaf and hearing audiences simultaneously. Taking their cue from Kane's play, where they found an interest in voyeurism, they introduced a video screen where actors signed text – but they marked this screen as different from, and not assimilable to, the live performance. In the latter the performers worked with simple actions and no props, whereas the former had costumes and props. The screens, never as it were fully 'present' in the flesh, offered a visually thickened experience. Similarly where an actor spoke text that was simultaneously displayed, part of the interest was in how these two elements cannot be exchanged for one another. The graphic patterns, the concreteness, of displayed text give it a presence not available to the spoken word. The staging of these points of difference, and the uncertainties around what is 'present', play back into a dramatic text that is deeply concerned about, and derived from, the mediation of real lives.

This mode of work is rather more than a house-style. For, in general, the theatrical dialogue around 'authenticity' and risk is not available to theatres which are constrainedly able-bodied. The aesthetic distinctiveness carries with it a political charge. For it is not seeking to make disability irrelevant to the art. It is instead suggesting that it is the very presence of every particular variant of ability, its material fact, which is the pre-condition for a theatrical aesthetic that is both powerful and autonomous.

'Community' and 'applied' theatres

Campaigning feminist or gay theatre faded from view as political movements during the 1990s. Some of their job seemed to have been completed, in that there were now laws around discrimination and a conscious stress on equality of opportunity. And their causes had apparently been transmuted into lifestyle choices, where girl power, regular clubbing and shopping as leisure allowed punters to feel 'good' about themselves, assisted by a range of highly effective party drugs. By whatever means such things as feminist and gay theatre ceased to be in the cultural spotlight. For those who were committed to forms of theatre that took their political and social responsibilities seriously, there was a new movement. This was characterised by an adjective that no longer carried any taint of affiliation: 'applied'.

Under the general heading of 'applied theatre' comes a range of names for related practices. These include Theatre for Development, Theatre for Social Change, Community Theatre, Community-based Performance, Engaged Art, Participatory Arts. Sometimes the practice is named after its domain of operation: for example theatre in education, theatre in prisons. All these names share some common features: they point to a theatre *for* something and a theatre that has a sense of public engagement (defined as that which is community, participatory, social). Judith Ackroyd suggests that these sorts of 'applied' theatre practice are all marked by 'intentionality' in that they are trying to address something which is outside of their own domain of theatre (in Nicholson 2005: 3).

Scholars of applied theatre trace its roots back into earlier decades, to the Workers' Theatre Movement and other theatres of the left, to theatre in education and to community theatre. We have looked at the first of these above, but we should now, before going further, look at the other two.

Theatre in education

This started with Caryl Jenner at the Unicorn Theatre Club in 1948. Although the Young Vic had already been set up, that was for young performers playing established plays. It did not have Jenner's polemical educational mission to give children opportunities for 'imaginative gymnastics to counteract the passivity of television'. (in Hodgson 1971: 58) In the same great year – the year of the 'Theatre Parliament' (see p. 10) – two initiatives were launched in Birmingham, by John English and by Peter Slade. Their aim of rebuilding cultural heritage and developing interest in theatre gave the education projects a crucial function in the immediate post-war period. A second aim, of Slade's, was theatre as therapy.

These aims tend to position the children as recipients – which became the dominant attitude. But in 1953 Brian Way's Theatre Centre at St John's Wood offered new opportunities for researching the forms of drama suitable for children, and the emphasis shifted to teachers. They were to be given assistance in dealing with drama in educational settings. At this point we encounter another entity, 'drama in education', which concerned itself with the teaching of drama and the uses of drama in the classroom. The child here is more often learner than maker.

Theatre in education, by contrast, gave the child a more productive role. The potential is stated clearly in the programme adopted in the first post-war theatre to be built, the Belgrade in Coventry. In keeping with the reconstruction of the bombed town the theatre emphasised youth and education, and revisited a strategy formulated by John English ten years before, the involvement of children in the organisation and decisions. Theatre activity was to range wider than classrooms. Behind this approach was Gordon Vallins, who later headed up a specific theatre-in-education department which, in turn, led in 1966 to the Belgrade's unique theatre-in-education project in alliance with civic authorities. With Arts Council encouragement this set the model for developments in Bolton, Greenwich, Leeds, Liverpool, Sheffield, Watford and York.

The Belgrade theatre-in-education aims

1. to involve young people in the organisation through participation on committees
2. theatre sessions in holidays with young people's participation
3. regular drama sessions available to young people
4. establishment of a permanent children's theatre company.

Through the establishment of theatre in education three strands intertwine – the development of an interest in theatre (sometimes seen as a counterbalance to other media), experiments in uses of drama in teaching – 'drama in education', and the role of drama in the development of young people. This last can point two ways: to theatre as therapeutic or to theatre as model for involvement in organisation and decision-making. There is, clearly, a political narrative that can be told in relation to the models and emphases in any particular period or place.

Community theatre

In the 1970s there was a distinctively political edge to the term 'community theatre'. Under this name, a company run on collective lines was founded in 1972 and did one show, Steve Gooch and Paul Thompson's *The Motor Show* (1974) about the Ford car works at Dagenham. They were aided by trade union activists who, among other things, smuggled Gooch into the factory. In a non-urban setting Medium Fair worked in a participatory way with Devon villagers through the later 1970s. This model is perhaps the familiar one. Early on, however, 'community' theatre was also done by permanent companies in fixed buildings. Of these the two leading organisations were the Combination at the Albany Empire, Deptford (which had been founded in Brighton in 1967) and the Half Moon in London's East End. They reached out to a new community, rejecting, Gooch says, the classic fringe or 'alternative' audience (Gooch 1984: 43) and thus promoting new attitudes to the work and its audience. These included a valuing of the working process over the finished product, and development of new forms that took the playing out amongst the audience, classically in the meeting scene (see Audience). When The Association of Community Theatres (TACT) was founded in 1973 it recalled the manifestos and approaches of the Workers' Theatre Movement.

Aims of first draft TACT constitution

1. to deal with everyday suffering and show its causes
2. to perform in places where people socialise and as part of larger events
3. to sharpen understandings through post-show discussions
4. to develop a form which is direct and involving   (from Itzin 1980: 176)

But this political understanding of community work was short-lived. Only five years after the founding of TACT in London, in Dorset Ann Jellicoe embarked on her 'community' plays. Her emphasis was on 'participation', with a blend of mainstream and other techniques. One thing was not emphasised: 'Politics are divisive. We strongly feel that the humanising effect of our work is far more productive than stirring up political confrontation' (in Kershaw 1992: 190). The question hangs: productive of what?

Applied theatre

The strands that feed into later applied theatre practice link together in that they all share a view that the preparation for political action and social change involves the overturning of long-held beliefs and assumptions, the development of new consciousness. For example, much of the early work of the Women's Theatre Group was directed at teenage girls. Education was seen as a key site for the transmission of, and challenge to, those values which kept society stable. Furthermore the structure of education – the extent to which it was, or was not, 'top-down' – similarly inculcated attitudes and expectations as to one's place in the social order. Through the 1970s there had been debates about, and experiments in, various methods of 'progressive' education. One of the great media images of 1968 and the years immediately following was of university students forcibly occupying the offices of those who ran the institutions. The 'school' was seen as microcosm of society at large. So within this context the relationship between theatre and education appeared to offer considerable potency.

This relationship established the beliefs and practices which would characterise the various applied theatres. When performances were done in schools, and especially in streets and at rallies, they were apparently bringing theatre into a real world. Helen Nicholson suggests that 'applied drama is primarily concerned with developing new possibilities for everyday living rather than segregating theatre-going from other aspects of life' (Nicholson 2005: 4). But it may not follow that a segregated activity is necessarily a bad thing. Clothes shopping and flower gardening are variously attractive precisely because they are segregated from other aspects of life. I make this quibble in order to highlight the binary mechanism which seems so important to the applied, namely that, because the applied is sceptical about 'segregated' theatre, it consequently puts firmer value on the 'real', and is thus – to use a favourite school exam word – more 'relevant', and therefore, by further extension, more efficacious.

The world of segregated theatregoing is often bedevilled by two related issues: one is that the performance profession is difficult to enter and succeed in; the other is that the audiences for the performances can appear passive and uninvolved. By contrast in any sort of self-defined community theatre project, the drive is towards openness of access and inclusion. As Petra Kuppers explains, community performance practitioners 'have to facilitate an exchange, bring people together, enable ways for the group to find its ways of working, and allow a group to value all its members' (Kuppers 2007: 10). In applied theatre practices one of the key words is 'participation'. This breaks down the perceived barriers around segregated performance and creates an involved audience – indeed, it can work towards a situation where there is next to no audience as such, simply levels of project activity. Helen Nicholson describes 'a political concern to demystify the arts by encouraging people from many different backgrounds and contexts to participate actively in drama and theatre, whether as reflexive participants in different forms of drama workshops, as thinking members of theatre audiences, or as informed and creative participants in different forms of performance or theatre practices' (Nicholson 2005: 10).

But Kuppers also warns about the downside of this participation: 'It is easy to be caught up in the warmth of communal celebration, and to uncritically stop exploration and development too early.' Indeed participation has its own rhetoric, its own performed qualities: 'the "warmly persuasive" nature of community is similar to the great affective power of performance' (Kuppers 2007: 10). So lingering in here there is a set of questions: who does the including? Who sets the line for exclusion and on what basis? What are the terms of participating? What does participation agree to? How is participation understood and critiqued? How does it promote its own self-reflection? As the various experiments at collective organisation discovered, structure and values are intertwined and crucial. Participation alone doesn't guarantee that you're on the side of the angels. To those marching down Unter den Linden with flaming torches held aloft, the nature of the community of the Nazi party must have felt warmly persuasive.

While participatory persuasion is an important part of the educational work, practitioners are aware of its tensions and slipperiness. Applied theatre practices may do transformative work by creating situations in which individuals feel newly connected to others and by developing scenarios and stories in which individuals make new sense of their lives and societies. Yet these two elements may come into conflict when the business of making sense articulates truths which are incompatible with cosy participation. The participants experience, usually in supportive conditions, a point where their own cultural and personal assumptions break down. While the drive in much popular drama and film is towards final satisfying resolution, applied practices may take participants towards what Taylor calls 'ambiguous or incomplete moments' (in Nicholson 2005: 24). In many cases the individual comes to encounter the distinction between self and other, where the presence and sometimes pressure of others has to be negotiated without losing sense of self. Nicholson associates this with the project of developing citizenship. It may also, sometimes, one presumes, be therapy.

In summarising these processes, the notion of a separate audience has evaporated. Nicholson says that the subject of her book on applied drama is the 'Active and creative participation in performance practices that dislodge fixed and uneven boundaries between "self" and "other"' (Nicholson 2005: 24). The adjectives 'active' and 'creative' spell out the distance from a theatre form in which audiences are supposedly passive. And that distance is marked in another way. In her handbook for community theatre workers, Kuppers points out how 'conventional stage performance in a theatre' can be inhibiting for both performers and audiences: 'The theatre as an institution has a history of exclusion' (Kuppers 2007: 103). In order to be more inclusive the community project can select its own appropriate form of performance, and it can select its own audience. It may choose to show work simply to selected people who are known to the performing group. Or it may choose not to perform. This is a logically possible choice because the most productive work of the project, the transformation of individuals, happens as a result of participation. It is the process of doing the work, rather than the presenting of the outcome, which matters.

Through developing its range of practices applied theatre has moved on a step from the political theatre movements which largely preceded it. It has redefined the role both of the person who does it and the person to whom it is done. In 'institutional' theatre, as both the political and the applied theatres may define it, the actor and scenographer are trained to the job, and paid for a range of skills which may be applied to any project. By contrast, irrespective of their training, the political activists' defining characteristic is the political commitment which they offer to their audience. In the applied theatre the 'activist' is just as likely to be someone who enables the performance of others. And while it is a skilled role, facilitation doesn't necessarily require the skills of the actor, which may take second place because facilitation works with the 'real'.

In the 'institutional' theatre, again, the audience may be defined as – albeit incompletely – a consumer. Their part in the contract of the performance is largely discharged, supposedly, when they pay their ticket money. After that they may watch indifferent or passive. The political theatre assumes that the audience has at minimum an interest in understanding a real-world situation or, more likely, that it has responsibility to become active itself. Early gay theatre asked its audience to come out; feminist theatre invited women to take control of their own lives. The coming-out and taking control will be done after the show is over, in the real world. Applied theatre tends not to address an audience which is separate from itself. The prospective 'audience' are invited to become sufficiently active that they join in as participants. Through being participants they learn about themselves and their relationships with society. This real-world learning is done in the context of the theatre project. If an outcome is seen by a separable audience, it is not so much shown to them as shared with them.

As we have known all along, the experience of being taken 'out' of yourself, of encountering otherness, was and is the stock in trade of the most established of theatres. That intense moment of shared, indeed communal, attention, with the breath held, during a tragedy; the instances when laughter has them – us – literally on the edges of the seats: these are moments when the evidence of the bodies, the muscular spasms, tells you that these watchers are somewhere outside of where they normally exist. And they have got there by a particular and peculiar process, one where you watch someone else doing something on your behalf. Clearly then it is not a defining feature of applied theatre that it creates conditions which take you out of yourself and into the presence of otherness. Most theatre does this. What is distinctive about applied theatre is that it doesn't encourage the process to happen through a division of labour, where one group use their skills to show something to another group. Applied theatre's exploration of self and otherness tends to require 'active and creative' participation in the process of doing. For it is not the resulting piece of art, it avows, but the process – the work – that transforms.

In acknowledging its duties to the wider commonweal – or as it might say, 'real life' – applied theatre may be said to have learnt the basic lessons of the Whig tradition. It worries about the passive consumption of theatre art as something not simply improper but also, characteristically, not useful. It seems to turn its back on a specialised category of performer, the one trained to show persuasively. And it sternly reminds that the persuasive rhetoric of communal involvement comes at the price of realisations about personal responsibility. In developing these practices it has managed to step well away from the old theatre archetype of licentiousness and elitism – indeed it tells us that it knows that theatre's history is of 'exclusion'. So too it turns its back on the modern equivalents of licentiousness and elitism – commodity, celebrity and consumption. Offering the new millenium a re-evaluation of theatre's importance as useful process rather than imaginary artwork, the applied theatre movement sets about its ethical, if not quite protestant, duty. And thereby accommodates itself effortlessly to the mindset enshrined for centuries by the Whig tradition.

Making good theatre

For two-thirds of the modern period, as for nearly two centuries before it, the public performance of plays was subject to licence from the state censor. The role of censor was performed by the Lord Chamberlain, or rather by his office. This office consisted of a number of readers of plays, each one of whom exercised their personal judgement as to whether the work respected appropriate standards in politics, religion, sexual 'decency'. As Steve Nicholson has shown, the censorship was alert to expressions of left-wing opinion and sympathy in the inter-war period; post-war it increasingly legislated against breaches of supposed norms of behaviour, especially around sexuality. The censor's readers of plays had no specialist skill as such: their social upbringing and class status were sufficient to give them a confident feel for what could be regarded as allowable. In the censor's terms, 'good theatre' was theatre which was allowable, licensable; theatre which fitted with the perceived norms of a dominant class. Good theatre was the opposite of naughty – or as the censor might have said 'nasty' – theatre.

In 1968 the formal office of censor was abolished. By this stage, as Kershaw (2004) points out, it had ceased to have much useful effect and therefore could safely go. There had been challenges since 1909, and at the end defiance came from both page and stage. Kenneth Tynan's 1965 piece 'The Royal Smut Hound' described the censor's 'paternal need to protect his flock' from exposure to anything in the genital area (Shellard 2000: 137). And, not exposing but more shockingly covering, Osborne's *A Patriot for Me*, with its scene of a drag ball, was put on as a 'club' performance by the English Stage Company, exploiting a legal loophole. They tried it again, unsuccessfully, with Bond's *Saved* and its baby stoning. When in 1966 the court conditionally discharged the accused and imposed a nominal fine, it was clear the end was near.

The end of the formal office of censor, that is, not the end of censorship … The most notorious example of attempted post-censor censorship came from a campaigner for all things Christian, Mary Whitehouse, who used the Sexual

Offences Act to bring a charge against the director of the National Theatre's production of Howard Brenton's *The Romans in Britain* (1980), which contained a depiction of anal rape. Mary Whitehouse had not seen the play and her case collapsed after three expensive days. But its work was perhaps then done – it had staged the public Christian voice. For more effective censorship other methods were available. These were a combination of media panic and local refusal of licence. Thus for example Gay Sweatshop's tour of Noël Greig's peace play *Poppies* ran into difficulties: a performance in a school in Avon led to condemnation from Tory councillors (because it was about homosexuality and opposition to war); the leader of the Tory group on Bristol Council claimed the company was 'sinister and subversive'; Devon's Chief Education Officer then got wind of the planned tour dates and banned the play; later a spokeswoman for Women and Families for Defence, one Angela Browning (let her be known to history), wrote to *The Sunday Times* attacking peace studies in schools and cited the performance of *Poppies* as an example of indoctrination (all details from Osment 1989: liii). In effect, then, possibly to a wider degree than before, the process of censorship was predicated upon the expression of individual opinion as to what was proper and what not. Without any clear criteria in place, theatre was exposed to the uninspected ideological judgements of those who had power to close it down or shut it off. Often that power – as in the case of newspapers and 'public opinion' – had no basis in law.

Concern for the health of others by those who know what's good for you has for a long time been an effective, caustically well-meaning, basis for censorship. But there is an even more efficient tool, namely self-censorship. There was a rash of this following the passing into law of Section 28 of the Local Government Act in 1988, which prohibited the 'promotion' of homosexuality in particular public domains. Even bodies to whom the Act was irrelevant, such as publishers, went into panic: Manchester University Press pulled the plug on a planned publication of a book about gay politics and culture. The vagueness with regard to the exact application of the Section's wording allowed plenty of room for individuals and groups to interpret as they saw fit. Where the prospect was possible prosecution, they erred on the side of safety.

Self-censorship has often been the most workable form of theatre censorship. Managements, attuned to the possible dangers, either refuse to produce work or ask for alterations. The wider the range of opinion that might be offended, the more vigilant the management must be. Thus the expansion of a world of that 1990s thing – 'stakeholders' – promulgates the likelihood of offence and, more serious than prosecution, withdrawal of funding. A famous, if difficult, example preceded, and possibly went much deeper than, the Section 28 activities. This was the case of Jim Allen's *Perdition* in January 1987. The play was drawn from a court case in London in 1967. It concerned allegations that Zionist leaders collaborated with Nazis during the war in the removal of the Jewish community in Hungary to Auschwitz. The play was put into production by the Royal Court Theatre Upstairs but pulled, at the last moment, by the theatre's artistic director, Max Stafford-Clark. There had been extended rows in the press, both on letters and leaders pages, about the 'facts' depicted in the play. Allen was accused of left-wing anti-Zionism and perpetrating stereotypes of Jews. But Stafford-Clark gave as his reasons the argument that he could not support a work which was 'distorted and distressingly incomplete' (Allen 1987: 139). The terminology of course begs questions – at what point does a play become 'complete'? But the tactic is clear: the production had to be aborted because people had discovered, after all, that this was a bad play.

This takes us into interesting territory. Censorship works on the basis of discriminating between what is allowable and acceptable and what not. Usually it mobilises vague, if potent, ideological concepts such as 'public decency' or 'nature'. But a whole set of discriminations, especially ones made through self-censorship, are based on whether the work is good art or not. Trevor Griffiths used to tell a story of friendly chaps in the BBC canteen pointing out helpfully that his latest political script was a bit old-hat. It's a deft tactic, because a concern with art – and with what makes 'good' theatre – often seems thoroughly altruistic. Both the makers of theatre and its scholars and commentators regularly engage in conversations about the quality and characteristics of the art-form to which they are committed. The business of making discriminations about art is a natural, so to speak, part of the activity of doing theatre.

In the modern period the business of artistic discrimination has been assisted by a framework of binary oppositions. There are two main sets of these: new against old; periphery against centre. There was the New Drama of the Edwardian period and the New Wave of the 1950s (together with the New Left). These generated their own explicitly value-laden associates – 'serious', 'vital': *Encore* magazine was subtitled 'The Voice of Vital Theatre'. This basically chronological binary has at the back of it an assumed historical map which shows where the points of 'new' activity are. Thus most accounts of post-war British theatre have in them three key dates – 1956 (because of *Look Back in Anger*), 1968 (because of counter-cultural explosion), 1979 (because Thatcher won her first election victory, often rather significantly misdescribed as a 'landslide'). The attention to these dates as moments of importance will tell you something about the structure of values that inhabits the account in which they figure, including this one.

Connected to the adjective 'new' there is an interesting cross-over word, 'experimental'. This adjective takes us into the second binary, for 'experimental' often designates that which is outside the dominant. The mapping of the dominant and its alternatives inhabits the language of theatre for the whole period. Borsa in the Edwardian period talked of theatre 'à côté', theatre to the side, on the edge, on the fringe as it were. The word 'fringe' itself only came to be consistently used in the early1970s. When Catherine Itzin in 1975 tried to sort out the various words that designated alternatives to the dominant she attributed 'alternative' to the mid-1950s, 'underground' to the early 1960s, 'fringe' to the late 1960s, whereas Jim Haynes suggests the underground began in about 1965. Itzin's own preferred word, as for many of her politically committed contemporaries, was 'alternative'. For 'underground' and 'fringe' suggest spatially marginalised positions, whereas 'alternative' suggests different values. These terms all have their significant others – which might be 'establishment', 'mainstream', 'dominant', 'commercial'. As Itzin suggests, there is, again, a politics in the naming, which has to do with being able to identify, or claiming the position to be able to identify, what is truly emergent, demonstrably free of mercenary compromise, principled or radical.

Following on from these quite general terms, more precise pairs of opposites have been attached to the forms and practices of the theatre. Brecht began the process by listing the features of Aristotelian theatre and opposing to them his Epic theatre. Howard Barker repeated the exercise with Humanist and Catastrophic theatre. Charles Marowitz did something similar for the 'modern' actor. Binary opposites are handy not just for polemical discriminations but also, more generally, for making things clear. As such they have been deployed by a number of academic commentators on developments in modern theatre art. Here the binaries are not intended to allocate value – as with, say, Brecht and Barker – but simply to make sense of processes. Bull (1984) characterises work after 1968 as falling into two traditions, avant-garde or agit-prop; Kershaw suggests traditions of live art and community plays, and Jones suggests physical theatre and identity theatre (Kershaw 2004: 372; Jones 2004: 458–9). The lowest common denominator here is that art is placed against politics, community, identity.

Much more explicitly value-designating in journalistic and academic discourse are two other pairs. One of these is performance versus theatre. Back in 1985 Rob La Frenais noted that 'in certain quarters it is now highly unfashionable to describe live, visual, and (seemingly) ad hoc events as performance art. In the thriving subculture of warehouse, party, fashion-show and theme club, the happening, old-style, has made the two decade jump' (1985: 6). Nevertheless in 2009 either word, now with academic disciplines in tow, can be a damning indictment. The other pair, easier to focus because now dead, is political versus non-political. In the late 1980s some theatre academics reviewed the impact of Thatcherism. Quite properly alert not only to the economic damage done but also to the ideological corrosion, there was vigilance about maintaining an ideal of committed anti-Thatcherite theatre. Or, rather, what it might look like. This was a generation who had started their careers in the late 1960s and the 1970s. They were part of the audience for the emergent state-of-the-nation plays, for the work of Portable and Women's Theatre Group, for the strategic penetrations. Thus later, when they reviewed Thatcherism in a discussion sponsored by *New Theatre Quarterly*, they discriminated confidently between properly 'political' theatre that opposed Thatcherism and looked like work by Brenton, Hare, Griffiths, McGrath, Edgar and, on the other hand, work by people such as Howard Barker. While they worried that there were no new plays and that the young were anarchists they ignored visual theatre and performance art. The silence, or at most worry, about the emergent is a value judgement: the emergent is problematic because it is not political in a way which might be recognised.

In reaching an academic symposium we seem to have journeyed a long way from state organisations that practise discrimination in relation to allowable theatre, or from theatre-makers who have polemical views on what makes relevant art. But all are, in their separate ways, engaged in the activity of distinguishing valuable from not valuable, allowable from not allowable, good from bad. It's one of the main things students learn. And the discussions, let's remember, are not free of consequences. In the row about *Perdition* the Royal Court's co-producer withdrew; there were allegations of theatres being refused to those who might want to do the play; the actors became worried about losing jobs and employability. The discussions about what is valuable and allowable – the definitions of 'good' theatre – provide the terminology with which decisions can be taken, and justified, in regard to funding and employment. All those bricks-and-mortar things with which this book began have been there all the time, because they too are thoroughly interested in the sort of theatre which can be designated – for whatever reason – 'good'.

Theatre as Mask: attempting to stage that which is other to the daily; but also the rhetorics of removing the mask, communicating authentically. Being among the familiar and being other than the familiar: making indeterminate the line between familiarity and strangeness.

16. Group Theatre, *The Ascent of F6* (1937) by W. H. Auden and Christopher Isherwood: towards the end the mountaineer Ransom gets to the summit and meets his mother.

17. Impact Theatre Co-op, *A Place in Europe* (1983) with Claire MacDonald, Nikki Johnson and Richard Hawley: a fragmented verbal text delivered through microphones, an extensive musical score, movement.

18. North West Spanner, *Just a Cog,* performed at the works canteen at Moderna Ltd, Mytholmroyd, Yorkshire (January 1977), with Penny Morris, Ernie Dalton, Newman Smith, Elsie Hallsworth.

19. Unity Theatre, *Where's that Bomb?* by Roger Gullan (Herbert Hodge) and Buckley Roberts (Robert Buckland) (1936): a set of fictional stereotypes summoned from Hell by Money-Power (on the left): a poor devoted mother, a romantic boss's daughter, a manly hero, and a bomb-carrying Bolshevik.

20. Cunning Stunts, *The Odyssey or Homer Sweet Homer!*: Erin Steele, Iris Walton, Margo Random (Circe) on guitar and Jan Dungey. 'Hello my name is Circe and these are my dancing pigs, we tour the Grecian Islands doin' all these gigs ...'

Afterword

It is a given, I think, that every age of theatre thinks about performers, audiences, writers, buildings – and why it does theatre. What then can I suggest is significant about that which is modern and British?

Schematically here are some tentative suggestions:

1. The period saw the emergence and perhaps decline of the director as a defined role.
2. It has seen a growth of the idea that performers can and should embrace a range of modes of performance, sometimes within the same show.
3. It has repositioned the writer once again in relation to the art of the theatre.
4. Even while shows have become a more efficiently consumed and disseminated market commodity, it has begun to abolish the audience.
5. The period has redefined theatre as an art that is not based in mimesis.

Bibliography

Ackland, Rodney 2000. *Strange Orchestra*, in *Plays Two*, intro. Michael Hastings. London: Oberon.

Adams, Robert 1947. 'Problems of the Negro in the Theatre', *New Theatre* 4.5: 11.

Allen, Jim 1987. *Perdition*. London and Atlantic Highlands: Ithaca Press.

Anonymous 1982. 'Making the World Vertical', *Performance Magazine* 15: 11, 27.

Ansorge, Peter 1975. *Disrupting the Spectacle: Five Years of Experimental and Fringe Theatre in Britain*. London: Sir Isaac Pitman and Sons.

Archer, William and Barker, Harley Granville 1907. *A National Theatre: Scheme & Estimates*. London: Duckworth & Co.

Artaud, Antonin 1970. *The Theatre and Its Double: Essays*, trans. V. Corti. London: Calder and Boyars.

Auden, W. H. and Isherwood, Christopher 1972. *The Ascent of F6 and On the Frontier*. London: Faber and Faber.

  1986. *The Dog Beneath the Skin or Where is Francis?* London: Faber and Faber.

Ayckbourn, Alan 1979. *Absurd Person Singular*, in *Three Plays*. Harmondsworth: Penguin.

Bailey, Peter 1996. ' "Naughty but Nice": Musical Comedy and the Rhetoric of the Girl, 1892–1914', in Booth and Kaplan 1996, pp. 36–60.

Baker, Elizabeth 1913. *The Price of Thomas Scott*. London: Sidgwick & Jackson.

  1991. *Chains*, in *New Woman Plays*, ed. Linda Fitzsimmons and Viv Gardner. London: Methuen Drama.

Baker, Roger and Griffiths, Drew 1997. *Mr X*, in *Gay Sweatshop Plays*, ed. Brian Roberts. London: Goldsmiths Plays.

Bannister, Winifred 1955. *James Bridie and his Theatre*. London: Rockliff.

Barker, Clive 1980. 'Theory, Practice, and Analytical Methods', *Theatre Quarterly* 9.36: 6–8.

Barker, Clive and Gale, Maggie B. (eds.) 2000. *British Theatre Between the Wars, 1918–1939*. Cambridge: Cambridge University Press.

  1977. *The Madras House*. London: Eyre Methuen.

Barker, Howard 1989. *Arguments for a Theatre*, intro. David Ian Rabey. London: John Calder.

  1990. *The Castle*, in *Collected Plays*, vol. I. London: John Calder.

Barrie, J. M. 1933. *The Admirable Crichton*, in *The Plays in One Volume*. London: Hodder and Stoughton.

Bartlett, Neil 1990. *A Vision of Love Revealed in Sleep*, in *Gay Plays: Four*, ed. Michael Wilcox. London: Methuen Drama.

Beckett, Samuel 1965. *Waiting for Godot*. London: Faber and Faber.

Benston, Kimberley W. 1987. 'The Aesthetic of Modern Black Drama: From *Mimesis* to *Methexis*', in *The Theatre of Black Americans: A Collection of Critical Essays*, ed. Errol Hill. New York: Applause, pp. 61–78.

Berman, Ed (ed.) 1975. *Homosexual Acts: Five Short Plays from The Gay Season at The Almost Free Theatre*. Ambiance/Almost Free Playscripts 1. London: Inter-Action Inprint.

Bond, Edward 1971. *Early Morning*. London: Calder and Boyars.

1971. *Saved*. London: Methuen & Co.

1972. *Lear*. London: Eyre Methuen.

Booth, Michael R. and Kaplan, Joel H. (eds.) 1996. *The Edwardian Theatre: Essays on Performance and the Stage*. Cambridge: Cambridge University Press.

Borsa, Mario 1908. *The English Stage of Today*, trans. and ed. Selwyn Brinton. London: John Lane The Bodley Head.

Bourne, Bette, Shaw, Paul, Shaw, Peggy, Weaver, Lois 1996. *Belle Reprieve: A Collaboration*, in *Split Britches: Lesbian Practice/Feminist Performance*, ed. Sue-Ellen Case. London and New York: Routledge.

Bramble, Forbes 1973. 'Crucible Theatre Sheffield – a Thrust Stage That Works', *Theatre Quarterly* 3.11: 71–84.

Brenton, Howard 1970. *Christie in Love*. London: Methuen & Co.

1976. *Weapons of Happiness*. London: Eyre Methuen.

Brenton, Howard and Hare, David 1974. *Brassneck*. London: Eyre Methuen.

Brenton, Howard, Clark, Brian, Griffiths, Trevor *et al.* 1972. *Lay By*. London: Calder and Boyars.

Browne, E. Martin 1946. 'Poets on the Stage', *Theatre Today* 1: 21.

Bull, John 1984. *New British Political Dramatists*. London and Basingstoke: Macmillan.

Burns, Elizabeth 1972. *Theatricality: A Study of Convention in the Theatre and in Social Life*. London: Longman.

Calder, John 1977. 'Editorial', *Gambit: International Theatre Review* 8.31: 3.

Callow, Simon 2004. *Being an Actor*. London: Vintage Books.

Chambers, Colin 1989. *The Story of Unity Theatre*. London: Lawrence and Wishart.

Cheeseman, Peter 1970. *The Knotty: A Musical Documentary*. London: Methuen & Co.

1971. 'A Community Theatre-in-the-Round', *Theatre Quarterly* 1.1: 71–82.

1977 *Fight for Shelton Bar!* London: Eyre Methuen.

Childs, Nicky and Walwin, Jeni (eds.) 1998. *A Split Second of Paradise: Live Art, Installation and Performance*. London: Rivers Oram Press.

Churchill, Caryl 1983. *Fen*. London: Methuen London (with Joint Stock Theatre Group).

Cole, Marion (ed.) 1967. *Fogie: The Life of Elsie Fogerty, C.B.E.* London: Peter Davies.

Collins, Jeffrey 1992. 'The Fine Rats International: Performance Art and Post-industrial society', *Performance* 65/66: 67–77.

Common Ground 1985. *The Fence*, in *Peace Plays*, selected and introduced by Stephen Lowe. London and New York: Methuen.

Complicite 2003. *The Street of Crocodiles*, in *Plays: One*, intro. Simon McBurney. London: Methuen Drama.

Cooper, Emmanuel 1980. 'Acting It Out: Gay Community Theatre', *Gay Left* June: 38–9.

Corrie, Joe 1985. *Plays, Poems and Theatre Writings*, ed. Linda Mackenney. Edinburgh: 7:84 Publications.

Coult, Tony and Kershaw, Baz (eds.) 1983. *Engineers of the Imagination: The Welfare State Handbook*. London and New York: Methuen.

Coveney, Michael 1990. *The Citz: 21 Years of the Glasgow Citizens Theatre*. London: Nick Hern Books.

Coward, Noël 1979. *This Happy Breed*, in *Plays: Four*, intro. Raymond Mander and Joe Mitchenson. London: Eyre Methuen.

  1979. *Present Laughter*, in *Plays: Four*, intro. Raymond Mander and Joe Mitchenson. London: Eyre Methuen.

  1979. *Hay Fever*, in *Plays: One*, intro. Raymond Mander and Joe Mitchenson. London: Eyre Methuen.

Craig, Edward Gordon 1980. *On the Art of the Theatre*. London: Heinemann.

Craig, Sandy (ed.) 1980. *Dreams and Deconstructions: Alternative Theatre in Britain*. Ambergate: Amber Lane Press.

Crimp, Martin 2007. *Attempts on Her Life*. London: Faber and Faber.

Culler, Jonathan 1986. *Structuralist Poetics: Structuralism, Linguistics and the Study of Literature*. London: Routledge and Kegan Paul.

Davies, Andrew 1987. *Other Theatres: The Development of Alternative and Experimental Theatre in Britain*. Basingstoke: Macmillan Education.

Dixon, Steve 2007. *Digital Performance: A History of New Media in Theatre, Dance, Performance Art, and Installation*, with contributions by Barry Smith. Cambridge, Mass: The MIT Press.

D'Usseau, Arnand 1947. 'There is No Place for Neutrality in the Theatre', *New Theatre* 4.2: 12–15.

Earl, John 2005. *British Theatres and Music Halls*. Princes Risborough: Shire Publications.

Earl, John and Sell, Michael (eds.) 2000. *The Theatres Trust Guide to British Theatres 1750–1950: A Gazetteer*. London: A&C Black.

Edgar, David 1979. 'Towards a Theatre of Dynamic Ambiguities', interview with Clive Barker and Simon Trussler, *Theatre Quarterly* 9.33: 3–23.

Eliot, T. S. 1962a. *Murder in the Cathedral*, in *Collected Plays*. London: Faber and Faber.

  1962b. *The Family Reunion*, in *Collected Plays*. London: Faber and Faber.

  1999. 'A Dialogue on Dramatic Poetry', in *Selected Essays*. London: Faber and Faber, pp. 43–58.

Elsom, John and Tomalin, Nicholas 1978. *The History of the National Theatre*. London: Jonathan Cape.

Etchells, Tim 1996. 'Diverse Assembly: Some Trends in Recent Performance', in Shank 1996, pp. 107–22.

1998. 'Valuable Spaces: New Performance in the 1990s', in Childs and Walwin 1998, pp. 31–40.

1999. *Certain Fragments: Contemporary Performance and Forced Entertainment*. London: Routledge.

Findlay, Bill (ed.) 1998. *A History of Scottish Theatre*. Edinburgh: Edinburgh University Press.

Fitzsimmons, Linda and Gardner, Viv (eds.) 1991. *New Woman Plays*. London: Methuen Drama.

Fry, Christopher 1950. *Venus Observed*. London: Oxford University Press.

Gaskill, William 1988. *A Sense of Direction*. London: Faber and Faber.

Giannachi, Gabriella 2004. *Virtual Theatres: An Introduction*. London and New York: Routledge.

Giannachi, Gabriella and Luckhurst, Mary (eds.) 1999. *On Directing: Interviews with Directors*. London: Faber and Faber.

Gielgud, John 1963. *Stage Directions*. London: Heinemann.

1979. *An Actor and His Time*, in collaboration with John Miller and John Powell. London: Sidgwick & Jackson.

Gooch, Steve 1984. *All Together Now: An Alternative View of Theatre and the Community*. London: Methuen.

Gooch, Steve and Thompson, Paul 1975. *The Motor Show*. London: Pluto Press.

Goodman, Lizbeth 1993. *Contemporary Feminist Theatres: To Each Her Own*. London and New York: Routledge.

Granville Barker, Harley 1930. *A National Theatre*. London: Sidgwick & Jackson

Greig, Noël 1994. *Plague of Innocence*, in *Gay Plays: Five*, intro. Michael Wilcox. London: Methuen Drama.

1997. 'Foreword' to *As Time Goes By*, in *Gay Sweatshop Plays*, ed. Brian Roberts. London: Goldsmiths Plays.

Greig, Noël and Griffiths, Drew 1997. *As Time Goes By*, in *Gay Sweatshop Plays*, ed. Brian Roberts. London: Goldsmiths Plays.

Griffiths, Malcolm 1977. 'The Drama Panel Game: An Inside View of the Arts Council', *Theatre Quarterly* 7.25: 3–19.

Griffiths, Trevor 1977. 'Author's Preface', in *Through the Night/Such Impossibilities*. London: Faber and Faber.

Guthrie, Tyrone 1961. *A Life in the Theatre*. London: Hamish Hamilton.

Hall, Peter 1972. 'Is the Beginning the Word?', *Theatre Quarterly* 2.7: 5–11.

Hall, Stuart 1970. 'Beyond Naturalism Pure', in Marowitz *et al.* 1970, pp. 212–20.

Hamilton, Cicely 1991. *Diana of Dobson's*, in *New Woman Plays*, ed. Linda Fitzsimmons and Viv Gardner. London: Methuen Drama.

Hamilton, Patrick 1947. 'Art Is Never Neutral', *New Theatre* 4.5: 2.

Hanna, Gillian (ed.) 1991. *Monstrous Regiment: A Collective Celebration.* London: Nick Hern Books.

Hare, David 1976. *Fanshen.* London: Faber and Faber.

Harrison, Tony 1991. *The Trackers of Oxyrhynchus.* London: Faber and Faber.

Haynes, Jim 1984. *Thanks for Coming!: An Autobiography.* London: Faber and Faber.

Heddon, Deirdre and Milling, Jane 2006. *Devising Performance: A Critical History.* Basingstoke: Palgrave Macmillan.

Hedley, Philip 1998. 'A Theatre Director's Journey to the Obvious', in Ikoli 1998, pp. 7–25.

Hoban, Russell 1984. 'Working with Impact', *Performance Magazine* 32: 12–14.

Hodgson, John 1971. 'Theatre in Education', *Theatre Quarterly* 1.1: 57–60.

Holdsworth, Nadine 2006. *Joan Littlewood.* London and New York: Routledge.

Howe, P. P. 1910. *The Repertory Theatre: A Record and a Criticism.* London: Martin Secker.

Hunt, Albert 1974. *Arden: A Study of His Plays.* London: Eyre Methuen.

1976. *Hopes for Great Happenings: Alternatives in Education and Theatre.* London: Eyre Methuen.

Hunt, Bampton (ed.) 1906. *The Green Room Book.* London: T. Sealey Clark.

Ikoli, Tunde 1998. *Scrape off the Black.* London: Oberon Books.

Innes, Christopher 2002. *Modern British Drama: The Twentieth Century.* Cambridge: Cambridge University Press.

Itzin, Catherine 1975. 'Alternative Theatre in the Mainstream', *Theatre Quarterly* 5.19: 3–11.

1979. 'Spanner at Work 1: Shop Floor Theatre', *Platform* 1: 8–13 (reprinted in Itzin 1980).

1980. *Stages in the Revolution: Political Theatre in Britain since 1968.* London: Eyre Methuen.

Jellicoe, Ann 1968. *The Sport of My Mad Mother.* London: Faber and Faber.

Jennings, Gertrude 1985. *A Woman's Influence,* in *Sketches from the Actresses' Franchise League,* ed. Viv Gardner. Nottingham: Nottingham Drama Texts.

Jones, D. A. N. 1971. 'Silent Censorship in Britain', *Theatre Quarterly* 1.1: 22–8.

Jones, Simon 2004. 'New Theatre for New Times: Decentralisation, Innovation and Pluralism, 1975–2000', in Kershaw 2004, pp. 448–69.

Kane, Sarah 2001. *Blasted,* in *Complete Plays,* intro. David Greig. London: Methuen Drama.

2001. *Crave,* in *Complete Plays,* intro. David Greig. London: Methuen Drama.

Kaye, Nick 1996. *Art into Theatre: Performance Interviews and Documents.* Amsterdam: Harwood Academic Publishers.

2000. *Site-Specific Art: Place, Performance and Documentation.* London and New York: Routledge.

Kennedy, Dennis 1985. *Granville Barker and the Dream of Theatre.* Cambridge: Cambridge University Press.

Kershaw, Baz 1992. *The Politics of Performance: Radical Theatre as Cultural Intervention*. London and New York: Routledge.

1999. *The Radical in Performance: Between Brecht and Baudrillard*. London and New York: Routledge.

(ed.) 2004. *The Cambridge History of British Theatre*, vol. III: *Since 1895*. Cambridge: Cambridge University Press.

Kuppers, Petra 2007. *Community Performance: An Introduction*. London and New York: Routledge.

Lacey, Stephen 1995. *British Realist Theatre: The New Wave in Its Context 1956-1965*. London and New York: Routledge.

La Frenais, Rob 1982. 'Art on the Run', *Performance Magazine* 19: 14–20.

1985. 'Happenings', *Performance Magazine* 36: 6–8.

Landstone, Charles 1953. *Off-Stage: A Personal Record of the First Twelve Years of State Sponsored Drama in Great Britain*. London: Elek.

Lavender, Andy 2006. 'Theatre and Technology', in *A Companion to Modern British and Irish Drama: 1880-205*, ed. Mary Luckhurst. Oxford: Blackwell, pp. 551–62.

Leacroft, Richard 1947. 'Design for a Civic Theatre', *New Theatre* 4.2: 18.

Littlewood, Joan 1970. 'Goodbye Note from Joan', in Marowitz *et al.* 1970, pp. 132–4.

Lukács, Georg 1969. *The Historical Novel*, trans. Hannah and Stanley Mitchell. Harmondsworth: Penguin.

MacCarthy, Desmond 1907. *The Court Theatre 1904-1907: A Commentary and Criticism*. London: A. H. Bullen.

MacColl, Ewan 1986. *Uranium 235*, in *Agit-prop to Theatre Workshop: Political Playscripts 1930-50*, ed. Howard Goorney and Ewan MacColl. Manchester: Manchester University Press.

Mackey, Sally 2007. 'Performance, Place and Allotments: Feast or Famine?', *Contemporary Theatre Review* 17.2: 181–91.

Malcolm, Richard 2005. 'Making Space, Marking Time: Station House Opera's *Mare's Nest*', *Performance Research* 10.4, *On Techné*: 45–57.

Malleson, Miles 1925. *The I.L.P. Arts Guild: The I.L.P. and Its Dramatic Societies. What They Are and Might Become*. London: I.L.P. Publications Department.

1927. *The Fanatics*. London: Ernest Benn.

Mander, Raymond and Mitchenson, Joe 2000. *Theatrical Companion to Coward: A Pictorial Record of the Theatrical Works of Noël Coward*, with an appreciation of Coward's work in the theatre by Terence Rattigan, updated by Barry Day and Sheridan Morley. London: Oberon Books.

Mann, Charlie 1985. 'How to Produce Meerut', in Samuel *et al.* 1985, pp. 106–8.

Marowitz, Charles 1967. 'Notes on the Theatre of Cruelty', in Marowitz and Trussler 1967, pp. 164–85.

1973. *Confessions of a Counterfeit Critic: A London Theatre Notebook 1958-1971*. London: Eyre Methuen.

Marowitz, Charles and Trussler, Simon (eds.) 1967. *Theatre At Work: Playwrights and Productions in the Modern British Theatre*. London: Methuen & Co.
Marowitz, Charles, Milne, Tom, Hale, Owen (eds.) 1970. *The Encore Reader: A Chronicle of the New Drama*. London: Methuen & Co.
Marshall, Norman 1947. *The Other Theatre*. London: John Lehmann.
Martin, William 1972. 'Theatre as Social Education', *Theatre Quarterly* 2.8: 18–25.
Maschler, Tom 1957. *Declaration*. London: MacGibbon & Key.
Matura, Mustapha 1992. *Welcome Home Jacko*. London: Methuen Drama.
Maugham, William Somerset 1961. *The Summing Up*. London: Heinemann.
  1999a. *For Services Rendered*, in *Plays: Two*, intro. Anthony Curtis. London: Methuen Drama.
  1999b. *Home and Beauty*, in *Plays: Two*, intro. Anthony Curtis. London: Methuen Drama.
Maynard Smith, Julian 1983. 'Documentation', *Performance Magazine* 22: 24.
  1994/5. 'The Bastille Dances: Station House Opera', *Scroope: Cambridge Architecture Journal* 6: 60–2.
McDonald, Jan 2004. 'Towards National Identities: Theatre in Scotland', in Kershaw 2004, pp. 195–227.
McGrath, John 1977. *The Cheviot, the Stag and the Black, Black Oil*. Breakish: West Highland Publishing Company.
  1981. *A Good Night Out: Popular Theatre: Audience, Class and Form*, foreword Raymond Williams. London: Eyre Methuen.
McMillan, Michael 1995. 'Fishing for a New Religion (for Lynford French)', in *Let's Get it On: The Politics of Black Performance*, ed. Catherine Ugwu. Seattle: Bay Press, pp. 190–209.
Morgan, Edwin 1970. 'That Uncertain Feeling', in Marowitz *et al.* 1970, pp. 52–6.
Morley, Robin 1983. 'Multi-Storey-Minimalism', *Performance Magazine* 24: 25–6.
Murray, Gilbert 2005. *Gilbert Murray's Euripides: The Trojan Women and Other Plays*, intro. James Morwood. Exeter: Bristol Phoenix Press.
New Theatre Quarterly 1989. 'Theatre in Thatcher's Britain: Organizing the Opposition', *New Theatre Quarterly* 5.18: 113–23.
Nicholson, Helen 2005. *Applied Drama: The Gift of Theatre*. Basingstoke: Palgrave Macmillan.
Nicholson, Norman 1946. 'Poetry and Realism in the Drama', *Theatre Today* 1: 22.
Nicholson, Steve 2003. *The Censorship of British Drama, 1900–1968*. Exeter: University of Exeter Press.
Nuttall, Jeff 1979. *Performance Art: Memoirs*, vol. I. London: John Calder.
Norton-Taylor, Richard (ed.) 1999. *The Colour of Justice*. London: Oberon Books.
Osborne, John 1976. *Look Back in Anger*. London: Faber and Faber.
  1991. *Almost a Gentleman: An Autobiography*, vol II: *1955–1966*. London: Faber and Faber.
  1995. *The Entertainer*. London: Faber and Faber.
Osment, Philip (ed.) 1989. *Gay Sweatshop: Four Plays and a Company*. London: Methuen Drama.

Owusu, Kwesi 1986. *The Struggle for Black Arts in Britain: What Can We Consider Better than Freedom.* London: Comedia.

Paget, Derek 1990. *True Stories? Documentary Drama on Radio, Screen and Stage.* Manchester: Manchester University Press.

Pearson, Mike and Shanks, Michael 2001. *Theatre/Archaeology.* London: Routledge.

Phillips, Mike [1981]. 'Black Theatre in Britain', *Platform* 3: 3–6.

Pickering, Kenneth 2001. *Drama in the Cathedral: A Twentieth Century Encounter of Church and Stage.* Colwall: J.Garnet Miller.

Pinter, Harold 1966. *The Birthday Party.* London: Methuen & Co.

    1968. *The Homecoming.* London: Methuen & Co.

    1976. 'Writing for the Theatre', in *Plays: One.* London: Eyre Methuen.

Platform [1982]. 'Editorial', *Platform* 4: 1.

Priestley, J. B. 1947. *Theatre Outlook.* London: Nicholson & Watson.

    1981. *An Inspector Calls,* in *Time and the Conways and Other Plays.* Harmondsworth: Penguin.

    2004. *They Came to a City,* in *Plays Two,* intro. Tom Priestley. London: Oberon Books.

Priestley, J. B. and Dean, Basil 1947. 'A National Theatre Authority?', *New Theatre* 3.12: 12–13.

Quick, Andrew 1998. 'Time and the Event', *Cultural Values* 2.2 and 3: 223–42.

Ratcliff, A. J. J. 1941. 'Are You a War-time "Hamlet"?', *Theatrecraft* 31: 10.

Rattigan, Terence 1977a. *The Collected Plays of Terence Rattigan,* vol. II. London: Hamish Hamilton.

    1977b. *The Deep Blue Sea,* in Rattigan 1977a.

Ravenhill, Mark 2001. *Shopping and Fucking,* in *Plays: One,* intro. Dan Rebellato. London: Methuen.

Rebellato, Dan 1999. *1956 and All That: The Making of Modern British Drama.* London and New York: Routledge.

Reckord, Barry 1966. *Skyvers,* in *New English Dramatists 9,* intro. Michael Billington. Harmondsworth: Penguin.

Red Ladder 1980. *Strike While the Iron Is Hot,* in *Strike While the Iron Is Hot: Three Plays on Sexual Politics,* ed. Michelene Wandor. London and West Nyack: The Journeyman Press.

Rees, Roland 1992. *Fringe First: Pioneers of Fringe Theatre on Record.* London: Oberon Books.

Reinelt, Janelle 1994. *After Brecht: British Epic Theatre.* Ann Arbor: The University of Michigan Press.

Rideal, Liz 1984. 'Mainbeam On! Charlie Hooker Discusses His Work', *Performance* 31: 9–12.

Ritchie, Rob 1987. 'Joint Stock: "Asking Basic Questions"', in *The Joint Stock Book: The Making of a Theatre Collective.* London: Methuen London, pp. 11–32.

Rogers, Steve 1983a. 'Profile: Impact Theatre', *Performance Magazine* 22: 5–8.

    1983b. 'High Kemp', *Performance Magazine* 26: 12–16.

1988. 'Showing the Wires', *Performance Magazine* 57/58: 9–14.
Rowell, George and Jackson, Anthony 1984. *The Repertory Movement: A History of Regional Theatre in Britain.* Cambridge: Cambridge University Press.
Rudkin, David 1963. *Afore Night Come*, in *New English Dramatists 7.* Harmondsworth: Penguin.
1986. *The Saxon Shore.* London: Methuen London.
Sachs, Edwin O. 1898. *Modern Opera Houses and Theatres*, vol. III. London: B.T. Batsford.
Saint-Denis, Michel 1960. *Theatre: The Rediscovery of Style*, intro. Sir Laurence Olivier. London: Heinemann.
Samuel, Raphael, MacColl, Ewan and Cosgrove, Stuart (eds.) 1985. *Theatres of the Left 1880–1935: Workers' Theatre Movements in Britain and America.* London: Routledge & Kegan Paul.
Schafer, Elizabeth 2006. *Lilian Baylis: A Biography.* Hatfield: University of Hertfordshire Press.
Settle, Peter 1941. 'Their Art Also is a Weapon', *Our Time* 1.6: 1.
Shaffer, Peter 1977. *Equus.* New York: Penguin.
Shank, Theodore (ed.) 1996. *Contemporary British Theatre.* Basingstoke: Macmillan Press.
Shaw, Bernard 1967. *Major Barbara.* Harmondsworth: Penguin.
Shellard, Dominic 2000. *British Theatre Since the War.* New Haven and London: Yale University Press.
Shiels, George 1945. *Paul Twynyng*, in *Three Plays.* London: Macmillan & Co.
Sidnell, Michael 1984. *Dances of Death: The Group Theatre of London in the Thirties.* London: Faber and Faber.
Silvera, Frank 1948. 'The Negro Actor – A Summing-up', *New Theatre* 4.8: 18–19.
Singer, Ben 2001. *Melodrama and Modernity: Early Sensational Cinema and Its Contexts.* New York: Columbia University Press.
Slater, Montagu 1936. *Easter: 1916.* London: Lawrence and Wishart.
1937. *New Way Wins: The Play from Stay Down Miner.* London: Lawrence and Wishart.
Sobieski, Lynn 1996. 'Breaking the Boundaries: The People Show, Lumiere & Son and Hesitate and Demonstrate', in Shank 1996, pp. 89–106.
Station House Opera 2008. www.stationhouseopera.com/Introduction/index. html (accessed 22 October 2008).
Stoppard, Tom 1976. *Travesties.* London: Faber and Faber.
Stourac, Richard and McCreery, Kathleen 1986. *Theatre as a Weapon: Workers' Theatre in the Soviet Union, Germany and Britain 1917–1934.* London and New York: Routledge & Kegan Paul.
Stowell, Sheila 1992. *A Stage of Their Own: Feminist Playwrights of the Suffrage Era.* Ann Arbor: The University of Michigan Press.
SuAndi 2002. *The Story of M*, in *4 for More.* Manchester: Black Arts Alliance.
Tanner, Doreen 1974. *Everyman: The First Ten Years.* Liverpool: The Merseyside Everyman Theatre Company.

Terson, Peter 1975. *Zigger Zagger*. Harmondsworth: Penguin.

Test Dept 2007. www.testdept.org.uk/td/history.1.html (accessed 10 July 2007).

Theatre Workshop, Charles Chilton,and the members of the original cast 1977. *Oh What a Lovely War*. London: Eyre Methuen.

Thomas, Tom 1985. *Their Theatre and Ours*, in Samuel *et al.* 1985.

Thompson, James 2005. *Digging Up Stories: Applied Theatre, Performance and War*. Manchester and New York: Manchester University Press.

Time Out 1971. 'Guide to Underground Theatre', *Theatre Quarterly* 1.1: 61–5.

Tomlinson, Richard 1982. *Disability, Theatre and Education*. London: Souvenir Press (E & A).

Travers, Ben 1979. *Rookery Nook*, in *Five Plays*. Harmondsworth: Penguin.

Tushingham, David 1994. *Live 1: Food for the Soul: A New Generation of British Theatre Makers*. London: Methuen Drama.

Twitchin, Mischa 2008. 'Shunt', *Théâtre/Public* 191: 54–2.

Ugwu, Catherine 1995. 'Keep on Running: The Politics of Black British Performance', in *Let's Get it On: The Politics of Black Performance*, ed. Catherine Ugwu. Seattle: Bay Press, pp. 54–83.

van Gyseghem, André n. d. *'The Theatre is our Weapon!'*. London: Russia-Today Society.

1947. *Theatre Old and New*. London: *Bureau of Current Affairs*.

Verma, Jatinder 1996. 'Cultural Transformations', in Shank 1996, pp. 55–61.

Wade, Allan 1983. *Memories of the London Theatre 1900–1914*, ed. Alan Andrews. London: The Society for Theatre Research.

Wallis, Mick 2004. 'Social Commitment and Aesthetic Experiment, 1895–1946', in Kershaw 2004, pp. 167–91.

2006. 'Drama in the Villages: Three Pioneers', in *The English Countryside between the Wars: Regeneration or Decline?*, ed. Paul Brassley, Jeremy Burchardt and Lynne Thompson. Woodbridge: Boydell and Brewer, pp. 101–15.

Wallis, Mick and Philip Kiszely forthcoming. 'Margaret Cropper 1886–1980: Fields of Practice in English Interwar Rural Amateur Theatre'.

Walter, Aubrey (ed. and intro.) 1980. *Come Together: The Years of Gay Liberation 1970–73*. London: Gay Men's Press.

Wandor, Michelene 1986. *Carry On, Understudies: Theatre and Sexual Politics*. London and New York: Routledge & Kegan Paul.

Wansell, Geoffrey 1995. *Terence Rattigan*. London: Fourth Estate.

Wardle, Irving 1970a. 'Comedy of Menace', in Marowitz *et al.* 1970, pp. 86–91.

1970b. 'There's Music in that Room', in Marowitz *et al.* 1970, pp. 129–32.

1979. *The Theatres of George Devine*. London: Eyre Methuen.

Wesker, Arnold 1971. *Chicken Soup with Barley*, in *The Wesker Trilogy*. Harmondsworth: Penguin.

Whitworth, Geoffrey 1951. *The Making of a National Theatre*. London: Faber and Faber.

Williams, Heathcote 1978. 'Corrugated Iron in the Soul: The Community Plays of Rough Theatre', *Theatre Quarterly* 8.29: 3–6.

Williams, Raymond 1980. 'Social Environment and Theatrical Environment: The Case of English Naturalism', in *Problems in Materialism and Culture*. London: Verso, pp. 125–47.

Willis, Ted 1946. 'The Labour Movement's Challenge', *New Theatre* 3.2: 18–20.

1947a. 'Theatre in the Second Battle of Britain', *New Theatre* 3.10: 2.

1947b. Editorial: 'The Next Steps', *New Theatre* 3.12:1.

Women's Theatre Group 1980. *My Mother Said I Never Should*, in *Strike While the Iron Is Hot: Three Plays on Sexual Politics*, ed. Michelene Wandor. London & West Nyack: The Journeyman Press.

www.arthurlloyd.co.uk (accessed 22 October 2008)

Yarker, James 2004 'Technology and Perception', www.stanscafe.co.uk/helpfulthings/technologyandperception.html (accessed 10 July 2007).

Zephaniah, Benjamin 1989. *Job Rocking*, in *Black Plays: Two*, ed. Yvonne Brewster. London: Methuen Drama.

Index

Cambridge Introductions to...

AUTHORS

Jane Austen Janet Todd

Samuel Beckett Ronan McDonald

Walter Benjamin David Ferris

J. M. Coetzee Dominic Head

Joseph Conrad John Peters

Jacques Derrida Leslie Hill

Emily Dickinson Wendy Martin

George Eliot Nancy Henry

T. S. Eliot John Xiros Cooper

William Faulkner Theresa M. Towner

F. Scott Fitzgerald Kirk Curnutt

Michel Foucault Lisa Downing

Robert Frost Robert Faggen

Nathaniel Hawthorne Leland S. Person

Zora Neale Hurston Lovalerie King

James Joyce Eric Bulson

Herman Melville Kevin J. Hayes

Sylvia Plath Jo Gill

Edgar Allen Poe Benjamin F. Fisher

Ezra Pound Ira Nadel

Jean Rhys Elaine Savory

Shakespeare Emma Smith

Shakespeare's Comedies Penny Gay

Shakespeare's History Plays Warren Chernaik

Shakespeare's Tragedies Janette Dillon

Harriet Beecher Stowe Sarah Robbins

Mark Twain Peter Messent

Edith Wharton Pamela Knights

Walt Whitman M. Jimmie Killingsworth

Virginia Woolf Jane Goldman

W. B. Yeats David Holdeman

TOPICS

The American Short Story Martin Scofield

Comedy Eric Weitz

Creative Writing David Morley

Early English Theatre Janette Dillon

English Theatre, 1660–1900 Peter Thomson

Francophone Literature Patrick Corcoran

Modern British Theatre Simon Shepherd

Modern Irish Poetry Justin Quinn

Modernism Pericles Lewis

Narrative (second edition) H. Porter Abbott

The Nineteenth-Century American Novel Gregg Crane

Postcolonial Literatures C. L. Innes

Postmodern Fiction Bran Nicol

Russian Literature Caryl Emerson

The Short Story in English Adrian Hunter

Theatre Historiography Thomas Postlewait

Theatre Studies Christopher Balme

Tragedy Jennifer Wallace